1985

STRASBERG'S METHOD

For Lorrie Hull
With thanks for
all your efforts
Lee Strasberg
Jan 10, 1981

Lee Strasberg

STRASBERG'S METHOD
As Taught by Lorrie Hull

A Practical Guide for Actors,
Teachers and Directors

S. LORAINE HULL

Foreword by Susan Strasberg

Ox Bow Publishing, Inc.
Woodbridge, Connecticut 06525

Published by
OX BOW PUBLISHING, Inc.
P.O. Box 4045
Woodbridge, Connecticut 06525

Library of Congress Cataloging in Publication Data

Hull, S. Loraine, 1928–
    Strasberg's method as taught by Lorrie Hull.

    Includes index.
    1. Acting.   2. Theater—Production and direction.
3. Strasberg, Lee.   I. Title.
PN2061.H85   1985   792'.028   85–2968
ISBN 0–918024–38–2
ISBN 0–918024–39–0 (pbk.)

Printed in the United States of America

Dedicated
To my children: Dianne,
Donald and Debra Hull
and
To my parents and brother:
Myron, Vera and Byron Boos

Contents

PART 3: DIRECTING

APPENDIXES

14. *Listing of Other Handouts for Teachers*   295

Acknowledgments

I express my sincere gratitude to those who helped me in the preparation of the manuscript. Special thanks go to Dr. Howard Mauthe for his assistance with the structure and organization of this book.

There are others who helped me with the many details of this endeavor: my daughter Dianne Hull, Noah Morowitz, Julie Jeffery, William Smithers, and Dr. Delia Salvi. I am also grateful for advice and encouragement from Dr. Jane Hamilton-Merritt and Shelley Winters. And most of all my thanks are due to Lee Strasberg himself. Mr. Strasberg was truly unique, and contact with him was an experience to be treasured. During the ten years I taught under his supervision, he was always helpful and generous in answering my many questions and especially willing to discuss the finer points described in this book.

My son Donald Hull, my daughter, and my parents and brother, Myron, Vera and Byron Boos, gave me the inspiration needed to fulfill this goal.

Foreword

by Susan Strasberg

"The finest words of the dramatist are dead without the actor's heart."
—Edmond Rostand, *Cyrano de Bergerac* (1897), act 1

"Acting is the ability to react to imaginary stimuli—to create real thoughts and feelings under imaginary circumstances."
—Lee Strasberg, 1982

When I was a little girl I was sure we had the biggest family in town. They seemed to be there weekdays, weekends, holidays alike. They ate in our kitchen; my mother, the actress Paula Miller, was also a wonderful cook. They read the books that lined our walls. ("Where are we," a friend from first grade asked, "in the public library?") They listened to the constant classical music my father played. (Franchot Tone once turned to my three-year-old brother Johnny at a Passover service and said, "Do you know what we're celebrating?" "Sure," Johnny piped up. "It's when Mozart passed over the Red Sea.") I heard them talking nonstop, in person, on the phone—arguments, discussions and questions.

As I grew up I realized that these visitors were not my blood relatives but my adopted "theatre" family and that what drew them to our home was their love, fascination, and passion for the creative process—writing, directing or acting. Everything they talked about—music, art, theatre, philosophy, politics, sex, literature, psychology—was related to the human experience that lay at the heart of the creative one. "It's your life— put your soul in it," poet Kenneth Patchen wrote. This was my father's life work. How proudly, almost reverently, he would unroll an antique Japanese scroll that told a story in pictures. "You see," his eyes would light up, "this was the very first moving picture." And if my father insisted that we listen to five different recordings of, say, Beethoven's Ninth, it was so he could urge us: "Listen, you'll see the difference that this pianist makes, the interpretation is completely original."

Later, when I began acting with no formal training, at the age of thirteen, I was grateful that I had absorbed some of those conversations by osmosis. This carried me through the first six years of my career before I actually had the opportunity to study.

Over the years, my father began expanding on Stanislavski's work in Russia, which had been his original inspiration as a young man in the theatre. He developed his own way of training actors, using his experiences as co-founder of the Group Theatre, as a director, as a teacher in his own private acting classes, and at the Actors Studio. This forms the basis for Strasberg's Method.

People tried to keep track of it all. Actors took longhand notes in class. Later the work was taped. Books were written about the Actors Studio describing the work there but not explaining it. (In my case the work in the private classes was often different from the more loosely structured work in the Actors Studio sessions. These continue today under the leadership of Ellen Burstyn, Paul Newman, Elia Kazan and others.) Myth and miscomprehension surrounded "The Method." People begged my father to write down the exercise work, and while he did do some writing about acting, including a book on his life work which he completed just before his death, he expressed doubts: "I'm not sure anyone could get all my work, especially the exercise work, on paper." It wasn't just that it was complex; over the years the system kept changing and evolving. He didn't intend it to be the Ten Commandments. It was a living process, a craft. In describing the development of the various techniques, one of my father's directing students commented, "Stanislavski defined the work, but Lee translated the impersonal in Stanislavski into personal experience, tools any actor could use."

When I read Lorrie Hull's book I thought, "My God, she's done it. She's caught so much of the work that's never been set down before." And for the first time I understood aspects of the process that had never been clear to me. I remember asking my father to explain "one more time" until finally embarrassed at my lack of comprehension I stopped asking. Fortunately, Lorrie, a Leo, was more persistent than I was. She not only asked, she got the answers, wrote them down, used them in her own twelve years of teaching for my father and then translated it all into an understandable, explicit, practical book that offers valuable tools for any actor (beginner to professional) as well as for writers, directors, teachers and anyone interested in the human potential: in such fields as psychology, the behavioral sciences, the mind/body/spirit connection and holistic medicine (stress relief techniques including relaxation and visualization).

I'm sure a lot of the major misconceptions about my father's work will be cleared up by *Strasberg's Method*. First, Lorrie Hull shows that my father defined the acting process as a craft, not an attempt at psychoanalysis or therapy. Also the book illustrates that these techniques work as well for the classics as for modern material. (Read Shakespeare's "Advice to the Players" in *Hamlet* to see how he wanted his plays performed.) My father often told his young actors, "You're being natural, but that's not enough. Natural I can see on a street corner. What we ask is that you be real. Art is both more beautiful and terrible than life." And as Tennessee Williams said, "You've only got two and a half hours to create an entire life."

My father was sometimes accused of focusing on the emotions to the exclusion of the intention of the author. My own work in his class illustrates this was not the case. As a young actress I was already so emotional and volatile that he never let me do any of the affective memory work. When I was young I tended to feel that if I was not emotional, I was not acting. My father said, "Susan, every time you come up to bat, you can't hit a home run. Sometimes what the team needs is for you to bunt." He pointed out: "You always want to play Beethoven when all this scene requires is Strauss. So please just play the best Strauss you can." In most of my work in class he encouraged me to look for the logic and intention behind the scene and to be more specific in my choices. Although I had played Juliet, Cleopatra and Anne Frank, I had to start at the beginning of the exercise work: a glass of orange juice, mirror and sunshine, which did not exactly thrill me—until I saw that without concentration, relaxation and will the actor was at the mercy of his prayers for inspiration.

The Method supposedly encouraged a lack of discipline. I remember my father yelling at some actor during exercise work. Afterward I asked, "Why were you so angry? He was trying so hard." (I, of course, identified with the young actor.) "Darling," he said (his "darling" could be a caress or a slap; this time it was kind), "I wasn't angry. I was trying to awaken his will. Without it, he will never be an actor." Always he emphasized will and discipline. The actor had to have full control over his body, mind and feelings. The exercises were equivalent to a pianist's

Susan Strasberg with her father, Lee, taken at their New York City home when Susan was performing in *The Diary of Anne Frank*.

hours of practice. A piano player takes for granted that in order to play he has to practice. The exercises described in this book are the actor's keys and notes. My father used these exercises flexibly, so that they were individually tailored to each actor's problem. If it wasn't broken, he didn't try to fix it.

Strasberg's Method also shows that an *affective memory* is a specific, disciplined process, not the production of some general uncontrolled emotion. The example my father used to illustrate affective memory was from *Swann's Way,* when Proust eloquently described the evocative power the smell and taste of tea cakes, madeleines, from his childhood had on him: "The smell and taste of things remain poised a long time, like souls ready to remind us, waiting and hoping for their moment . . . and bear unfalteringly, in the tiny and almost impalpable drop of their essence, the vast structure of recollection." This is such stuff as an actor's dreams are made of, the essence of his work. Everything the actor has seen, heard, touched, tasted, smelled and experienced are money in his emotional bank. "Darling," my father said to a young actress, who was weeping uncontrollably, complaining of the pain of remembering, "Be thankful you're an actress. You can use this pain. It makes you a Rockefeller, a Getty, because you can transmute it, transform it and use it."

The most popular misconception leads to the question I have been asked the most over the past thirty years. If you're a Method actress, aren't you supposed to live your part? If that were true, I would have died at fifteen when I played Juliet. My father used to tell a story describing the amount of faith or belief the actor needs:

> A Texas oilman went to heaven. "Sorry," said Saint Peter, "you can't come in."
>
> "Why not?" the oilman demanded. "I lived a virtuous life just so I could get into heaven. It's unfair."
>
> "It's not that," said Saint Peter. "There's no room. Our quota for oilmen is filled, so you'll have to go down there."
>
> "Please," the oilman pleaded, "let me into heaven for five minutes. If I can't make a place for myself, I'll go to hell."
>
> Intrigued, Saint Peter agreed: "But only five minutes."
>
> The oilman made a beeline toward the congregation of oilmen, whispering to each one. Suddenly it was bedlam. The oilmen en masse ran out of the gates of heaven. Collaring the instigator, who was running as fast as the others bringing up the rear, Saint Peter demanded, "Where are they going?"

> "To hell," replied the oilman.
> "Why, what did you tell them?"
> "I told them they struck oil in hell."
> "Then why are you going?" asked a puzzled saint.
> "Because," the oilman replied, *"maybe it's true."*

I've always felt that was the heart of the commitment of both actor and audience: "Maybe it's true."

It's amazing to realize that for thousands of years the actor had to work on a hit-or-miss basis, with no technique or body of work to sustain him. One renowned ancient Greek actor so longed to re-create real grief that in his desperation he brought an urn with the ashes of his dead son onstage in *Oedipus*. As recently as one hundred years ago a standard Italian acting textbook included these directions on how to portray *fury*: "Rise, put hat on, jam it on the head, fling it on the ground, pick it up, tear it to pieces, pause briefly . . . strike fist hard on furniture, stamp the foot, wheel around . . ." How fortunate is today's actor that men like Stanislavski, Vakhtangov and my father finally created a craft so that he or she no longer needs to depend on the fickle muse of inspiration or the vagaries of his or her own emotional ups and downs. Besides, it is never enough just to be inspired. Inspiration doesn't always show up at 8:30 every evening, eight performances a week, or at 6:30 in the morning on a film set.

Reading this book reaffirmed my admiration and respect for actors. Who else has to be so totally private in public? Nowadays taking your clothes off can be easy, but to bare your soul is another matter altogether. I am awed at what courage actors have; I am awed by their willingness to take risks with themselves, to be vulnerable, to create and live inside another person's mind and soul. I know how it's done, but it still seems magical to me. And the actor is the magician, the rabbit and the hat. I agree with writer Ben Hecht who once said, "If I were to die and go to a heaven entirely populated by actors, I would not be unhappy." That is a sentiment my father and I shared.

Shortly before he died, my father asked Al Pacino to approach a well known actor about a project my father longed to do. Al reported back to my father, "He said it was impossible and to tell you you must be dreaming." "Darling," my father retorted, "I may be dreaming, but he's asleep." And still the waking dream goes on. Shakespeare wrote in

Hamlet: ". . . the purpose of playing . . . now, was and is to hold, as 'twere the mirror up to nature."

True. But the dream promises that the actor may do more than just reflect life, he may also illuminate it.

After my father died, Francesca De Sapio, an actress from the Actors Studio, wrote about his work: "It is that constant search of the actor for the thread that unites body, heart, mind and soul—that search which is essential to the art of acting."

After reading *Strasberg's Method* (for Lorrie Hull has captured so much of the work so extraordinarily well) I feel sure that my father, "Pop," would be enormously pleased. Once, when he was given one of his numerous awards, a reporter asked, "How do you feel about all this?" He thought for a moment before replying: "Doing the work is my greatest reward." And it was.

Introduction

Is it not monstrous that this player here,
But in a fiction, in a dream of passion,
Could force his soul so to his own conceit
That from her working all his visage wann'd,
Tears in his eyes, distraction in's aspect,
A broken voice, and his whole function suiting
With forms to his conceit?

—Hamlet II, ii

Aristotle, one of the foremost Greek philosophers, once said that dramatic ability is a natural gift and can hardly be taught. But in this Aristotle has been proved wrong. The art of acting *can* be taught.

Lee Strasberg, a founder of the Group Theatre, artistic director of the Actors Studio, and founder of the Lee Strasberg Theatre Institute has been the greatest single influence on the art and craft of acting in the United States. Strasberg is recognized worldwide for having taught and nurtured three generations of actors, directors and playwrights whose careers in theatre and cinema have been outstanding.

Julie Harris eagerly acknowledges her debt:

> I remember being present at the first meeting of all the members of the New Actors Studio . . . Harold Clurman, Tennessee Williams, Elia Kazan, Lee Strasberg, Cheryl Crawford, Bobby Lewis . . . All were there talking to us . . . telling us their hopes and plans for this new group. It was a dream for me . . . a home . . . a beginning . . . with the most inspired people I could imagine. Mr. Kazan was my first teacher, then Mr. Strasberg, and I was in heaven all the way.[1]

The gratitude of yet another generation of actors is expressed by Ron Liebman:

> The Studio was a place for me to work out when there really was no other. There was no other because the Studio had Lee Strasberg and it was FREE and I had no money and that was a great deal for a young actor fighting the furies . . . the theatre's and his own.[2]

Strasberg's "Method" is a practical acting technique that was first defined by Stanislavski in Russia and later developed by Strasberg and others in the United States. The American Method recognizes great actors of the past and defines what they do when they are good. The technique trains actors so that there is evenness in their work. But the Method is not a rigid, static system. Rather, it seeks to add new elements to Stanislavski's basic principles by means of experimentation. This is accomplished by making use of our expanding knowledge of human psychology, the process of conditioning, the role of habits, the interaction between the conscious and the subconscious and the process of creative imagination.

The theatre world today, as Lee Strasberg explained many times, is filled with discussion about acting—the Stanislavski system, the Method, the laboratory work of Grotowsky, the experiments of the Living Theatre and the theories of Artaud, Brecht and others. Nonetheless, it remains true that for over two thousand years the problem of the actor in developing an inner technique has been misunderstood and superficially divided into an external or an internal.

The author and Lee Strasberg at the Actors Studio discussing the direction of a scene. Photo by Jonathan K. Rout.

The American Method is particularly associated with Lee Strasberg, a controversial figure whose philosophy and practice has been much discussed. But such writings have not adequately explained the evolution of Strasberg's teaching methods or described those methods in usable form. The Method is a path of discovery to guide actors and directors toward what works for them. Delia Salvi, professor of theatre at UCLA, noted: "Lee's exercises are much more specific than other instructors' because they deal more directly with the problems created by a lifetime of conditioning. One of the results of the training is to open up the instrument."[3]

Strasberg was for many years aware of the need to offer his training in acting and the theatre arts to a wider public. But the very special and individual nature of the work confined his instruction to the membership of the studio and to professional classes. This book, based on my experience and personal studies with Strasberg, attempts to broaden that audience. I present my understanding of Strasberg's method for the actor, teacher or director who wants to hone his craft.

Although voice, speech, movement and dance are important areas of training for the actor, this book will not touch those fields. I do not intend to slight such training. Good speech instruction can clear up speech defects, poor articulation and undesirable native accents as well as expand vocal range and volume. Classes in movement and dance are equally valuable, for they free an actor whose body is restrictive. These important areas are often addressed in separate classes. This book deals only with techniques of teaching acting and directing.

I was a faculty member at the Lee Strasberg Theatre Institute, Los Angeles, for over twelve years. I was the first and only instructor ever asked by Lee Strasberg to organize and teach the course "Understanding of the Method." I have effectively used the techniques described in this book in teaching and directing at every level of the American theatre: creative dramatics and children's theatre; elementary, junior high and high school theatre; college, university, extension and community theatre; professional theatre; national and international workshops; national competitions; and coaching acting for motion pictures and television. Strasberg's Method may not be the only way to teach and learn acting and directing, but it is a way that works. Witness the success of many of the artists who have studied with Strasberg at the Actors Studio: Edward Albee, Joseph Anthony, Lou Antonio, Beatrice Arthur, Bar-

Lorrie Hull coaching her daughter Dianne for the role of Ellen in *The Arrangement,* written and directed by Elia Kazan. Phot © Warner Bros.– Seven Arts, Inc. All rights reserved.

bara Bain, Carroll Baker, James Baldwin, Martin Balsam, Anne Bancroft, Herbert Berghof, Richard Boone, Jocelyn Brando, Marlon Brando, Beth Brickell, Roscoe Lee Brown, Ellen Burstyn, Zoe Caldwell, Lewis John Carlino, Lonny Chapman, Dane Clark, Jill Clayburgh, Montgomery Clift, Michael Conrad, James Dean, Robert De Niro, Sandy Dennis, Mildred Dunnock, Robert Duvall, Betty Field, Sally Field, Jane Fonda, John Forsythe, Anthony Franciosa, James Frawley, Martin Fried, Jack Garfein, Ben Gazzara, Michael Gazzo, Scott Glenn, Allen Garfield, Charles Gordone, Lee Grant, Barbara Harris, Julie Harris, June Havoc, Pat Hingle, Dustin Hoffman, Celeste Holm, Dianne Hull, Kim Hunter, Israel Horovitz, William Inge, Anne Jackson, Lainie Kazan, Shirley Knight, Diane Ladd, Martin Landau, Arthur Laurents, Cloris Leachman, Jack Lord, Norman Mailer, Karl Malden, E. G. Marshall, Walter Matthau, Kevin McCarthy, Steve McQueen, Peggy McCay, Burgess Meredith, Marilyn Monroe, Michael Moriarty, Patricia Neal, Paul Newman, Jack Nicholson, Carroll O'Connor, Gerald S. O'Loughlin, Al Pacino, Geraldine Page, Estelle Parsons, Arthur Penn, George Peppard, Anthony Perkins, Frank Perry, Sidney Poitier, Sydney Pollack,

Chatting with Burgess Meredith at the Actors Studio in Los Angeles. Photo © Demetrios Demetropoulos.

José Quintero, Steve Railsback, Martin Ritt, Jerome Robbins, Cliff Robertson, Mark Rydell, Eva Marie Saint, Alan Schneider, Madeline Sherwood-Thornton, William Smithers, Kim Stanley, Maureen Stapleton, Rod Steiger, Anna Sten, Susan Strasberg, Rip Torn, Jo Van Fleet, Christopher Walken, Eli Wallach, Leslie Warren, David Wayne, Dennis Weaver, James Whitmore, Gene Wilder, Shelley Winters and Joanne Woodward, among others.

Part 1
Background

1 The Rewards of Studying Method

The violinist Yehudi Menuhin, a child prodigy who made his debut at 10, began having trouble with intonation at age 22. (Intonation is getting the exact note desired—neither sharp nor flat—through finger placement.) Since Menuhin's former teacher had retired, he sent a letter to the great violinist, Eugene Ysaye. "I would like to play for you," he wrote, but he meant, "I would like to study with you." Ysaye replied, "I don't take students, but I would like to hear you play." So Menuhin played something very difficult. When he was finished Ysaye said, "Wonderful! Marvelous! But if I were you I would practice my scales."

Menuhin left confused and hurt. He was one of the world's leading violinists and he was being told to go back to basics. He called his former teacher and told him what had happened. His teacher said, "Of course! When you were a child of 6 or 7 and I gave you an assignment that would take someone else a week to accomplish, you often came back the next day with a finished piece, technically wrong but complete. I could not possibly criticize it." Now that Menuhin was older and his fingers not so supple, he had to relearn fingering and master the technique he had failed to acquire as a child. Menuhin, like most young people, was more interested in accomplishment than in the means by which that accomplishment might be reached. Just as there are child geniuses, there are also children whose hard work, effort and training *make* them into concert violinists.

In all the other creative arts, such as painting, writing or dancing, we recognize that the individual must train himself in order to perfect his craft. Only in the art of acting do we hear people say that the way to learn to act is to walk on stage and act. If that were true, then the way to learn to play a Chopin étude would be to sit down and play a Chopin étude. Of course, we know that is impossible. You must sit down and study the notes and the simplest scales first. *The artist's first task is to master his instrument.* In the case of the pianist it is the piano; in the case of the actor it is himself. Once an actor has achieved self-mastery, he is ready to interpret a role, just as a trained pianist is able to interpret an étude or sonata.

Let me take this analogy one step further. When a person starts learning to read notes and plays them on a piano, he or she can very quickly learn simple pieces. As training continues, the pianist learns more complex runs and fingering and advances to more complex pieces. The progression should be the same for the actor. The budding pianist can play when he starts to study—so can the actor. But he or she must grow with knowledge of the craft. You do not play Lear without solid grounding in the basics.

So it is evident that the actor needs technique. He or she cannot be given talent, but good training can realize potential. Why then the Method? The basic problem of the actor is repetition. If I am good, what makes me good? Can I do it again? *Inspiration is not enough, precisely because it is unpredictable.* The Method is a composite of the acting processes great actors have employed over the centuries to help them conquer the various problems that arise in performance. Stanislavski was the first to recognize the universality of these techniques, and, influenced by the works of Pavlov and modern psychologists, he formulated a modern approach to acting.

Acting a role is not just learning lines, cues, stage business and set responses, imitating what you did before; it means creating the inner life of the character, including the character's ongoing thoughts, sensations, perceptions and emotions.

Method is not used *instead* of any other form of acting—it is an adjunct to other forms. If you have been trained in other forms or even if you have not been formally trained at all, it does not matter. Method starts with the individual, with his or her body, background and senses. It trains the actor to respond quickly and fully to all stimuli in an effort to create reality in acting and spontaneity in all types of performance. Barbra Streisand reported, "After studying with Strasberg, I gave myself more wholeheartedly to my songs."[1]

Those who begin training while still young usually have an advantage because of their greater flexibility and susceptibility. The young are unspoiled; they are physically, mentally and emotionally more receptive and capable of learning faster than older people in general, although there are some notable exceptions.

Anyone who seriously contemplates acting as a career must realize that it is necessary to study and learn not only for the present but also in order to set up a pattern for future growth. You are developing your craft to last a lifetime.

2 The Evolution of Strasberg's Method

Strasberg's Early Life and Training

Nothing in Strasberg's family background indicated that he would develop an avid interest in theatre and eventually become one of the most influential theatre men in the world. Born in Austria in 1901, the youngest child of Ida and Baruch Meyer Strasberg, Strasberg came from a family that had never been involved in professional theatre.[1]

The Strasbergs immigrated to the United States in 1909 when Lee was a young child. He was casually involved in drama as a youth on New York's East Side and appeared occasionally in Yiddish amateur productions, but he had no contact with professional productions until his early twenties. "Why are you worrying?" he once asked a young actress who was concerned about starting her career late. "When I was your age, I wasn't even an actor. I was in the human hair business."

The young Strasberg had an insatiable appetite for reading, evident in later life in his New York apartment, where bookshelves lined every room from floor to ceiling. His retention of what he read was phenomenal, and he had vast knowledge in all areas of the arts. As a youth he read much about the theatre, and in the early twenties he joined the Students of Art and Drama, an amateur group that met and performed at the Chrystie Street Settlement House. He worked with them sporadically until 1927. He often referred to the influences from those years in the course of his teaching: Jeanne Eagels in *Rain,* John Barrymore's *Hamlet,* Eleanora Duse's farewell appearances, performances by Chaliapin and Giovanni Grasso and Stanislavski's first American visit with the original troupe of the Moscow Art Theatre.[2] Gordon Craig's book *On the Theatre* (1911) made Strasberg realize that theatre was not just a place of entertainment: theatre held the imaginative possibilities of a great art.

Not until Strasberg saw Stanislavski and the Moscow Art Theatre perform in 1923 did he realize that his dream of theatre art could actually be created on the stage. Strasberg then sold his share of a manufacturing firm that made women's hair pieces to his partner and decided to try to work professionally in the theatre.

In 1923 Strasberg auditioned for and was accepted by the American Laboratory Theatre, a school founded by two of the most outstanding teachers of the Stanislavski system, Richard Boleslavsky and Maria Ouspenskaya, the latter referred to by Strasberg as "the Madam." Boleslavsky had spent fifteen years studying and acting with Stanislavski, and Ouspenskaya was an outstanding actress whom Stanislavski regarded as one of the best teachers of his system. Both of these individuals had also studied and worked with Eugene Vakhtangov in the Third Moscow Art Theatre Studio. They transmitted to Strasberg Vakhtangov's formulations and evolution, based on Stanislavski (see appendix B).

Strasberg's training in the Laboratory Theatre had a profound and lasting effect on him. He often recommended Boleslavsky's *Acting: The First Six Lessons*[3] to his students. In 1977 he referred to his notes from Boleslavsky and Ouspenskaya's teachings and was amazed at how detailed and explicit they were. "They [the notes] obviously meant more to me than to anyone else," he said.[4] He learned from them the discoveries by Stanislavski and Vakhtangov about the psychological nature of the actor and he studied the training methods they had developed.

It was typical of Strasberg that he tested what he learned, just as Stanislavski and Vakhtangov had before him. Strasberg observed professional directors and actors and tried the Method for himself. Between 1923 and 1931 he used and tested Stanislavski's discoveries and Vakhtangov's concepts in his acting for the Theatre Guild, in his directing for the Chrystie Street Settlement House and finally as head of actor training and as a director for the Group Theatre, which opened in 1931. As a result, Lee Strasberg, as actor, director and teacher, passed the experience and discipline of Stanislavski's approach, and Vakhtangov's adaptations of that approach, to countless actors, directors and writers. For over fifty years Strasberg developed, tested and constantly adapted Stanislavski's method, as well as his own concepts, for the modern theatre.

After studying with the American Laboratory Theatre, Strasberg began his professional theatrical career in 1924 in the early Theatre Guild productions. He worked in the Theatre Guild's *Green Grow the Lilacs* and with the Lunts in *The Guardsman*.

Founding the Group Theatre

After working in many capacities (including stage manager) for the Theatre Guild, Strasberg founded the Group Theatre in 1931 with Harold Clurman and Cheryl Crawford. In order to develop an ensemble group Strasberg took responsibility for the program of actor training. The *Encyclopaedia Britannica* states that he coached the actors in the principles of naturalistic acting formulated by Stanislavski.[5] Through the Group Theatre Strasberg helped develop actors, directors and playwrights, including Luther Adler, Stella Adler, Maxwell Anderson, Morris Carnovsky, Lee J. Cobb, John Garfield, Elia Kazan, Sidney Kingsley, John Howard Lawson, Robert Lewis, Karl Malden, Sanford Meisner, Paula Miller, Clifford Odets, Martin Ritt, Franchot Tone and William Saroyan.

In Robert Hethmon's introduction to *Strasberg at the Actors Studio,* he delineates the Group Theatre's contribution to American theatre:

The Group Theatre made a permanent contribution to our theatrical life.

The author with Elia Kazan on location for *The Arrangement* in Malibu, California. Hull observed Kazan's directing. Photo © Warner Bros.–Seven Arts, Inc. All rights reserved.

They were the first American company fully trained to perform as an ensemble, and as Clurman later wrote of their first production, they "succeeded in fusing the technical elements of their craft with the stuff of their own spiritual and emotional selves. They succeeded in doing this because, aside from their native character and habit, they were prepared by the education of their work together before and during rehearsals." Quite apart from the Group's discovery of fine playwrights and gifted actors, this was its gift to our theatrical tradition—this successful realization of a theatrical art which can be achieved only by a trained ensemble theatre. It introduced to the American theatre a vision of reality and truth in acting and production which has served as a standard of judgement ever since.[6]

The *Encyclopaedia Britannica* claimed that with the launching of the Group Theatre a U.S. director for the first time could enjoy a "continuity of creative purpose among the anarchy and waste of the long-run system."[7] This experiment of developing a permanent ensemble of actors had an important influence on the American theatre, for the Group Theatre led the way in the development of permanent ensemble repertory companies as we know them today.

The Strasberg-directed first production of the Group Theatre, Paul Green's *The House of Connelly,* stirred much excitement in New York.[8]

The production was greeted with mixed reactions but the positive qualities of the acting ensemble were singled out for praise. While Stanislavski had no direct hand in the formation of the Group, his pupils influenced its directors . . . The New York Public was impressed by the high level of performance and the artistic integrity of the actors.[9]

In addition to encouraging Paul Green, the Group Theatre, through its training, gave the playwright Clifford Odets his first opportunity, gave Irwin Shaw his first Broadway success (*The Gentle People*) and brought William Saroyan into the theatre with "the boldly experimental" *My Heart's in the Highlands.*[10]

Tracing the beginning of the Method, Paul Gray wrote of Strasberg's method of training actors for the Group Theatre's productions:

Concentrating on the "actor working on himself" through improvisation, Strasberg put extraordinary emphasis on the creation of "true emotion." He introduced a series of emotional memory exercises designed to stir up or create mood. . . .

. . . Strasberg insisted upon truth and integrity, and he was determined to overcome clichés and to prevent actors from relying on gimmicks and playing to the audience.[11]

Originally, the Method or System were terms used to describe the totality of Stanislavski's ideas. In the *Encyclopaedia Britannica* Strasberg wrote:

> The Method represents a development of his [Stanislavski's] procedures based not only on his writings but also on his actual achievement in his major productions. It includes the work of Vakhtangov, who demonstrated that Stanislavski's ideas apply to the essential problems of the actor in any style and not only the realistic style most often associated with them. The Method became widely known in mid-twentieth century largely through the work in films of such actors as Marlon Brando, Rod Steiger, and Geraldine Page, who had studied at the Actors Studio in New York City. These actors made a powerful impression and showed a remarkable ability to bridge the gap between stage, screen, and television to an extent that aroused excitement and interest in the rest of the world. So strong was the fusion of performer and role that many of the traits of the character were confused with those of the actor, which led to serious misunderstanding. But at mid-twentieth century an American style of acting was being born.[12]

In recent times the Method is a term typically associated with Strasberg's teaching, as described by Sylvie Drake in the *Los Angeles Times* in an article concerning Los Angeles Theater Alliance meetings:

> But the meat and potatoes of the weekend discussions came in the exploration of dramatic acting—the serious stuff that Constantin Stanislavski sought to formulate into a training process early this century and whose process has given rise to numerous interpretations, distortions, deviations and what has also become known as the Lee Strasberg "method" which virtually gripped American theater in the '50's.[13]

The development of an inner technique in acting, to the exclusion of external theatrics, is based on much historical observation beginning with the "modern" theatre of Shakespeare. Strasberg elaborates as follows:

> Modern theatre starts with the Shakespearian theatre. Other influences before it have valuable lessons to teach us. The Greek theatre has had a vital effect on our own. The Oriental theatre and the pre-literary *Commedia dell'arte* offer instructive suggestions. But the Elizabethan theatre or primarily Shakespeare—the master playwright—is still the central pillar of living theatre throughout the world. The rise of the modern theatre is also

the rise of modern acting, to an extent hitherto unsuspected. We are accustomed to quote Hamlet's speech to the players as an abstract universal
statement of what acting is . . . It was not intended as an abstract statement.
It was the fighting speech of a protagonist taking sides vigorously in the rise
of modern acting. . . .

He sees all life in terms of action and character, not as acting and bellow-
ing. . . .

"Suit the action to the word, the word to the action." In other words: do
not act to overawe and excite your audience, but act in order to create for
them the image of truth, of nature of a man, "in gait and accent."[14]

Artistic Director of the Actors Studio

Attempting to carry on the tradition of the Group Theatre, which had
ceased to exist in 1941, Elia Kazan, Cheryl Crawford and Robert Lewis
established the Actors Studio in 1947.[15] Strasberg was teaching at the
American Theatre Wing in the late forties but joined the Actors Studio
in 1949 when Kazan asked him to teach there.

Strasberg was artistic director of the Actors Studio, East and West,[16]
from 1951 until his death in February 1982. He was responsible for the
studio's artistic policies and its units for actors and directors. An actor
became a member of the Actors Studio by auditioning for a committee;
if the actor passed the preliminary audition, he or she then had a final
audition for Lee. If the auditioner did not pass, he was accepted as an
observer or was asked to audition again in a year, after he had grown in
his craft. The rumor was that Geraldine Page auditioned several times
and that the studio goofed when it did not accept numerous talented
actors, like George C. Scott. Lee also approved professional courtesy
observerships, which numerous established artists in the industry as well
as a few professors and Ph.D.'s (including myself) received.[17]

The Actors Studio, East and West, has produced plays continuously
to the present time[18] in its own buildings (*Richard III* in New York, *Old
Times* and *The Caretaker* in Los Angeles and New York as well as other
plays and original works such as *As It Was—And Is* in Los Angeles and
The Secret Thighs of New England Women in New York[19]). The productions are open to the public. The Los Angeles Actors Studio through

Margo Albert's leadership presented a special on Chicano history which later aired on CBS television.

Plays acted and directed by Actors Studio members have been part of the studio's work, East and West. Through critiques Strasberg guided the direction of most of these plays, many of them original. Numerous projects of the Actors Studio have become television or movie productions and/or commercial plays, for example, *The Zoo Story* and *A Hatful of Rain* with Ben Gazzara, Shelley Winters and Tony Franciosa.[20]

In the introduction to *Famous American Plays of the 1950's* Strasberg relates the Actors Studio involvement with *A Hatful of Rain*.

> Michael Gazzo's *Hatful of Rain* grew out of a project started at the Actors Studio. The ideas of the play are in no way representative of the studio, but the process by which the play was helped into being is. The close interrelation between the playwright, director, and actors served to define characters and events and to give each moment the character of life. This was especially useful in creating a vividness of dialogue and a relation between word, gesture, and behavior which contributed enormously to the success of the play and its distinguishing characteristic.[21]

Bruce Dern expresses the meaning of the Actors Studio when he says, "It meant hope to me in all those early years as an actor. The studio gave me a feeling of growth and security that I never felt commercially. It gave me a place to belong, and still gives me the feeling I'm in the struggle constantly to be an artist."[22]

Founding the Lee Strasberg Theatre Institute

Similar projects "helping plays into being" were nurtured at the Lee Strasberg Theatre Institute in New York City and Los Angeles. Since 1969, when the institute was founded in New York and Los Angeles, until Strasberg's death, his training was open to any interested theatre person. Work and membership in the Actors Studio is by selection, but the founding of the institute provided an opportunity for any actor or director to gain firsthand knowledge of the fundamental concepts of the Strasberg work.[23] According to Strasberg, professionals and nonprofessionals enrolled in the institute classes, workshops and seminars were pushed toward the development of their art and themselves through class activity, exercises, scene work, demonstration, commentary and discussion. Both the institute and the studio continually presented plays free for the public.[24] Strasberg managed to spend considerable time on both coasts with the Actors Studio and the Lee Strasberg Theatre Institute in his efforts to guide the development of American theatre, continually nurturing and honing the talent of actors, directors and writers.

Basis of the Method

Strasberg has always explained that the Method is not based on isolated ideas that he developed himself. Rather, it is a summation of the best that has been achieved worldwide on the professional level. Strasberg claimed that both he and Stanislavski used in their training what great actors had achieved, sometimes without being aware of it. Stanislavski and Strasberg discovered what actors had already done through the unconscious use of memory. The Method consists of procedures to help find the road to creativity, to allow the actor to work creatively rather than mechanically. Strasberg always stressed that he followed in the footsteps of Stanislavski and Vakhtangov. The Method is thus not Strasberg's private achievement but the achievement of great actors put into a form usable by all interested actors.[25]

Strasberg emphasized that the Method is a procedure, not a series of rules to be applied specifically.[26] He believed that what was new about his approach is basic to understanding acting of any kind: the actor deals with living material. "Therefore, the problem of training the actor or working with the actor derives not from the greater problem of dealing with the play but from the problem of dealing with [the actor's] own instrument."[27] Strasberg explained that the actor's "instrument" is his own body and impulses; the actor must be able to make this instrument do what his mind conceives.

This new understanding of the basics of acting was only possible because of advances in the fields of medicine and psychology. Strasberg clarified the link with psychology:

> . . . until modern psychology came into practice, we really could not understand why the actor had [certain] problems . . . When the inspiration was not there, the best thing [he] could do was to learn voice, speech, and to

train the body. These elements are not unimportant, but these elements train only the external elements of the actor . . . not the talent of the actor. . . . Use of memory is essential to understanding the entire process that goes into acting. In acting everything is done unconsciously as a process of memory. The important thing in Stanislavski and our approach is that we point to the fact that there is a third kind of memory which we all are aware of and yet which we have not recognized. That may be called affective memory, which means memory of sensation, memory of emotion. . . . This is, by the way, what is new . . . because otherwise, experiencing on the stage cannot be done night after night . . . without an inner technique, which previously was left up in the air when the actor did not stimulate the emotions.[28]

Concluding the interview Strasberg asserted again, "Even though I stress the newness of the knowledge, the facts are not new."[29] Great actors, insofar as they achieve good results on the stage, are unconsciously using the elements Stanislavski, Strasberg and others have tried to define.[30]

Part 2
Actor Training

1 Relaxation

Value of Relaxation

The principle of relaxation is at the heart of the Strasberg method of teaching acting. Strasberg considered the emphasis on relaxation one of Stanislavski's most important discoveries and made it the foundation of his own approach. He termed relaxation one of "the elements basic to all acting in any period and in any kind of play."

Physiologists tell us that when we are awake, all of our muscles possess a constant small amount of contraction, which is called *tone*. In addition to basic tonic contraction, we are all subject to increased contraction of certain groups of muscles, even when we are not doing anything in particular. This excessive muscle contraction while we appear to be at rest is appropriately referred to as *tension*. Tension may be caused by mental apprehension (such as fear of harm or stage fright), or it may simply be habitual (produced by habitual ways of walking, talking or sitting). Tension is the occupational disease of the actor; it stands between him and the character he hopes to create onstage. Tension blocks and distorts thought, emotion and action, a point Strasberg illustrated with the following story:

> If you give an individual an easy problem, one that is not simple but that he can solve—something like 12 × 13—an ordinary person has to take a little time to do it, but he will usually come up with the answer. If you ask the same person to pick up a piano—something that definitely tenses him— and you give him the same problem, no thought can permeate his mind. He'll have to drop the piano in order to answer you. In order to act, the actor must relax.[1]

Of course actors are not the only performers who must learn relaxation. Have you ever watched Olympic athletes prepare for events that require a supreme effort? They move about, shaking their arms and legs loosely to get the relaxation necessary to let them concentrate on the action to come.

Many problems in acting disappear when the actor learns to relax.

When he reduces muscular tension, his technique is not evident and his thinking and emotions come through to the audience. Most talented actors in the past have found their own relaxation techniques, but years of experience were sometimes necessary to accomplish this. Now relaxation can be learned through exercise and practice, and once learned the technique becomes more than just a classroom exercise. Relaxation is a skill that must be practiced before any other work can begin, whether in the classroom, in rehearsal or in preparation for performance onstage or before the camera.

Teacher Guidance

Initially, in my acting class, the student is asked to take a seat and assume a position that he might take on a bus or train when he wished to sleep. The student is told to let his body go limp—"flop like a rag doll"—an instruction I have also used with children. The student should find a position in which he could go to sleep if he had to, but he should not lose control and actually sleep. After achieving this initial limpness, the actor begins to move groups of muscles in order to identify tension and then relieve it. If the student slips in the chair, he adjusts and squirms, never letting himself fall.

The instructor must actively assist class members with commentary as well as with physical tests for relaxation and trouble spots. The instructor may lift a limb to feel if it is tense or to see if it will drop and be limp when released, or the instructor might move the student's head into various positions, feeling for unsuspected muscle tension. The instructor may feel tenseness or see tenseness in the position of an arm or leg. He can then tell the student to recognize the tension by moving that part of the body in a wide circular arc from the large muscles of the shoulder or hip to achieve relaxation of the connecting part.

If tension is visible in other areas of the body, such as the fingers, the instructor simply advises the student to move or shake the fingers. He may also guide the actor to breathe deeply, stretch his arms out from the shoulders, move the arm and fingers, then move the neck and head. The instructor will pay close attention to the student's face and mouth, urging him to relax these muscles if they are tight. If there is tension in

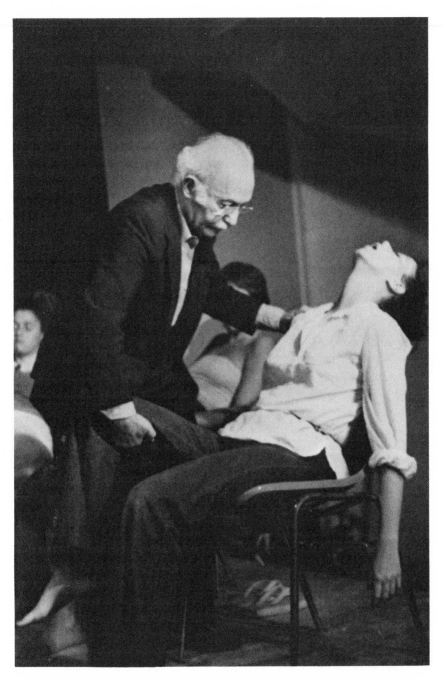

Strasberg checking a student's relaxation. Photo by Jonathan K. Rout.

the tongue, the instructor's thumb under the chin can help relax it at the time the instructor physically checks the student.

Tension resulting from habit is perhaps the most difficult to overcome, for it is the most difficult for the student to recognize. Certain casual body postures that have become habitual through the years may have elements of tension that the actor has never noticed. The student must beware of merely "getting comfortable." "Comfort" in fact can be diametrically opposed to relaxation, because in getting comfortable one tends to return to habitual body attitudes that can be restrictive rather than relaxing. Strasberg himself believed that "comfort is habit," so he often had students sit in straight-backed chairs while practicing relaxation in order to prevent the assumption of a "comfortable" attitude. At the same time Strasberg and other instructors also admonished students to move: "Do not remain in a habitual parallel position. Wiggle and move about, so you are sometimes shaped like a pretzel."

A competent instructor is invaluable to a student learning relaxation, particularly because the instructor can point out areas of tension that the actor had not known about. Sometimes the results are most unexpected. One girl announced triumphantly, "I have to leave the class because I'm pregnant. . . . I went to many doctors trying to get pregnant and couldn't. Then, with the acting relaxation techniques practiced every day, I became able to become pregnant."

If the student is unable to release tension—displaying uncontrolled emotion, making choking sounds or unable to make any sounds at all— the instructor may tell him to make noises to relieve tension or emotion while simultaneously moving.[2] The teacher can give precise commands, such as: "Take a breath with the lungs—hold it and now make a sound. Put your arms out level from the shoulders." Stretching the arms out allows some students to relax, and that can help them make the sound. After being told to stretch his arms out to the side, the actor is again guided: "Take another deep breath and make even and easy noises with good, relaxed in and out breathing. Let the sound vibrate from the lungs,[3] not from the throat, as the throat will tense if you use it. So keep the throat open, then the sensation will flow with ease and will also release the tension deep down."[4] To check a student an instructor may pat him just below the chest or hold his hand on the student's diaphragm while he holds the other hand on the student's back. Sustained, even and easy low-pitched sounds that cause the entire chest to resonate are especially effective. At a later stage in training the instructor may ask the student to coordinate the sound with feelings. If the student answers, "I'm not feeling much" or "I'm bored," then he can be told to make a sound that is bored. The student by himself, however, does not try to connect the sound to emotion. Often it just happens.

When an unforced sound does not relieve the actor's tension or emotion, then he is permitted to make full, explosive, sharp, abrupt sounds supported by deep breaths. If the sound is choked, the actor could be asked to make one or more abrupt sounds. "On the one hand the actor commits himself, and on the other hand he can show he's in control." Nevertheless, Strasberg stressed that the sound should usually be even and easy.

Another valuable relaxation tool is speaking aloud the mind's commands to the body. The student is encouraged in class or before rehearsal to verbalize his commands to his muscles. Obviously, such verbalization techniques cannot be used during performances.[5] By that time, the actor must have learned to achieve relaxation without making sounds or moving. The actor's goal is to will and control relaxation when needed so that in performance he achieves physical relaxation along with heightened energy and concentration.

The Use of Movement to Aid Relaxation

Movement does not achieve relaxation; rather, it draws attention to what must be done. When using motion to pinpoint tense areas that need relaxation, the instructor prescribes motions that are unconventional, "larger than life." This helps prevent the student from falling back into habitual motions that fail to produce the desired relaxation. Individuals trained in dance may be at a disadvantage here, for they are accustomed to controlled and graceful dance motions and may have trouble making the cruder movement desired in relaxation training.

To eliminate movement bound by habit, the student is instructed to extend his arm(s) straight from the shoulders or his leg straight from the hip, after which, sitting or standing, he may either move the limb in a wide circular motion or let it collapse limply in place. He turns his body to the right or left side when he stretches out the leg of that particular side. This too is to break "the habitual parallel position," face front.

Another technique is to stretch the limb in slow motion toward the sky and then let it go limp.[6] The student can then concentrate on an entire muscle group thus isolated and command it to relax—either from hip to toes or from shoulder to fingers. While commanding a certain area to relax, the student should move other areas of the body. For when an individual moves one part of his body, he guards against tensing another. The instructor also urges the student to check relaxation through movement while doing class sensory exercises. Through such training the actor learns where to relax and develops the control to achieve it.

Special Tension Areas

Strasberg identified four areas of the body that are important in achieving relaxation. He argued that when the four basic mental areas are relaxed the rest of the body is ready to relax.

The first of these areas is the brow and the muscles at the temples, where tense people often press their fingertips in times of stress. Of course, the actor must learn to relax this area without the use of his fingers for he cannot interrupt an important scene to rub his temples! When relaxation comes to this area, people often speak of feeling a great weight lifted.

The second important area is the bridge of the nose leading into the eyes. The instructor guides the student: "Let the eyelids droop slowly until they close" or "Let all the energy ooze out of the eyelids." Here, too, the actor may actually feel a weight lifted when he lets his eyelids close in this manner.

The third area includes the muscles along the side of the nose which lead into the mouth and chin. These are some of the most active muscles in the body and a great deal of tension may build up here. Our use of the muscles around the mouth in such actions as speaking, eating or kissing results in habitual patterns that interfere with relaxation. The student is first encouraged to move his mouth in unaccustomed ways: perhaps grimacing, yawning so widely that it seems grotesque, making a big grin like a jack-o'-lantern or moving the mouth first to one side as far as possible and then to the other side. He should feel the pulling of facial muscles and then let them relax. Such means are often sufficient to produce relaxation; the mouth should be relaxed or numb, as it would be if the person were drunk and not concerned with verbal coherence. The jaw should be slack. The student is told to simultaneously relax all his facial muscles.

The fourth area is behind the neck and down the back. Tension often builds up in the thick muscles of the neck and manifests itself by reduced mobility of the head. Sometimes tension of the chin and tongue also comes from the back of the neck. If the neck is tense, the instructor can feel this directly or can detect resistance when he attempts to move the student's head. When the student's neck is relaxed, the instructor will be able to move the head easily in a circular motion in any direction. The student may work on neck relaxation by letting his head fall back on the chair, by holding his head toward the tense side of the neck, by moving his head in a circle both ways or by letting it drop on his chest. The best approach, however, is to rest the back of the neck against the top of the chair, move the head around in a circular fashion and then let the neck relax.

Recently I have incorporated the following advice into my teaching:

> An overall image [useful] during sensory exercise work might be that the pelvis is a foundation into which is set a flexible fishing pole (spine) with a melon (head) impaled on top of it. Letting the head fall forward momentarily, as a relaxation device to break tension, is very beneficial but remaining in that forward position too long is bad for a number of reasons: it could promote more tension, pinching the nerves that feed into the spinal cord and inhibiting respiration or it can induce psychological withdrawal. An upright posture during exercise work will enhance concentration, respiration and the optimum use of the nervous system. Think of the head as growing out of the spine, hold it up straight by balancing it when doing an exercise (e.g., the drink).[7]

Too many students try to do an entire exercise with their heads thrust forward rather than balanced in an upright position. If not corrected in exercise work, this lifetime habit can carry over into performance where some actors habitually thrust their heads and shoulders forward.

Another area deserving special attention is the back,[8] which must move or float freely. Its tension can be tested while the student is sitting or standing. If the student stands, he holds his arms out in front of him or to the side. The teacher may touch the lower back muscles, then move up the back. Touching these muscles allows the instructor to aid the student to determine which muscles are tense and often releases emotion and tension.

Arched shoulders are evidence of back and neck tension. Whether the individual is standing or sitting, the shoulders should not be held tensely because that can also result in back or neck tension. To relax the shoulders, raise them as high as possible to the ears and rotate them backward and downward, repeating five times slowly; then repeat the procedure, rotating them forward and downward five times. Some students relax this area better if the instructor manually guides the rotation of the shoulders, with a backward and forward motion like kneading dough.[9]

Another technique that promotes muscle relaxation is to tense and then relax each muscle of each section of the body. This exercise can be done in class or at home (in bed, for instance). Begin with the toes and work progressively up the body, alternating from the left to the right side. If this exercise is done while standing, the student can stretch up to the sky and/or shake his hands. Sometimes he is told to let all the energy go out the fingertips. Applying the above technique, the actor becomes aware of the muscles that are tenser than others and he develops area control leading to full body relaxation.

Relaxation in Preparation and Performance

As the student progresses through his training, through exercises in concentration and sense memory[10] and in rehearsal, he always begins his work with relaxation. And relaxation should always begin preparation for performance. Shelley Winters has told how she often began relaxing at home at 3 P.M., especially before an evening performance when she was younger, while at other times she willed the relaxation just before she entered a scene.[11]

Relaxation is just as important in preparing for a tense or highly emotional scene as for a quiet, peaceful one. A skilled actor will be full of emotion inside while at the same time commanding outer ease. If an actor works himself up only physically for an emotional entrance, the scene is usually tense and forced. It is better to do psychological or emotional preparation but remain completely relaxed muscularly. A trained actor realizes that muscular tension is not the same thing as intensity.

Relaxation is the tool that enables the actor to make the fullest use of his instrument—himself. Strasberg illustrated while demonstrating relaxation:

> By training relaxation an actor can achieve control over himself, so he can repeat it later on. When an actor relaxes, sometimes things that are there come through (e.g., when does wine pour? When you open the cork). There's a definite relation between physical [relaxation], mental and emotional. If an actor can control physical aspects, then he has the key to control the mental and emotional . . .
>
> How does one use the relaxation process on a set? All you do are a few notes, like a violinist, and then you are ready to play. Whatever you can do is a result of training. An actor can improv at home by himself, so when he comes on the set, he can do it. Things we train to do are meant to work at the moment of production, so you can do for yourself the work that has to be done. . . . There are times you can sit in a chair and no one will know you are doing relaxation. . . . Your training has to be long enough and go far enough to give you control over yourself. There has to be daily work over a period of four years—three years can maybe give the groundwork. [12]

I emphasized that verbalization and movement cannot be used as aids to relaxation when the actor is actually performing. Ultimately, the actor must learn to relax and concentrate without such aids, even under the pressures of production. Through constant practice in relaxing, actors develop a kind of internal monitor that instantly recognizes abnormal tension during performance and automatically issues the command to relax muscle groups not actually being used.

Strasberg compared tension to a violin that is out of tune or not played properly—"one gets screeching."[13] He further maintained that after an actor had achieved relaxation, he often displayed real talent for the first time in a full and startling manner:

> The actor becomes completely responsive. His instrument gives forth a new depth of resonance. Emotion that has habitually been held back suddenly gushes forth. The actor becomes real—not merely simple or natural. He becomes fully concentrated. He unveils totally unsuspected aspects and elements of himself but with such a degree of ease and authority that he seems

literally to have taken off a mask, to have emerged from a disguise that previously had smothered his true personality. Yet all he did was relax.[14]

Is it any wonder that we teachers constantly urge students to relax, repeating the command over and over again? Luther Adler, who was in the Group Theatre when Strasberg was head of actor training, met Strasberg on the street several years later and told him a wonderful story: It seems Adler dreamed that he had died, and when he approached the pearly gates, there was Lee Strasberg, who slowly raised Adler's arm and said . . ."Too tense."[15]

2 Concentration

Concentration is the second element in the Stanislavski triad relaxation/concentration/sense of truth. Stanislavski felt that in order to create a sense of reality on the stage the actor must learn to treat scenery and other objects on the stage as if they were real, even though most are not. Furthermore, Stanislavski believed that the actor must be capable of creating imaginary objects and treating them as if they too were real. He must be able to look out a stage window or up into a stage tree and visualize a real object. The actor accomplishes this by means of concentration.

Concentration is the process of focusing one's mind on an object or objects. The term *object* means anything an actor can focus on; this can be a real object, an object the actor remembers, a situation or sensation the actor recalls from his own experience or even a totally imaginary idea. Real objects such as lamps, chairs, pictures or garments may be used as objects of concentration. Or the actor may choose his remembrance of such things as his object of concentration. Sensations such as heat, cold, sound or odor can also be reexperienced and used as objects of concentration. This process is called *sense memory*.[1]

Relaxation is an important prelude to concentration, for it releases muscle tension and allows the mind to focus on the object of concentration. At the same time, concentration helps the actor develop and maintain relaxation by preventing extraneous thoughts that produce muscle tension. Relaxation and concentration thus support one another; the two processes must go hand in hand.

Many exercises are useful in developing the ability to concentrate. The beginner actually starts during his earliest relaxation practice; the teacher encourages the student to concentrate on areas of his body that appear tense and to move these parts and then relax them. The student is also taught to concentrate successively on the important relaxation areas as previously described.

A good class exercise that demonstrates what happens when an actor concentrates specifically is to ask several new students to go onstage or to the front of the room so they may be observed as actors. Almost invariably the students wander about aimlessly or try to "indicate" their acting. Then the teacher asks them to concentrate on something specific (for example, a favorite book, the last ten movies recently seen: the plots, who was acting). Almost immediately, the class members perceive that the "actors" become believable as persons when they have something on which to concentrate.[2]

Sight and sound exercises, especially in youth classes, can be effective in teaching concentration. In one sound exercise, after preliminary relaxation, the student is asked to concentrate for five minutes or more on the sounds he hears around himself and to distinguish whether they originate in the classroom, in the hall or outside the building. He then relates all the sounds he heard and their location. In a sight exercise an object, such as a candy wrapper or matchbox, is placed in front of the student, along with a pencil and paper. After preliminary relaxation, he is asked to concentrate on the object, carefully observing its size, shape, color, texture, borders, odor or other characteristics; then he is either asked to put the object aside and draw it or to close his eyes and to recreate the reality of the object's appearance, describing it from memory. When asked to place the object next to his drawing or to open his eyes again to concentrate on the real object, the student is usually surprised at the number of details he missed on his first observation. Continued practice along these lines serves to sharpen the student's awareness and makes it possible for him to recall objects and situations so vividly that he can better create a sense of truth as an actor.

On one occasion in the classroom a woman insisted she could recreate perfectly a painting hanging in her home; she loved it and had looked at it every day for years. She was told she could describe it in class if she would then go home, concentrate on it fully as she had now been taught and report back any details omitted from her description. She was amazed to find that she had overlooked many of its colors, forms and textures. The student can be guided to practice such simple sight and sound exercises at home, filling his memory bank with images that can be called up and used in the future as the need dictates.

The student begins to improve concentration and sense memory by focusing on sensations (see part 2, chapter 4). He will be asked to practice sensory exercises at home with a cup or glass filled with liquid. In class, as he tries to recreate the sensations through imaginary stimuli, he may be questioned: "How does the outside of the cup feel?" "What is inside the cup?" "Is it hot?" "Do you feel the heat entering your grasping fingers?" As he raises the cup: "Do you feel heat on your lips?" "Do you feel the steam against your face and in your nose and eyes?" For a first sensory concentration exercise, liquids such as tea, coffee, tomato juice or orange juice may be used, whether hot or cold, sweet or sour.

Improvisation is a valuable technique for developing concentration. Classes are broken up into pairs, and each pair of students is asked to prepare a sketchy beginning, middle and occasionally an ending of an improvisation, concentrating on one object or objective. The object used is generally a physical activity or a sensory experience like seeing a ship, smelling a flower, hearing waves or music or eating a specific food. The student is instructed to concentrate on the assigned object as the improvisation begins, but when the partner responds he or she must concentrate also on thoughts and feelings about the partner. Thus, the two partners must react both to the assigned or chosen object and to each other, concentrating on both at the same time. After the conclusion of the improvisation, the teacher's critique focuses on how well concentration was maintained. The student may be asked: "Did your mind wander?" "Did you find yourself thinking about how the scene looked to someone else?" "Did you find yourself thinking about what you were going to say or do next?" Obviously, if the student responds affirmatively to any of these questions, he is losing concentration. Sometimes this lapse is so considerable that the student cannot continue the scene, in which case the teacher must stop the improvisation and explain what has happened. Extensive practice at improvisation is especially valuable to the stage performer, who must often improvise to get a scene back "on track" when things go wrong or a memory lapse occurs onstage.

Another technique to improve the actor's concentration is the narrative monologue (see glossary and part 2, chapter 9). In the narrative monologue the actor speaks out his character's thoughts in addition to speaking his own lines. He speaks out between the lines as well as sometimes during his partner's lines. This rehearsal procedure helps the actor think and behave in a logical way for the character. An actor should be able to focus his thoughts, eliminating those that do not pertain. Shelley Winters accomplishes this objective by selecting specific thoughts for her character and writing them in the margins of her script (always realizing that some thoughts will be changed according to what occurs in individual performances).

Although the concentration exercises described above and in chapter 4 are planned and progressive, the teacher must continually adapt assignments to the rate of progress and the special needs of each student.

The importance of observing minute detail in objects can hardly be overemphasized. In Albee's play *The Zoo Story,* for example, one of the actors looks at and reads from a street sign that is some distance away. On one occasion during the rehearsal I noted that the actor involved was only glancing toward the sign in a general way and was not very convincing in appearing to read the sign. He was asked to pick a specific spot for the sign and to concentrate on visualizing a sign he had seen and known. He was told not just to see a mark on the wall or a spot in the auditorium but to "see" a street sign he had known and recreate the reality of that sign. His first response was, "I know what a sign looks like and what I should see." But I told him, "No, that isn't real enough. You must decide what kind of post the sign is on, how it is made, what color it is, what the printing looks like and so on so that you see a real object, not just a vague generalization in your mind's eye. It is not true concentration to merely define the sign in your mind; you must believe in it and see it so accurately that you are convinced you see a real street sign." As Strasberg said, "The object and the concentration that results from attention to the object are the basic building blocks from which the actor works. The objects on which the actor concentrates . . . produce a sense of belief and of faith and involvement in what he is doing, and this in turn leads to unconscious experience and behavior."[3]

Concentration on concrete objects will usually produce reliable results. Strasberg commented that there is "more reliability in a real object than in a fantasy object." But when the object itself is not available the actor must create one as close as possible to the real thing. This makes it necessary for the well-trained actor to have numerous objects available in his memory. Strasberg told student actors, "Various kinds of objects . . . for concentration are needed only because you cannot depend on one magic key to unlock every scene." And what works for one actor may not work for another! Each actor must develop his own concentration techniques. A simple imaginary physical or sensory object may work at one place in a role while a more complicated nonmaterial object may be needed at another place. The actor should practice with the object as part of his homework until he gets consistent and reliable results. The actor must experiment, testing the degree to which focusing on an object works. (This technique avoids the vague or inflated approach to a scene, which often merely serves to confuse the actor.) The actor might also try a series of objects until he finds the sequence that produces the desired results.

As Strasberg told us: "All of our work leads to what to put concentration on: during relaxation exercises, sensory exercises, onstage or before the camera—whatever the commitment is."

3 Sense Memory

What Is Sense Memory?

Sense memory is reliving sensations that were experienced through the five senses. Strasberg stressed the term *reliving*, not just remembering, explaining that the difference is between knowing something and truly recreating it. That difference, between mental activity—remembering—and reliving the experience, Strasberg explained, was not made up by Stanislavski or his modern interpreters but is substantiated by psychology (see appendix C).[1]

How to Practice Sensory Exercises

Practicing beginning sensory memory exercises can be compared to memorizing a poem. An English student will hold a copy of the poem and read the words over and over, trying to remember, hiding the words and referring to the printed page to check his remembrance. The actor follows the same procedure with sense memory. He concentrates on the actual object (for example, drinking from a glass or cup, putting on shoes and stockings, combing the hair, putting on makeup or shaving) and then tests himself by putting the object aside to see whether he can recapture the experience without actually using the object. When the actor repeats the action by going back to the real object, he concentrates on those sensory aspects that did not work or were not full for him.

"Work with objects and sense memory are as fundamental to [an actor's] art as are daily finger exercises to a pianist,"[2] Strasberg wrote. In beginning sensory work the instructor can demonstrate to students how work with actual physical objects contributes to faster sensory growth. Actors who practice with real objects at home usually progress faster in recreating their sensations, and this is evident to their classmates.

The actor should never strive for physical reactions. He should just let reactions happen. The actor never worries about the end result. He uses his will and effort to keep his concentration on the proper object and lets results happen. If other sensations not connected with the object come into play, the actor lets them happen but does not let them carry him away from the object of concentration. Strasberg told one class, "An actor without control in exercises is like a car that veers off without [anyone's] steering."[3]

Why a Sequence to Exercises

Method acting courses teach specific exercises to stimulate the actor's imagination and to instill the proper procedure to unleash the actor's creativity. The first exercises I assign are habitual daily activities involving external sensory experiences. Strasberg stated that practicing daily activities, such as drinking a breakfast drink, getting dressed, looking in the mirror, applying makeup or shaving, lead to the creation of sensory reality. "People are more aware of things close to their bodies," Strasberg noted. The sequence of exercises is important (see below, chapter 4),[4] but the instructor may introduce minor variations to suit individual problems. Exercises done in class are assigned by the instructor. Students are not assigned exercises in combinations (see chapter 4) until they get two single exercises working simultaneously. The exercise work gradually increases in complexity. If at any stage the instructor sees the actor unable to handle the number of sensory realities assigned, he or she should take the actor back to a smaller number of sensory exercises or even to a single exercise.

In class a student is never allowed to abandon the assigned exercise to try another, since flitting from one exercise to another involves loss of concentration. Everything taught is cumulative. The student adds each new object to those already working. This build-up is important to remember when the work involves adding a second sense memory to an original and then progressing to threes, fours, fives and more. Often an actor must concentrate on several elements at the same time in exercise work, as when he is performing. The sensory and affective memory exercises are to prepare the actor for times during performance when he has more than one object of concentration.

In the beginning exercises the student is cautioned not to try to imitate what he does literally, such as gulping the morning drink. Nor should he make a conscious effort to convey his reactions to the class. Rather, the actor's concentration should be focused on recapturing the physical sensations generated and the muscular efforts involved in a simple daily activity. The student is encouraged to investigate and explore thoroughly a simple object that he has dealt with many times in his daily routine. Working with such a common, objective and unemotional object develops the actor's imagination so that he can deal with far more complex and difficult realities, such as those he ordinarily will face onstage. The beginning exercises, as well as later ones, develop the actor's imagination, but they also test whether he can create emotional and other realities.

The sense memory innate in every human being leads to strong responses from some students but requires much practice and work from others. Initial exercises therefore use objects that have a material existence in order to develop the actor's awareness. This will ultimately lead to greater awareness in memory and more responsive senses. Strasberg explained:

> The senses are thus trained to remember more and to remember more vividly. But if the actor tries to bypass the work with material objects and to proceed immediately to objects such as pain, which involve only memory, he will find that the sense memory is not really trained.[5]

Real-life Sensory Memory

Real-life sense memory can be compared to stage sense memory. Sense memory is experienced in life when an individual comes to a particular place where he experienced a sensation or emotion and reexperiences the original feelings. A stimulus sets off the reaction, such as blushing, growing angry, becoming depressed or happy. Onstage, real-life reactions and behavior must be created in response to imaginary stimuli. Sensory exercise work develops this skill. Strasberg wrote in *Producing the Play*:

> Acting, technically speaking . . . from a purely craft point of view, is the ability to respond to imaginary stimuli. We expect of the actor not that he do something unusual but that he react as he himself would if he were the character. . . . Therefore, the actor's real problem is not concerned with his

reactions, but rather consists in training himself to make these imaginary objects or stimuli real to himself, as they would be in life, so they will awaken the proper sensory, emotional or motor response.[6]

Also in *Producing the Play* Strasberg emphasized the role of the senses:

> You can directly control the functioning of your mental and muscular energy, but there is little you can do with your senses and emotions in life. Yet our senses are our "windows to the external world." Not only is it through them that we acquire our actual (not verbal or mental) knowledge of the world, but it is through them that we react to our environment.[7]

What Is Good Acting?

Strasberg answered this question in 1977 in a lecture on truthfulness in acting and the training methods that produce that quality: "The use of affective and sense memory is the discovery of Constantin Stanislavski, and it is the cornerstone of the modern method of training the actor."[8] In the lecture he elaborated:

> The thing that makes the difference [in truthful acting] is the conscious or unconscious use of sense memory. Stanislavski observed and saw actors use it and some who did not. The first thing Stanislavski discovered was the working of the unconscious—the way in which an actor's activity stimulates experience, and how the actor has to create a foundation for what he has to be concerned with onstage. If you taste an orange and a lemon, you will know the difference better than I can explain. The same is true in acting. You will know if you experience the reality. . . . Acting deals not with remembering, but with experience. The greatest thing when you see an actor performing is to think, "That's the way it is" and recognize the reality of it. An actor creates onstage experience living through reality. What Stanislavski emphasized was not making believe or imitating something, and not indicating, but the ability to experience.[9]

Sense-Memory Substitution for Character Situations and Real Sensations

Most teachers do not advocate living every situation in life that might have to be created on stage. Actors are encouraged to substitute their own truth for what is needed when performing. Actors would be burned-out, neurotic messes if they tried to live what must be portrayed.

One actress found an ingenious method for re-creating the role of the prostitute junkie in *Catcher in the Rye*. During the scene when the prostitute comes to the boy's room, she continually wiped her eyes and sniffed her nose. After the scene Strasberg told her he had really believed she was hooked on drugs and asked her what she had used. "The common cold," she answered. Her nose and eyes had really been running. Strasberg considered that was all that she needed to prepare for and to use in the scene in order to portray the drug aspect of the role. Of course, other elements were used in working on the character. The point is that when playing similar roles the actress had trained herself to use the same sense memory. She also used this technique to create a prostitute junkie role for the pilot of "Police Story" and for other film and stage work. Strasberg always encouraged his students to do homework so that each could develop a repertoire of what worked sensorily and emotionally for himself or herself.

Simple examples of creating substitute sensations while performing include eating mashed potatoes but creating the reality of ice cream; drinking colored tea but creating the reality of whiskey—the smell, taste, burning in the throat; taking a sugar pill but creating the taste, smell and subsequent pains in the stomach of poison; or handling glass jewelry as if holding precious stones and not worthless junk. Boleslavsky's famous example of a substitute sensation is that of an irritating mosquito driving an individual frantic. The actor substitutes his familiar desire to kill a mosquito for the scenic motivation to kill a person or commit a crime of passion. The actor uses his imagination as he builds on his own sense of truth—what he knows (his rage to kill a mosquito). The reality of many acts, such as dying or murder, can never be created onstage but a sense of their actually taking place is imparted to the audience by the actor's substitution of realities from his own life. He imaginatively uses his mental, physical, sensory and emotional resources.

Sense Memory and Concentration

Concentration combined with effective sense memory generates truthfulness and reality in performance. Without concentration the actor is unable to focus on his task and maximize his sense memory. "Lack of concentration," Strasberg stated, "causes stage fright." Strasberg developed a battery of sense memory and other exercises to enable the actor to enrich his own awareness of life around him, to provide a source for his stage life and to increase his powers of concentration.

Strasberg, his peers and followers all embraced sense memory exercises to stimulate an actor's imagination in order to re-create sensations and enhance creativity. The actor explores his reactions and impulses in order to strengthen the existing senses so they can be called on whenever necessary for the requirements of a character, place, time or event. Training in sensory exercises involves learning how to relate the sensory exercises to activities, words and outside influences without showing the sensory work. "You don't wear a tailor-made suit inside out, showing the work. You wear the seams on the other side. This is like sensory work—you don't show it."[10] In other words, after practicing sensory exercises a trained actor knows what buttons to push, so the desired sensation is just there!

An actor's practice of sense memory exercises, whether at home, in class or in rehearsal, should include a search for the proper objects and means to concentrate on. After finding the proper objects, the actor should practice diligently so that the impulses and imaginary stimuli become real to him.

When an actor creates an imaginary object, he gets more than that object. He gets his response to the object, so he has in effect created a particular aspect of himself. When the actor creates the object's reality, he knows he has succeeded if he is visualizing the object and feeling the sensations. The body will perceive the object as real because the person gets the same sensations from the physical object. In acting, the source is imaginary but the responses are real. That is what creates a belief or sense of truth in the actor. He knows the responses are real, and that he created them, so he can believe in his own truthfulness. When an actor develops a belief in himself through his re-creation of sensory reality, then he can begin to create a truthful, believable life for the character he is portraying.

Exercise work enhances scene work. Even one truthful sensation at the beginning of the scene can add to the believability of the whole effort. Lee himself quipped, "A little bit of real coffee is worth a ton of watered down." One truthful sensation can lead to the creation of others so that new elements are added with credibility.[11]

The actor's fundamental training begins with work on himself—with the exercise of his will, concentration and sensory response. He learns to think, to behave and to experience. Exercise work leads the student from a purely mental understanding to the total mental, physical and emotional experience of which he is capable. All of the relaxation, concentration, sensory, affective memory and improvisation work leads to an ability to design the sequence of an entire scene or play, and portray a believable, truthful character.

The sense memory techniques of the Strasberg Method are difficult enough to frighten even veteran professionals. Lee once twitted Altovise Davis, who was enrolling in Strasberg's classes for the third year, "You'll be off making another movie soon and will not be in class long, but you can send Sammy in your place." Altovise responded, "Sammy says he would be scared to death to be in your acting class. He wouldn't know what to do." Later Altovise told my class that Sammy had observed her patience and perseverance in practicing the exercises but feared he would not be able to do them. Altovise Davis realized that practicing the exercises allows the actor to develop his sense of seeing, touching, hearing, smelling and tasting, a lifetime process that provides any actor with ever-expanding resources.

4   Sequence and Description of Sensory Exercises

Sequence of Basic Sensory Exercises

The following sequence of sensory exercises[1] was developed by Lee Strasberg after his training with Richard Boleslavsky and presents an overall view of the sensory exercise work as taught in my classes. Descriptions of specific exercises, suggestions of how to work on the exercises and sample guidance from instructors follow the listing. The exercises with asterisks are designed to be assigned in order. Those without asterisks may be assigned according to the individual student's needs. Some exercises may also be omitted, depending on the progress of the student and the discretion of the instructor.

*1. *Breakfast drink*	The student creates his usual breakfast drink (commonly orange juice or coffee). All of the objects in the exercises are created imaginarily.
*2. *Mirror*	The student creates a common mirror activity, such as shaving or putting on makeup. The goal is an awareness of self. The instructor notes if the student has an introverted subjective quality or an objective awareness of self.
3. *Putting on and taking off shoes and socks*	The student creates putting on and taking off shoes and socks. He is using well-defined objects to recapture the stimuli and muscular effort involved in this simple habitual act.
4. *Getting undressed*	The student creates putting on and taking off underclothes.
5. *Three pieces of material*	The student creates the touch of three pieces of cloth of differing texture.

*6. *Sunshine*   The student creates the feeling of
                                  exposure to the sun. The instructor will
                                  be able to see if the senses are working
                                  when the student is not reproducing a
                                  motor activity.

*7. *Sharp pain*   The student creates sharp pain in a
                                  localized area of the body.

†8. *Sharp taste*   The student creates a sharp taste and/or
    Sharp smell   smell, such as lemon or vinegar. Sharp
                                  taste and/or sharp smell are sometimes
                                  assigned in combination with sharp pain
                                  as well as separately before or after pain.

†9. *Sound or sight*   The student creates a familiar
                                  composition of music, a painting, or
                                  various sounds, such as waves, a fog horn
                                  or a train whistle. Other familiar objects
                                  can be created just from the sight aspect
                                  (if a student creates a picture on the wall,
                                  he should be concerned with the frame,
                                  size, shapes, colors, forms, shadows and
                                  the like). (See also part 2, chapter 6.)

*10. *Place*   All sensory aspects of a particular place
                                  are created (see chapter 8, "Where Am
                                  I?," chapter 9, "The Actor's Task," and
                                  appendix G, no. 7).

*11. *Overall sensations*   The student experiences overall
     Bath   sensations, such as hot or cold water over
     Shower   the entire body, wind or rain. The actor
     Wind   should, where appropriate, create the feel
     Rain   of soap, the element of nakedness and
     Sauna   similar sensations.
     Extreme heat
     Extreme cold

*12. *Personal object*   The student creates sensorily an object
                                  that has special significance for him (e.g.,

†These above four exercises—taste, smell, sound or sight—can be assigned earlier if a
student has problems.

*13. *Combination of two:*
     overall sensation and
     personal object

*14. *Combination of three:*
     overall, personal object
     and memorized words
     or other
     assigned sound

*15. *Combination of four:*
     overall, personal object,
     sound, daily activity

*16. *Private moment*

17. *Private moment with*
    overall sensation

18. *Private moment,*
    overall, personal object

19. *Private moment,*
    overall, personal object,
    words

20. *Private moment,*
    overall, personal object,
    words, daily activity

21. *Private moment,*
    overall, personal object,
    words, more daily activities

an object given him by someone special or an object with sentimental meaning). Eventually he can also create two personal objects.

There can be other combinations of two or more (see appendix G for more exercise suggestions). If the student first creates the overall sensation, he then adds another object, and then another and so on. Sometimes an actor creates a personal object or sensory object first, and then adds the overall sensation. The order can vary. Everything is cumulative. Assigned sounds can be memorized words sung or spoken, a song sung or spoken or gibberish. The song may be hummed also. The words or sounds come out through the sensations; if hummed the sound should be strongly heard. Daily activities can include brushing teeth, dressing, other personal activities, cleaning the house, mowing the lawn and similar tasks.

The student recreates being alone, using his own room or a familiar room. The exercise goes beyond ordinary concentration.

This exercise may also be combined with others in the following manner: imaginary and real objects, daily activity, sound and different adjustments. Initially, the adjustments are ordinarily sensory objects brought into the exercise after it has started and at different points of the exercise. But the adjustment can be a sensation, such as sharp pain or an affective memory. An emotional adjustment is often used if the private moment is used for preparatory work before a scene. Various daily activities, as all objects, can be added in a cumulative way.

22. *Private moment,*
    overall, personal object,
    words, daily activity,
    adjustment

23. *Private moment,*
    overall, personal object,
    words, daily activity
    or activities, adjustment,
    then second adjustment,
    third and so on

*24. *Animal exercise*

*25. *Standing up the*
     animal

*26. *Bring the animal*
     fully upright: now
     human, retaining
     certain animal
     characteristics

27. *Human with animal*
    characteristics with
    a phone call or other
    adjustment

28. *Human with animal*
    characteristics with
    phone call, overall
    sensation

29. *Human with animal*
    characteristics with
    phone call, overall
    sensation, personal
    object

The student recreates the animal. The exercise develops observation, awareness and control. The adjustments can be similar to private moment adjustments: sharp pain, more sense objects, affective memory or two affective memories.

As with the private moment, the various combinations with sense and affective memory adjustments are limitless and can continue through years of actor growth.

30. *Human with animal
    characteristics with
    phone call, overall
    sensation, personal
    object, daily activity*

31. *Private moment with
    animal exercise*

32. *Private moment with
    animal exercise with:
    overall sensation*

33. *Private moment with
    animal exercise with:
    overall sensation,
    personal object*

34. *Private moment with
    animal exercise with:
    overall sensation,
    personal object,
    memorized words*

35. *Private moment with
    animal exercise with:
    overall sensation,
    personal object,
    memorized words,
    daily activity*

36. *Private moment with   Adjustments can include sense memory
    animal exercise with: or affective memory (emotional) or two
    overall sensation,   different affective memories.
    personal object,
    memorized words,
    daily activity or
    activities, adjustment(s)*

37. *Affective memory*   This exercise can be utilized at any
    (emotional memory)   level of training (see chapter 5).
38. *Song and dance*   The song and dance exercise is effective
                                              only when done in front of the class and
                                              when the instructor has the ability to
                                              perceive if the student is in touch with
                                              himself. It is also an excellent exercise to
                                              cure acting problems (inexpressiveness,
                                              inhibitions, etc.). The exercise does not
                                              demand that the student have any kind of
                                              experience, and the instructor and actor
                                              will not know what they will discover
                                              when the student does the exercise. At
                                              the beginning of the exercise the body is
                                              relaxed and still, so the impulse has to
                                              come out through the sound. The student
                                              commands the tone, controls his body and
                                              yet is free and responsive on stage. In the
                                              dance or movement part of the exercise
                                              the student responds spontaneously and
                                              then tries to recreate the spontaneity, as is
                                              necessary in all acting. The exercise and
                                              the ability to do it are tied to
                                              expressiveness (see part 2, chapter 6).

The instructor must use good judgment in assigning exercises and monitoring progress. Each assignment can in fact be adapted to a student's problems. If a hot drink does not work in the first exercise, the next assignment can be a cold drink, or vice versa. Difficult as this may be to grasp, in all these exercises the actor is being asked to really feel, see, hear, taste and smell and *not to merely imitate* the physical actions of these experiences. If the actor shows a particular tendency toward imitation (for instance, in the mirror exercise), his next assignment can be an exercise like putting on and taking off shoes and socks, which brings him closer to his own bodily sensations. An actor may fail to create all or even any of the sensory aspects of a particular exercise; regardless, he may be assigned a new exercise so that the problem exercise does not become a challenge.

Some teachers ask students to repeat an exercise up to five consecutive class times. Strasberg, however, advised his faculty not to stay with the same exercise for such a long period. "The general rule is to go on, for staying too long on the same exercise can create a negative effect on individual work."[2] As recently as 1981 Strasberg cautioned the instructor not to frustrate the student:

> The instructor must use his own judgment about a student's repeating an exercise in subsequent classes: to go on to other exercises to avoid frustration in the actor, to go back to the problem exercise later, or to go on to other exercises and add the problem exercise as an adjustment to another exercise. Even though extra exercises can be added throughout the work, and actors sometimes need to go back to exercises previously completed (often as adjustments), the sequence is eventually covered if an actor trains for an ample period of time—approximately three years.[3]

Description of Basic Exercises

Breakfast Drink

The student receives the following instructions:

> Remember, you are not doing this exercise in order to learn stage physical actions. The things you do in practicing this exercise you may never do when playing a role. The purpose of this exercise is to experience and fix in memory the reliving of all the sensory aspects of the breakfast drink.
>
> Choose what you habitually drink in the morning (e.g., a cold fruit juice or a hot drink like tea or coffee). As with most sensory exercises, you will practice at home at least one-half to two hours or more each day.[4] Begin by relaxing (as you would for most exercises). Take as much time as you need. Then start with the cup or glass you usually use filled with the liquid. Take the cup or glass in both hands and concentrate on your five senses—one at a time. Run your hand slowly and repeatedly over the outside of the container. Feel the texture, weight and balance of the container and the heat, steam or cold. Smell the aroma. See the color, size, shape, grooves and nicks of the container and the liquid. Hear the sloshing of the liquid, the sound of sipping or the clink of ice cubes. Taste the liquid, preferably several times. While you are concentrating on the taste, also be aware of the touch

of the container against your lips and tongue, the temperature of the liquid, the texture of the liquid and container and all other sensory aspects. This whole procedure should be done slowly with thorough investigation and exploration of all sensations.

Now, set the container down, turn away and repeat the entire procedure without the breakfast drink. If you find that you are not able to recreate some of the sensations experienced with the actual cup or glass in your hand, go back to the physical object itself and explore it again. Concentrate on weak sensory aspects as you work with the container (for example, if you cannot relive the odor, return to the drink and focus on the odor in particular). By thus alternating between the actual drink and imaginarily reexperiencing the drink, weak sensory aspects may be strengthened and the experience relived.

These directions are merely suggestions to guide beginners. All exercise practice is flexible, and each student experiments and explores in his own way. The student is cautioned, however, never to just imitate the drinking of a liquid in the morning; he or she must investigate thoroughly all sensory aspects of the procedure. The senses, in recalling the breakfast drink, already have the memory; the exercise taps that memory. The breakfast drink exercise deals with a familiar, simple, nonemotional object and involves all the senses. Such a small object, like the glass or cup, is also easier to focus attention on and thus it is easier for the student to create the details.

After home practice, the student does the exercise in class under teacher guidance. The real object—the full cup or glass—is not utilized in class. After relaxation, the student attempts to recapture all of the sensations he explored in his work at home. The instructor checks the student's relaxation and observes and guides the exercise. The teacher must be sure the student is not merely going through the motions but instead is reexperiencing the sensations. If a student is watching how he holds his hands or the shape they take, then he is usually only imitating what he does with the drink with just a mental image of it. Constant hand motions may indicate a lack of sensory exploration to really experience all the five senses. In such instances, the instructor can guide by asking questions (for example: "How rough is the texture?" "Is it rougher than ——— or ———?" "Are there any grooves?" "How heavy is it?" "Do you feel the coolness or the heat more on one part of the hand than another?").

If the actor can sincerely answer questions about the temperature (for example, he might be feeling the temperature of the drink more strongly in his index finger), he is beginning to work well. If he cannot, he becomes aware of where to put more concentration and draws his attention to the type of exploration that is sensory. After being asked a question like "How hot is it?" the student can then start exploring with his hand around the cup or mug and through the handle of the cup to test for warmth. The feeling can occur when the warmth comes through the cup to his hand and when his lips come closer to the liquid. At first concentration may only be mental, but eventually it transfers itself to the senses. An actor may get the mental and sensory both in a flash, after which real sensation will continue to occur.

The student is usually asked to describe his re-creation of the object, noting all specific detail: color, size, shape, designs and texture. Sometimes to aid a student's concentration he is asked to trace the cup from the rim down to the bottom and back up the side. When the student has the index finger through the imagined cup handle, the index finger and thumb do not touch, for room must be left for the handle between them. The correct amount of space between the fingers and thumb must be judged for a cup or glass. The student should try to recapture the particular muscular effort of holding the object and the sense of its weight. There should be a shift in balance when the liquid sloshes or when the cup is tilted or slowly lifted. The student should feel the liquid as it moves from side to side, concentrating on the weight not only in his hand but also in his whole arm and shoulder. The container will become lighter as the student drinks.

Some students are asked to feel the rim of the cup on their lips, to gently run the tongue around the rim of the cup or to trace the rim again, but with their other hand. The liquid can then slowly be felt on the lips, as the student continues to concentrate on heat or cold, smell and taste. The liquid may be felt under the tongue, against the cheeks, in the mouth, at the back of the mouth and then along the throat. It may just be felt in one of those areas, for sometimes just one or two sensations will work. The student may next focus on the sensation of the liquid in his stomach. Before beginning this exercise, the student will have decided the specific taste and texture of the liquid (e.g., if the orange juice had pulp in it or was smooth, if the tea had spice or lemon, or if the coffee had cream or sugar).

Occasionally, after the exercise has begun, the student may need to move his arms to relax. He can then switch the object to the other hand or set it down on a re-created surface, such as a table or counter. He should take care to keep the visual image of the object alive as the object sits on the surface. Thus, while he relaxes, the object and its reality continue for him. There is no set way of creating the reality of the object. What works for one person may not work for another. Some may hold the object to the cheek, on the arm or on the knee. Because minds and responses work differently, the order of concentration on sensory aspects in any exercise varies with the individual.

If the exercise does not work in all of the sensory aspects just described, the student is told not to worry. Sometimes one sensation will come first or sensations will come and go. If there are no sensations working at all, the instructor may vary the assignment, using a cold drink if hot was the first assignment, or vice versa, or assigning a transition in the exercise itself from a hot to a cold drink or from a cold to a hot one. Students are encouraged to be pleased when one sensory aspect begins to happen; with practice at home and full concentration other sensations will inevitably follow.

Students working with a hot drink often feel the heat of the liquid's steam as their first actual sensory breakthrough. One skeptical doctoral student enrolled in my classes at the Lee Strasberg Theatre Institute had a surprising experience when her work with a hot drink caused her eyes to water and her nose to run. She was thrilled, exclaiming, "Now I am beginning to understand why we do sense memory exercises!" She then began to appreciate the difference between simply remembering something mentally and actually reliving the experience sensorily and making it happen in the present. She now understood when students were merely imitating and when they were re-creating and reliving an experience through recall of one or more of the five senses. She was developing her own sense of truth and returned to her university a convert to Method.

Mirror

This exercise, like all the exercises involving literal objects, is first done at home in a manner similar to the breakfast-drink exercise. Men generally shave and women apply makeup. While carrying out this procedure before a real mirror with real objects, the student should carefully examine all aspects of the head, neck and hair as well as all objects being used, noting facial blemishes, hairline, textures, odors, weights, touch, size, shape, color, contour and similar qualities. At least ten to fifteen minutes should be spent in this activity. Then the student repeats the exercise without the mirror or objects. As in the breakfast-drink exercise, if there are any sensory aspects the student is not able to re-create, he or she should return to the mirror and real objects, concentrating especially on those weak areas. This alternation between real objects and imaginary ones may take place only a few times or many times, depending on the student. Some actors use the alternating process successfully for years.

When the mirror exercise is done in class (after relaxation), the instructor watches to see that the student is not merely repeating motions involved in shaving or applying makeup but rather is attempting to re-create sensorily an image of his or her body as well as the objects used.

This exercise begins to awaken the student's awareness of himself as a physical object. Re-creating one's own image is much more personal than recreating a drink. In class a student is usually advised to strive to see himself in the mirror for ten or fifteen minutes and then begin to deal with the objects, whether he has created his own image or not. The objects used should be imaginarily created in all aspects: size, shape, weight, smell, color, texture, contour. By using containers of creams and lotions, a razor or similar material as well as his or her own body the actor has greater opportunity in this exercise to become specific.

An actor is never to observe his reactions in a mirror and then repeat them to the class. Such imitation is incorrect; it may train observation but it does not train the senses. After trying to see himself, the actor should go on to handle and re-create the objects used to apply makeup or to shave. When the actor goes on to re-create the reality of the objects and deals with them, sometimes they start to work sensorily. That can key other realities, so the student will look up into the mirror and occasionally actually reexperience seeing himself. By creating his image for the first time, the actor becomes involved on a personal level—he brings himself alive.

The mirror exercise is one of the most difficult. The eyes should remain open (they can be closed at first as in other exercises). Focusing in space, the actor must create an image of something that isn't there: himself. When asked if he sees himself, and to describe specifically what he sees, if the answer appears to be impersonal, the teacher may ask pertinent questions (for example: "What is the most attractive feature you have? The most unattractive? Where do you see wrinkles? Blemishes? Moles? When you smile, what impression does the right eye give or the left eye? Do you look tired under your eyes?"). These astute questions are to help the actor develop a more personal use of himself and to become specific. Sometimes creating one's own image is easy, for the actor taps his good sense memory of sensations that his body routinely lives. If the actor cannot see himself, there is usually not enough awareness of self.

In the mirror exercise, as in most others, if the actor is at the back of the stage or classroom, near the end of the exercise the instructor can ask him to come forward, as he keeps the exercise going, and describe the exercise to the teacher. Or the instructor goes to the student to guide him through the exercise.

If the mirror exercise works well, the next assignment is ordinarily sunshine, which is a nonphysical exercise allowing the instructor to determine to what degree or intensity the senses work.[5] But if the breakfast drink did not work and if the student is imitating in the mirror exercise, the next assignments are usually daily activities that involve direct contact with the individual, such as putting on shoes and socks and then underclothes.[6]

Shoes, Socks and Underclothes

If the actor needs more work with physical objects, assignments can involve putting on and taking off shoes and socks and subsequently underclothes. Tapping the sensations in these two exercises is usually easily done, for a person generally has a good memory of things done so regularly. First, as advised for most exercises, the student begins by relaxing. When the sensory work begins, the instructor should point out that these exercises are not movies in the mind; the actor should become aware of real sensations. Because of the deliberate action of hands and body, these exercises help focus concentration. The sensation of a stocking moving up the leg is a strong one and is easier to re-create.

The underclothes exercise, in which the student creates putting on and taking off underwear, deals with inhibitions and tests whether the student will have difficulty creating emotional and sensory realities through his imagination. The actor must not rush but work for the reality of his senses. The element of imaginary nakedness should be created.

The actor is encouraged in both exercises to admit when he is not getting the reality or when he is slipping in and out of reality. Some of the craft of acting is being able to recognize when the reality is gone and then attempting to regain it. The actor can say aloud or to himself, "I'm losing it. I must get it back again." Each instructor finds his or her own way to stimulate the actor's desire to get the sensation. At times an actor is working too generally, so the instructor's specific questions in the drink, mirror, shoes and socks, underclothes and material exercises should encourage specific sensations. If a student is not getting such sensations, the material exercise can be assigned next, in lieu of or before or after the two exercises just described.

Three Pieces of Material

The materials should be as different from one another as possible. Terry cloth, fur and a thin cotton are good examples. The actor should concentrate on the different textures of the three pieces as he works on improving his sense of touch. He should investigate the material thoroughly, holding it to his face, on his arm, around his neck, on his knee and in various areas and positions. Fingers can be run over the material to smooth it one way and then another, as with velvet or fur. The actor may keep his eyes closed during the beginning of this exercise. The sense of sight may be brought in by re-creating the colors and the lines of the materials and the precise texture with bumps and threads felt and seen. The student is encouraged, however, to put full concentration on working for the difference in texture of the three pieces through the sense of touch. The student goes back and forth between the three materials, comparing and contrasting. He is not to work with a garment, like a sweater, for associations could lead to emotional reactions. It is better to work with abstract pieces of material, preferably with all three pieces the same size.

The material exercise is good for the actor's sense of truth, for he can ascertain if he is getting real sensation through the fingers or merely imitating. If the actor does not check the touch moment-to-moment by exploring with his hands and if all touch appears the same, he is probably just going through the motions. It is important for the actor to get the reality of the touch and not be dependent on the way he moves his fingers. Some instructors tell students who are imitating, "Don't do what you would do if the object were real—do what you have to do to *make* it real."

Sunshine

The sunshine exercise should be practiced prior to class, preferably by using the sun itself. In class the actor does the exercise sitting in a chair. He moves in the chair and checks relaxation. He then adjusts and moves his body to receive sensation in a particular location, at the same time relaxing other areas. The eyes are usually closed as the actor strives to reexperience the feeling of the sun. Sometimes it helps for the actor to re-create a particular occasion when he felt the sunshine and then reexperience that sense impression. The muscular energy needed to recreate literal objects is not a factor in working for the rays of a good, hot sun.

The instructor can now determine if the senses are really working. He may ask, "Where, specifically, do you feel the sun's rays the strongest on your face?" The student may become aware that the feel of the sun on the crest of the cheekbones is different from the feel on the mouth, eyelids or other areas. Such a response tells the actor that all areas are not equal, that all sensations are not equal in all areas. The actor is thus guided to work more specifically, to be more differentiating, to work for a more truthful grounding.

Usually the first places to reexperience the sun are those most prominent: the forehead, the bridge of the nose and the upper lip. The actor keeps his concentration going in these areas as he lets the sensation of the sun seep through the rest of the body. As in relaxation work, if an actor is concentrating on one area of the body and loses the sensation of the sun in another area, he concentrates on bringing it back to the lost area. He always tries to keep the sensation going in the areas where it is working. The instructor can ask the actor to identify the places where the sun is working the strongest; the student almost always chooses the top of the legs and the arms and feet as well as the top of the head or face. He is encouraged to keep the sensation going in all of these areas as he lets the heat spread through his entire body. The instructor may probe with further questions: How does the sun feel through his clothes? How does the sun feel on his bare skin or his scalp? The actor should be led to an awareness of the different kind of sensations felt when the sunshine hits a clothed area versus the bare skin. Generally, places other than where the sun is working the strongest will feel a degree of heat ranging from mild body warmth to a muggy, hot, stifling kind of heat, depending on how long the actor lets full concentration work.

As the actor concentrates on the feeling of the sun in certain areas, other responses often occur, such as perspiration or redness of the skin. Perspiration often occurs on the nape of the neck, around the hairline on the forehead, on the upper lip, across the nose and under the eyes or on the chin, according to individual responses. Clothes sometimes cling to the body. Later in the exercise the actor should also concentrate on body areas that are not hit directly by the sun (for example, under the arm, the buttocks, the back of the leg, the nape of the neck). Continual exploration makes the student aware of the various kinds and degrees of heat experienced by the body. When one sensation of heat works, the student tries to keep it going as he concentrates on another.

The actor is cautioned not to substitute stage lights for the sun but to re-create the sun as he knows it so that he controls the stimulus, its placement and intensity. If the actor focuses his concentration on a certain placement of the sun he imprisons himself, restricting his movements and his possibilities, so it is important that he also be able to change the sun's position.

The sunshine may work fully, as the actor explores the experience all over his body. If there is discomfort, the actor should not stop but keep the sensations going until the instructor stops the exercise or the entire class exercise work ends. Beginning students have a tendency to want to stop an exercise just when it is beginning to work, just when they need to go into it more fully.

All individuals will react differently to these exercises. The procedures and questions I have suggested are examples, not rigid directions. All homework suggestions, class guidance and questions are to facilitate the actor's concentration by training him to become more specific and thus more real.

Since the sunshine and the mirror exercises do not always indicate if the work is intense enough, instructors are advised to assign next sharp pain or another exercise with an intense reaction. Strasberg told his faculty, "Some [students] do not react fully in the mirror or sunshine exercise. Pain is a good test, because the student goes from a simple sensory exercise to an intense sensory one."[7] Strasberg, however, advised teachers to leave out the pain exercise, or return to it later, for students

with psychological or emotional problems. In such cases Strasberg recommended daily activities that emphasize the sensory aspects and that
work for control "to become firm." If the sensory reality of daily activities does not work for a student, Strasberg advised using a personal
object out of sequence.

Sharp Pain, Taste and Smell

Exercises testing the intense reaction are also rehearsed at home.
Whereas sharp pain is practiced by remembering a sensation, sharp taste
and smell can be practiced with the real object. The pain exercise tests
the actor's ability to create sensation by reliving a memory of a particular
sensation rather than practicing with a literal object. At home or in class,
the student relaxes in a chair first.

The sharp pain exercise is assigned to be created in a specific bodily
area so that the actor knows exactly where to focus. A pain, such as a
toothache, not associated with anything emotional (like a birth or car
accident) is advised. The actor chooses a pain he has experienced; it
sometimes helps to remember a particular time when the pain occurred.
If it is a toothache, the actor must remember if it was a sharp or a dull
ache. As the student works for the initial sensation, he concentrates on
the area of the mouth involved. He will then explore with his tongue
and re-create the sensation felt when the tongue touched the tooth. The
instructor may ask, "Are the gums swollen? Do the gums or jaw hurt
along with the tooth? Is the pain affected when the mouth is opened,
when you talk, eat or when cold air strikes the tooth?" Some students
have related responses connected with the toothache, like a headache
or pain along the side of the face. The effects of this exercise, as in all
exercises, will differ with the individual, but the student should remember to just let it happen—*never* show, *never* perform.

An actor must be able to control the pain he creates. The instructor
encourages him to move the rest of his body (for instance, first the arms,
then the legs—one at a time) so "the pain spreads and he can express
himself more fully." The instructor may guide movement and deep, even
breathing during pain. The pain exercise not only tests the intensity of
a student's reaction but also allows the instructor to know if the student
is blocked. The instructor can also observe how much the student gives
in to the pain or how much he fights it.

If the pain exercise does not work, the instructor most likely will assign sharp taste and smell next. If taste and smell were assigned before pain, other variations can be created. Even if the exercise does work, the student can pursue other sharp taste and smell exercises, an overall sensation or a personal object, depending on the teacher's judgment. Some instructors include sound or sight exercises at this point, depending on the student's needs.

Most instructors know when a student succeeds with the pain exercise. Failure usually results from poor concentration. At times sharp taste and smell exercises will unlock something in the actor, allowing him to re-create a sensation. If the actor does not get sharp smell or taste, it is often because he is not specific. He must work with the real object for his homework. One technique is to compare the strong smell of soap to the more pungent, even rancid smell of cheese. The actor must re-create the specific nature of smells in order for work to become more specific and more real (he or she might also try a particular perfume, flower or spice).

If a student has problems with taste, another exercise involves taste transitions: from sweet to sour and then from sour to sweet. The actor can work with all kinds of foods and liquids. A hot dinner is sometimes assigned if necessary. The exercise of taste thus includes smell, touch and sight.

Sensations begin to work for some actors when they do exercises of sharp pain and sharp taste and/or smell in combination. If this does not work, the next assigned exercises—the overall sensations—by their very nature tend to unlock the actor. Sharp pain is one of the adjustments frequently assigned to an overall exercise and it often works well in conjunction with the overall sensation. Sharp pain is also a common adjustment assigned to private moment, animal and combination exercises.

Sight and Sound

Sight and sound exercises are detailed in chapter 6 and in the sequence of sensory exercises listed at the beginning of this chapter.

Overall Sensations

Overall sensation exercises include reliving such experiences as the bath, the shower, the steambath or the sauna. These sensations, plus those experienced in the rain or in extreme heat or cold, test the actor's ability to re-create sensation all over the body.

Whether practicing at home or doing these exercises in class the actor must take his time and let the sensations build. Feelings on different parts of the body will be different. In a shower, for instance, the water will feel different hitting the scalp, trickling down the body, hitting the shoulders, the genitals or the feet. In a bathtub the body will feel different when immersed in water up to the neck than when immersed in water up to the waist. The student works specifically to relive all sensations, such as how hot the water is, how the part of the body outside the water feels different from the part in the water, the touch and smell of the soap and the washcloth. If the person leaves the tub he or she will experience the sensory elements of dripping water on the body and the touch of the towel. In overall sensations the actor must thoroughly investigate *all* areas of the body. For overalls involving hot steam the exercise should reach an unbearable point before being stopped.

Inhibiting and confining factors in the student are often released in the overall sensation exercises. When nakedness is really created in the imagination, the actor may blush or giggle embarrassedly when describing to the instructor how the exercise is working. If the actor creates undressing in the exercise, he must be careful not to rush as he follows a physical sequence of undressing.

It is especially important for the actor to move constantly during the overall exercise so that he can assure himself that the muscles of his body are indeed relaxed while he is trying to experience the sensation of the shower, sauna or other overall. He must remain loose yet respond with physical logic (for example, getting into the bath) and strive to maintain his relaxation. If an actor does not relax with freedom, the body will react through habit rather than according to the senses. Overall sensation exercises are particularly important exercises, for many students have their first sensory breakthrough in this exercise. Strasberg explained that the overall sensation works through kinetic senses all through the body.[8]

When a personal object (see next section) or daily activity is added to the overall exercise, the body maintains the overall while the hand does the activity. The actor must think with his body. Several adjustments can be added to the overall exercise to train the actor to do more than one thing simultaneously, as he must when performing. Each ad-

Strasberg guiding sensory work. Photo by Mark Shahn.

justment is in addition to the previous exercise. The first additional exercise assigned with an overall sensation is usually the personal object, but sharp pain or another adjustment could be assigned first. Next follow words and daily activities. The order and selection can vary according to individual actor's problems.

Speaking out and expressing moment-to-moment what the actor is experiencing are encouraged in this and the other exercises. Additionally, when assigned words are added to the overall exercise, the student should understand that the words are intended to connect with the impulse and permit expression. Words are spoken or sung, but they should not follow a pattern. If the song or monologue does not release the actor so that there is spontaneous expression stemming from the sensory work of the exercise, gibberish often will. Gibberish (see chapter 6) is also encouraged if the actor is worried about fellow class members' opinions as he speaks out his thoughts. Thus, in the overall exercises with combinations of two's, three's, four's, or more, as well as in private moment or animal combinations, an actor is occasionally encouraged to speak gibberish.

I cannot stress enough that the actor in the overall, or any other exercise, must never work for the end result. Rather, he should let the exercise take him where it goes. Of course, if his mind wanders away from the object of concentration or the specific exercise, then the actor does *not* go with that but consciously uses discipline and will power to return to the object of concentration, the assigned exercise.

Personal Object

The object used should have sentimental value and a marked personal association for the actor. Examples of appropriate personal objects are jewelry, letters, a childhood toy or special gifts. If the literal object is not available to work with at home, the memory of an object is tapped. The object can derive from any time in the student's past. Strasberg told students: "Anything that is seven years or older should be able to be dealt with. If something is more recent and you feel it won't work or you are not ready for it, don't push it. You can use something else, as there is no reason to challenge yourself. On the other hand, you should not run away out of fear."[9]

Any of the previous exercises may result in an emotional response, depending on the prior conditioning of the individual. The personal object exercise, however, is the first exercise designed to seek an emotional response directly.

While practicing at home or creating the object imaginarily in class, the actor works for the physical sensations of the personal object. The instructor should caution him not to *seek* emotion. If there is emotion there—and there usually is if an appropriate object has been selected—the actor should let it happen. In this or in any other exercise the actor should always remain relaxed while letting the emotion out. In other words he laughs or cries, but he does not contort his facial muscles. In life one habitually tenses one's muscles to fight emotion, but an actor must let all his muscles, including facial ones, be at ease in the exercises.

Thus, the actor's instrument must be kept flexible during the exercise: the instructor should particularly monitor relaxation when the exercise is done alone, without adjustments. If the actor's behavior is contained or inhibited, it can mean that the emotional reaction or connection that often springs from the personal object exercise is blocked. Emotion should result spontaneously from experiencing the sensory aspects of the object. In this as in all the exercises the actor is encouraged to speak out if something is not happening. He can say exactly what he is thinking: "I don't know what to do" or "I feel like . . ."

When the sound of a song or monologue is added to the personal object, the instructor often has to tell the student to make the sound audible: "Let's hear the song more." "Hum it, sing it or whatever, but let's hear the sound stronger." This can also be the instruction for the next time the exercise is done in a class. A sauna or other overall sensation, with a personal object, song or monologue and eventually a daily activity, are subsequent assignments. Each new adjustment is added to the preceding exercise, so the actor works first with one element then two or three and so on.

Instructors often assign a personal object exercise as a detour from the regular sequence of exercises when a student is not succeeding sensorily. Because of the personal nature of the personal object the student could begin to get a sensory response. Strasberg suggested: "The student can stay with the personal object assignment at least four class periods, with a different personal object each time. Then he can be taken back to the exercise sequence."[10] If the personal object exercise works right away, then the student is taken back into the regular sequence of work. This could be the sunshine exercise, if cloths and the more literal object work were assigned after the mirror exercise, or the pain exercise or wherever he was in the sequence of exercises. If the personal object does not help the student focus his concentration and work sensorily, as it ordinarily does, then the teacher may resort to special guided exercises or further work with literal objects in the classroom (see chapter 6).

Some instructors assign overall sensations and personal objects separately or together as a regular part of the exercise sequence, even if the student is not proceeding well sensorily. Strasberg tied together these exercises:

> Overall sensations are useful not only when I can't tell if there is a block but they also help to unlock areas the student is totally unaware of—and without the student knowing it. In overall sensations, I deal with [the block]. . . . if the student can't move, I know there's a block without the student's knowledge. I deal with it not externally, but by making them move, and making contact with those [blocked] areas. . . . Sometimes, if this does not work, I give them a personal object. The personal object will sometimes work a first time, but the student should continue a second or third time, or I can't tell if there is still a block. Sometimes, when a personal object works the first time, the student will cry and say he doesn't feel anything sensory, but that doesn't matter, as obviously something is working if he is crying, so give the student a sense that this works.[11]

After the overall sensations exercise, a student will often be given a personal object exercise addition if he has not had this type of exercise before. Strasberg himself advised the instructor to assign the personal object exercise in combination with an overall as well as separately.

Advanced Sense Memory Exercises

Combination Exercises

Two sense objects of any combination may be assigned earlier than this point in the work, according to individual needs (see appendix G). Examples include drinking a beverage while sitting in the sun or reading a book, or listening to music while smelling a flower or eating something. The first element should already be working before the student adds another object of concentration.

Combination exercises usually begin with overall sensations and continue into private moment and animal exercises. Overall sensations often relax an actor, enabling a second exercise added to the overall to work more fully than originally.

Strasberg's special contribution to combination exercises is in releasing the student's inhibitions, freeing him from habits of containment or from individual mannerisms that block his instrument. According to Strasberg, if the instructor observes the student carefully during relaxation and during movement in the sensory exercises, he will recognize repetitious behavior—habits—and can deal with them. The whole effort of drawing the actor's attention to movement is based on a precise understanding of how habits function and how to free the actor from their constraints. The goal is not just to take away inhibitions but to generate a precise understanding of how the instrument functions when sensations are provoked.

Blocks sometimes do not occur until the actor has to make a sensation real that is not. A younger actor may not be real enough while an older actor may habitually be too emotional or melodramatic. The older actor may be striving just for emotions, and such emotion is sometimes expressed through habitual mannerisms. But combination exercises can aid the actor to avoid such programmed responses. In fact, such problems handicapping both younger and older actors can be helped with the same type of combination exercise involving an overall sensory experience plus an emotional exercise, such as a personal object or an affective memory (discussed in chapter 5). These kinds of combination exercises aid students and professional actors to get in touch with their own feelings and free their instruments of the extraneous.

Some actors do exercises every day to try to contact themselves emotionally, to become more aware of who they are as well as to get in contact with certain kinds of emotions. This kind of work aids in the natural expression of emotions. Emotional work alone can establish and confirm a habitual way of expressing emotion, so it is better to use combinations of sensory and emotional work. All parts of the body are involved in an overall, so when the emotion comes, the body itself is absorbed in an exercise exploring sensations unrelated to the emotional object. As a result the emotion has to find a unique way out every time.

Some instructors believe that combination exercises are the bread and butter of acting training. Any combination—twosomes, threesomes, foursomes or more—based on the overall, private moment, animal or any combination of exercises is valuable for the advanced actor, as long as one element is emotional.

In sum, combination exercises ensure emotional truthfulness and permit genuine emotion to express itself honestly. Strasberg was convinced that combination exercises, practiced diligently, develop an emotional honesty and truthfulness that is not trapped in habit.

Private Moment

The private moment exercise at first is only done in class, but eventually this exercise can be used as part of preparation before a scene, improvisation or performance (see chapters 7 and 8).

For the class exercise the student brings personal articles from home and arranges them in a corner of the classroom or onstage. He or she may bring records to play, a radio, books, makeup, mirror, scissors, papers or other articles. The student does not relax before this exercise. Even if he or she is tense, it is all right, for the individual could be tense when alone at home. The student re-creates through sense memory the familiar room in which the private experience occurs. He concentrates on bringing all sensations alive for that room. He works on creating the room until he can see, feel and smell furniture and other objects in the room (see "The Actor's Tasks—Creating a Place" in chapter 9 and appendix G, 7). By establishing belief in the place, the student increases concentration and belief in the private activity itself.

The student then proceeds to carry out some activity or activities in which he engages only if he is alone, something he would stop (or continue in a different way) if someone, even a husband or wife, entered the room (for example, cutting toenails, undressing, looking in a mirror, singing, talking to himself or dancing with wild abandon). The private moment exercise should not be confused with just being alone or being personal. Strasberg claimed that it does not necessarily follow that being alone means a person is private. At home a person knows something is private if he or she stops doing it when another enters; something personal he might continue to do, even if a little embarrassed. The exercise continues from one to two hours until it is terminated by the instructor.

After the student has once successfully completed the private moment exercise by creating aloneness, he is instructed for subsequent classes to add adjustments to it of another of the exercises he has done before (as suggested by numbers 16–23 and 31–36 on the list at the beginning of this chapter). If the additional work should be the personal object or an affective memory, the actor should *not* push for the emotion but rather work for specific sensory realities. Strasberg suggested adding an emotional exercise (on the spot or for a subsequent class) "in order to [reveal behavior] not ordinarily revealed or to feel emotion not originally felt in the private moment."[12] The instructor makes these assignments at the end of the exercise for the next class meeting, or the student may choose the adjustments himself.

The primary objective of the private moment is to create the sense of being alone, even though the student is surrounded by classmates doing their own exercises. If the student has problems with the private moment exercise (such as an inability to create the sense of aloneness), then the exercise can be explored under the instructor's guidance. The instructor encourages the student to speak out his frustrations and describe what is happening, enabling the instructor to be more astute in guiding the exercise.

The instructor at certain times may tell the student what to do in order to guide him toward revealing behavior he might not ordinarily reveal. The student can be advised to listen, sing or dance to music, brush hair or read, depending on the props available. The student may be asked to follow these instructions as fully as possible, without thinking and with complete will and effort. If a pupil tries to stop what he is doing, he should be forced to go on, as fear can block the student's work in other areas. The student is generally guided to take his time and avoid rushing. But some times he may be asked to do something as quickly as he can, without thinking, all depending on the actor's needs at the moment. Each actor must abide by his own sense of truth. The instructor ultimately has the option of stopping the exercise if the student is not creating the sense of aloneness.

This exercise is particularly valuable in determining whether an actor is private or not, whether his concentration is sufficient to exclude observers. If the actor cannot ignore the audience enough to let himself function, he is clearly not able to create imaginarily well enough to guarantee his own privacy. Consequently, the private moment exercise is often used for individuals whose previous exercises seem not to be working because of a lack of privacy.

The private moment exercise was devised by Strasberg after he reread Stanislavski's famous "public solitude" statement. Stanislavski had noticed that great actors performed as if they were not being observed. Strasberg concluded, "Acting is being private in public." Strasberg began to use the private moment variation of concentration exercises in 1956 and 1957 to combat the problem of inhibition in front of an audience. Strasberg reasoned that every actor must have had a moment in life when he was alone, when he behaved in a manner that required complete privacy, when even the sound of a door opening would be enough to stop the activity or alter behavior. This was a moment when the actor was private, not simply alone. Strasberg's theory of making use, in public, of the strong impulse and impetus of what happens only in private has led to fuller commitment, a release of emotions and more vivid expression in many students. As Strasberg said, "Some people are too concerned with what they would do in a scene. The private moment is for the purpose of bringing into the scene a certain absorption. The private moment goes one stage beyond regular concentration and eliminates the effect of the audience on what you [the actor] do."[13]

The actual private moment is further described by Strasberg:

> He [the actor] then says, "I am going to choose the moment in this room when I think this particular thing about myself, when I worry about my job or my home life or my relationship to people, when I carry on long speeches to people who aren't there, or dance wildly or sing or dress up or undress." He then does that moment as fully as he can—but does not imitate. The doing is left to happen as easily as it can. He says, "I am going to see how far I can go in that direction. I will not do things that good taste obviously will not permit on the stage, but I will try to get close to my moment of privacy. If I get too close to a part that good taste does not permit, I will walk off stage. I'm not sure I'll reach that point, but if necessary I'll walk off and complete that part off stage and then come back. I will see what will happen. I will see if I can create [the moment] as fully as if I were not being watched."[14]

The private moment exercise should enable the actor to develop a private kind of concentration, to engender via the exercise the sense of being unwatched. The ultimate value is that such a sense is portable and can be carried into actions, behavior, words and scenes unrelated to the actor's particular room. This portable privacy can be taken into any kind of scene, whether the actor is alone or with others, and the actor then is able to maintain a sense of privacy in front of an audience. The method of achieving this portable privacy is one of the most profound of Strasberg's inventions.

Private moment exercises are effective problem solvers. Many students conquer blocks and open whole new areas of expression. The student with a monotonous voice sometimes displays more vocal colors in a private moment, and his or her voice expressiveness and acting behavior change after the private moment works. In a private moment actors can begin to really think onstage. This is often evident when impulses are spoken out. Impulses can also be spoken out in gibberish. Gibberish in the private moment often releases emotion and expression when the actor is too embarrassed to speak out. The private moment exercise can also release an actor's inhibited movement onstage or before a camera. In life people move with much more vividness and with a wider scale of expression than they usually permit themselves onstage. A student performing a private moment often moves and behaves with unforeseen abandon. The improvisational nature of the exercise leaves the student free to follow through with his or her impulses, which can lead to a fullness of response. The private moment can also give an actor an unaccustomed belief in himself as a result of the freedom of behavior and emotion.

Strasberg related how the private moment opened new areas of expression when applied to arias, monologues, soliloquies and moments when a performer was left alone onstage. "People have wonderfully theatrical behavior when they're private," explained Strasberg, "much more so than when they're simply alone. They speak to themselves with such vividness, they argue, they tell people off. They carry on in a way which they immediately inhibit when somebody is there."[15] Thus Strasberg found that the private moment exercise suggested possibilities for behavior when an actor was left alone onstage. Strasberg compared this to a concert, when the violinist plays the cadenza:

> He can explore this moment to the fullest, unencumbered by other moments. Stanislavski calls that the Star Pause, and there are very important moments like that in plays. An actor is left alone on a stage, sometimes with no words, and yet the author makes some demands. He wants something to happen. During the pause the character comes to a decision. We found that these moments in life are enormously dramatic. I had never known that until we started with the private moment.[16]

Because of the intense personal nature of the private moment, Strasberg usually did not assign private moments to students in need of psychiatric help for fear of accentuating their personal problems.[17] Instead, he prescribed work on concentration, objectives and exercises with physical objects. He worked for clarity and definition in such actors but avoided emotional exercises that let the student feel too much.

Strasberg also found, however, that the private moment could help the troubled actor control his imaginative life:

> When you create these things within the events of the stage, you are able to deal with them in a way in which, if they happened in life, the complete reality would overwhelm you. So we have found that for some people who have an emotional problem, dealing with it in a private moment actually helps them to learn to deal with it in life—to control it, to handle it . . . The private moment actually has a good effect on their personal life.[18]

The same theory applies to role playing in counseling. Social workers and school counselors have joined my acting classes to learn to use improvisational and private moment techniques in role playing. The client may play someone else in his life while the social worker plays the client or vice versa. Social workers have reported that this type of role playing aids them and the client to understand and cope with problems.

The private moment has a special character because "nothing needs to happen." The private moment can be done over and over, for it is not just one exercise but many combinations of exercises. To a monologue can be added an exercise adjustment and then more adjustments. An adjustment or exercise can even be added in the middle of the private moment, but the student should be guided to continue to do everything as before, with the same monologue. Numerous combinations can be assigned according to the student's problems. Even though the private moment is done initially as a class exercise, it can eventually be done as part of the preparation before a scene or improvisation (as explained in chapters 7, 8 and 9). The freedom of expression, fullness of impulse or greater degree of theatrical energy released in the private moment often continues into the scene.

I once guided a student in a class private moment combined with an affective memory (sense and emotional memory work; see part 2, chapter 5, and glossary) to prepare her for an audition for the television show "Baretta." She got the role out of approximately a hundred actresses and then came back to class to ask for more guidance for a particular scene. After working on the scene in class, she filmed it at Universal, where the two leads in "Starsky and Hutch" observed her working. They were so impressed when she cried on cue and then controlled the crying on cue for seventeen takes that they asked her if they could visit her acting class. Later the student worked on another private moment in class with sense memories of a cold and tiredness, and another adjustment of an affective memory for a particular scene. When she finished, she thanked me for helping her, because she said she needed that work for the next "Baretta" filming. When I asked when she would be filming, thinking I could advise her about homework based on what we had done, she answered, "In a half hour"! She had asked her director at Universal if she could come to class first for help with the scene. The "Baretta" director told her he wished he could send all his people to the class, for no one else was as well trained.

Another student worked in class on a private moment, with an adjustment of an affective memory that stimulated the creation of fear. She applied this exercise for her television role in "How the West Was Won." She also worked on hysteria for a movie, beginning with a private moment and then adding an affective memory for an adjustment. First, she worked on the sequence in classes. She was able to re-create and control the hysteria for six or more takes, eliciting the praise of her director. Most teachers have many similar samples of how students use the private moment combination professionally with sometimes one affective memory, sometimes more, and usually adjustments of sensory work added to the basic private moment.

Concluding a faculty meeting, Strasberg confided:

> If someone has difficulty with the sensory work, I will give a personal object or sound, and if these still do not work, I jump quickly to the private moment. When a student realizes he cannot deal with an audience, the student may need to go back to basic exercises but nevertheless, make progress in the private moment exercise. It carries Stanislavski's idea [public solitude] into exercise form, and the actor can retain in the public eye a kind of behavior that not only is private but often exceeds in vividness anything that he would create by ordinary good acting. A sense of truth already trained in previous exercises becomes very clear in the private moment. If a student is not private, guide the student to realize he is not private.[19]

Animal Exercise

The student begins by observing an animal in the animal's environment, at the zoo or wherever possible. The student can make notes recording the animal's movements, his gait, his bulk, the location of power, his center of power, weight, and strength, his use of his paws (for example, has he a certain dexterity with his fingers different from other animals, as with a gorilla?), his knuckle movements, how he holds and moves his head, how he jumps and how he uses his mouth (for instance, do larger cats use their mouths in similar fashion? do they do things with their mouths that humans might do with their hands?). This meticulous observation should include all physical manifestations of the animal's actions. For domestic animals, some students try to match each movement with the animal, as in a mirror exercise. The student should also watch and record the animal's walk and rhythm, how the animal moves about his cage or environment (how does the animal relate to the cage?), how he eats, how the animal observes or watches objects around him, the way he sits, what sort of things attract his attention and how he concentrates on things around him. The student finally studies the causes or inner impulses that motivate the animal's actions, working from the outer actions of the animal to discover the animal's inner impulses. The actor's imagination should be stimulated by the image of the animal.

After careful study of the animal and his own notes, the actor then concentrates in practice at home on assimilating the animal's characteristics and peculiarities. The actor tries to become aware of the differences between his own and the animal's body, imagining the cause for the animal's behavior. The actor attempts to understand the logic behind the animal's actions (why does the animal move as he does or lumber or spring as he does? why does he turn his head in a certain way? why does he eat in a certain way?). The conditioned responses, instincts and inner life of the animal are re-created.

When doing the animal exercise in class, the student may use the entire classroom or just the stage. He can use the animal's imaginary environment or the reality of the stage or room. If he uses imaginary surroundings, sensory objects like the bars of a cage can be created. If the reality of the stage or room is used, everything in it can be utilized as the animal reacts to the objects. The latter method is encouraged, for the actor then avoids creating extra sensory objects for concentration.

The actor must see his surroundings from the animal's point of view. Encountering a real object in the room, the actor/animal will inspect for the smell, taste, sight, sound or feel of it, just as the animal would. The actor might react to a particular object as a plaything or as something dangerous; he might react to a classmate as an animal would react to a human. Because an animal relies on his senses to explain a moving form, the instructor might deliberately do something to get the actor/animal's attention, such as rustling paper, swinging jewelry, tossing a wad of paper or a small ball, stamping a foot, whistling or shuffling feet. This type of improvisation gives the student other ways to respond, to discover the animal more clearly and to explore the animal's behavior. By observing the actor/animal's reaction to such disturbances, the instructor can determine the actor's degree of concentration. If the actor is deeply involved, sudden movement should startle him, other gestures should catch his attention and produce a characteristic response.

After the student re-creates the outer characteristics of the animal, he is encouraged in later classes to make sounds like the animal. Even if he has never heard the animal make a sound, the student should use his imagination to explore vocally the kinds of sounds he thinks appropriate; the instructor can even pose questions for the actor/animal to respond to.

In subsequent classes the student stands the animal on two feet, adding human characteristics. Next, he or she makes the animal more human while retaining animal characteristics. In final assignments the actor/animal can make imaginary phone calls as a human displaying animal characteristics. Other exercises may be added to the basic animal exercise as the student's work progresses, but each addition should be developed over a period of several class meetings.

The primates are easier to re-create because their mannerisms are closer to a human being's, enabling the student to work more specifically. Sometimes the instructor suggests a specific animal to an actor with specific problems. A bird, for instance, is a good choice for an actor who has difficulty with body movements—for a bird moves deliberately. Some instructors suspect that the actor's choice of animal reveals a desire to be like that particular animal, so the student is usually allowed to make his own selection for this exercise. Choosing his own animal can also spark the actor's will to do the exercise.

The animal is a good exercise for those out of touch with themselves.

It takes the pressure off being themselves. The student/animal has to move and react deliberately and unhabitually. The exercise can thus break basic patterns determined by habit. The animal exercise is also good for people who are subjective and want only to feel. Work on the exercise requires scrupulous observation. In the early stages the actor gets away from feeling and concentrates on physical movement.

The animal exercise thus trains the external approach and develops the external characteristics of the actor. The goal is to make the muscles obey, depending on the type of movement and position of the animal. The actor learns to control himself physically in the exercise, then in subsequent classes adds sensory adjustments and the various combinations as listed in the beginning of this chapter.

Strasberg explained to his faculty about the use of the animal exercise out of sequence:

> When there is real difficulty sometimes, and I don't know what to do, I jump to an animal exercise. When people say they aren't feeling anything, it means they cannot contact with the body. But in an animal exercise they can say, "That's how you hold your hand." The animal exercise breaks basic patterns the body sets up and breaks blocks. The actor acquires certain habits and those dictate the way in which he expresses himself. This is Pavlov, not Jung. The animal exercise makes the actor do an entirely different kind of thing by making him observe, and do a totally different thing with his hands, for instance. The more aesthetic an individual, the more the animal exercise completely breaks the pattern of human behavior and breaks the actor away from habits he has acquired. The will is involved.[20]

The second stage of the animal exercise requires the actor to portray something of the animal's inner life. Eventually the actor will get to the stage where he re-creates emotional or mental as well as physical characteristics of the animal. For example, does the frisky young cat want to play? Does the older cat want to stretch and sleep? What does the animal want or fear in relationship to where it is, who or what it fears, touches, hears, sees, smells? By answering the above questions, the "why" of the animal is re-created. These inner emotional results, such as thinking, feeling and responding as the animal, usually come in later stages of the exercise. Basically, the animal exercise is used to teach the actor to carry out unemotional tasks with muscular control. The student should be warned that the exercise not only needs careful observation work in order to create the animal's movements but must also eventually involve the inner, physical and mental reality of the animal.

Strasberg credited his teacher Maria Ouspenskaya with making him aware of the value of animal exercises for the development of powers of observation, concentration and imagination. This particular exercise, which probably developed in Russia as a character exercise, works toward continuity of behavior, with all the details linked to form a complete personality, the animal's. Sometimes an actor begins the exercise by isolating the element most characteristic of the particular animal. Because the student knows he cannot just be himself—he must concentrate to do something in order to act the animal character—he is also assisted in losing self-consciousness.

The animal exercise thus functions as the beginning of character work, for the actor must begin to perceive the differences between himself and the character portrayed, animal or man. Some actors find it easier to develop a character by exploring an animal exercise first, for the exercise involves carefully finding the differences between himself and the character created.

The animal exercises can be the key to characterization. The actor creates a character with an independent life in the same way that a picture is separate from the painter. When the actor works on animals like monkeys or gorillas, who have qualities similar to man's,[21] he first becomes the animal with a different kind of walk, rhythm, behavior and attitude. Next, he becomes the character with those same animal characteristics. The final stage of the animal exercise, then, is to play a human being with the animal characterization within the human being.

When utilizing an animal exercise for a specific character, an actor may sometimes develop a believable character by completely altering his or her own normal body. For the original play *What Time Does It Get Dark?* by Travilla Deming, Felix Chavez worked on a gorilla to help him play an old man. Felix is a trained dancer with an uncompromisingly upright posture. But with the help of the animal exercise he developed the shoulders and stance of an older man. He learned to control himself physically as the character, then filled in with sensory work. *What Time Does It Get Dark?* was presented in a premiere production in 1978 as an outgrowth of my Teachers/Directors/Writers class at the Lee Strasberg Theatre Institute.

Lee J. Cobb once described how he used an elephant animal exercise to create the character of Willy Loman in *Death of a Salesman*. The lumbering gait and the burden of the oppressive weight of the world on his shoulders (possibly motivated by Willy's failure and guilt) made Cobb appear to be an older, heavier man onstage, even though Cobb himself was not a heavy individual. The outstanding characteristic of the elephant—its heaviness—appeared in nearly everything Willy Loman did suggesting the physical and spiritual burdens he carried.

Further Advice to Instructors

The prerequisite for all exercise work—except the private moment—is relaxation. The instructor usually checks individual relaxation before allowing the student to begin an exercise. Occasionally a student is instructed to continue working on relaxation rather than proceeding with the assignment. During the exercise itself the instructor should watch for tension in the body and apprise the actor of tension in specific areas. Often the student is not aware that he is tense in a particular area but he can usually identify tension himself after it is pointed out. He can then watch the location in future work.

Most basic exercises should be done in a sitting position. Except for exercises involving standing, like overall sensations, putting on or taking off underclothes, mirror, animal, private moment and combinations, the student is encouraged to stay in a chair with his head upright. If he is permitted to move at random, his impulses may be dispersed. In addition, he may engage in habitual movements that stifle creativity. Of course, exercise work must remain flexible. If a student feels the need to move out of the chair in order to relax or to get a sensation, the movement may be valid.

An actor should guard against being too concerned with the mechanics of an exercise, that is, the physical behavior. The goal is to concentrate on his instrument in order to create a specific sensation. If the student does not move at all in an exercise, he may be too tense, holding in energy. Sometimes a student does not move because he is afraid to disturb his concentration, his habits are reigning, he is too mental or he is just not looking for or aware of relaxation. The student should move during an exercise, as he did during initial relaxation, to test his relaxation, to dispel tension and search for sensations. But the instructor should advise actors that unnecessary movement diffuses concentration.

The reality of a sensory object should be there through at least one of an actor's senses. For instance, if the actor looks away from the glass in the drink exercise, the object should still be there through his sense of touch. Conversely, if the actor wants to relax both of his hands, he may first set the glass on an imaginary surface. Then the reality of the glass should remain there through sight. To facilitate concentration, many students prefer to keep their eyes closed when beginning an exercise.

But whether the eyes are open or closed, the student should not continually hold his hand with the imaginary object directly in front of his face or in any fixed position relative to his head and body. Beginners are more prone to do this, falling into a physical relationship between the head and the object. A fixed position between head and hands leads to establishing a set mental image making it difficult for the student to tell the difference between something conceived in his mind and something created through his senses. The actor moves the neck and head, then, along with his entire body, not only to relax, but also to break a relationship between the head and hands which accompanies a mental image. He should be able to feel the imaginary sensory object in his hands, as well as relive all the appropriate sensations, no matter what the rest of his body is doing.

The instructor monitors a student carefully to be certain that he does not hold his head in a fixed straight line with the object and does not hold the object consistently in the same position in relation to his body. An alert teacher is aware that if a student is in either of these fixed positions, he probably is not re-experiencing sensations. Keeping his head away from a set position in relation to the object, helps the actor's hands find sensory aspects of the object and helps his eyes create a fuller visual image. The instructor must be patiently aware that at first the student may create only one sensory reality or none, as the work may be mostly mental if the student is not reliving the sense experience. The teacher knows that as the actor works on exercises, he ultimately realizes that he can concentrate on many senses at once and that concentration can be used for multiple realities.

If the individual has used his senses in life—as he or she must have—the objects experienced are there in sense memory. Most instructors try to accustom students to the idea that everything they experience in life can be re-created. A student *knows* when the sensation he has re-created is real. Moreover, the instructor can often point out to a class the actual physiological changes in the actor's body as a result of his creating and using imaginary stimuli. Method exercises help actors find what works for them; they experiment in order to build a repertoire of imaginary stimuli to use at will as necessary. The task of the teacher is to guide students to train themselves to react to imaginary stimuli as they would to real objects.

The instructor's attitude is important. A positive approach encourages the student to keep on working and to go on to another exercise. If a particular sensation is weak, other exercises, perhaps assigned out of sequence, will strengthen that area. Once the area is strengthened, then the instructor can return to the sequence of basic exercises to profit from their logic and purpose.

Method exercises give the actor continual reinforcement and opportunity to work on weaknesses. Out-of-sequence work, as well as repetition of the early exercises at a later time, addresses problems, while adjustments to combinations coordinate basic beginning sensory work and advanced work. For instance, sometimes in the later stages of exercise work the instructor will ask the student to accumulate several exercises all together. If an advanced exercise, such as an overall sensation, has gone particularly well, the instructor might ask the actor to add to it an earlier exercise that the actor found difficult. The recent success may enable the actor to handle the earlier problem better. Conversely, if the actor is having trouble with an advanced exercise, such as an overall sensation or a private moment, the instructor might assign the addition of the breakfast drink or another simple exercise. Then the actor may not feel so frustrated about being stuck a long time on one type of exercise. In addition to creating the reality of the breakfast drink, some actors will actually increase the real sensations connected with the more advanced exercise.

Continual practice at home is extremely important, even after the actor has moved on to a new exercise. The instructor should maintain a sense of progress, which the flexibility of the Method encourages, for unless the actor is assigned a new exercise the existing one can become a source of frustration.

My final word on exercises is *practice*. I recommend that when practicing at home the actor alternate between exploring the real object and re-creating the object imaginarily. Elia Kazan once described how hard he worked as an actor when he was with the Group Theatre.[22] He said that he "peeled" an orange five hundred times for homework practice, sometimes using a real orange and sometimes not. By such practice he was finally able to actually "feel" the orange peels even when he was using an imaginary orange.

Actors realize the value of continuing exercise work even when they have "made it" as movie stars. When Shelley Winters moderates at the Actors Studio, she reminds actors to practice their sensory exercises, as she still does. She swears, "I'm still reviewing the breakfast drink." Steve McQueen brought Ali McGraw to meet Strasberg, his former teacher, and Lee cast his penetrating look at Steve, asking, "Are you satisfied with what you are doing, Steve?" McQueen became the insecure student again, answering, "No, I should be practicing my exercises."

5 Affective Memory

The term *affect* is used by physicians to describe a patient's emotional status. The concept of affective memory was introduced in 1896 by the French psychologist Theodule Ribot in *La Psychologie des sentiments* and later developed in his *Problèmes de psychologie affective* (1910). He used the terms *affective memory* and *emotional memory* interchangeably. In experiments with human beings Ribot found that the individual could feel the effect of some event in his or her past by reliving the event in the imagination.

Stanislavski believed that advanced psychology could teach the actor to be the master of his own inspiration and how to call it forth, especially through the technique of affective memory. The Russian actor and director had read of Ribot's theories and had also become acquainted with Pavlov's experiments with dogs. Pavlov sounded a bell whenever he gave food to dogs, so the animals associated the bell with food and were thus conditioned to salivate whenever they heard the sound of a bell. That sound became a conditioned stimulus. Whether they were given food or not, the dogs experienced the same sensations. Strasberg concluded, "We know from psychology that emotions have a conditioning factor. That's how we're trained . . . The emotional thing is not from Freud, as people commonly think. Theoretically and actually, it is Pavlov. By singling out certain conditioning factors, you can arouse certain results."[1]

"The use of affective memory and sense memory," wrote Strasberg, "is the discovery of Constantin Stanislavski, and it is the cornerstone of the modern method of training the actor."[2] Stanislavski adopted Ribot's concept for his theory of acting and Strasberg refined the definition, explaining that "affective memory has sense and emotional memory whereas sense memory may not have emotional memory but deals with objects and other specific stimuli."[3] Strasberg always stressed the difference between mentally or abstractly recalling a state of feeling (that is, intellectually rethinking a sequence of events) and using the affective memory to actually *reexperience* the entire occurrence. In using affective memory Strasberg had the actor choose a personal experience associated with the emotional state desired. Then the actor was to re-create sensorily the place, the light and temperature, his clothes and how they felt next to his skin, where he felt hot or cold, a person seen and touched, other sights, odors, tastes, sounds, voices, what was said, what was answered and so forth. As the senses were stimulated, the emotion associated with the sensations of the particular experience would be relived and take possession of the actor.[4]

Strasberg cautioned against trying to recapture emotion directly: "Emotion is not directly controllable." The process of remembering by concentrating on sensory objects is evident in Marcel Proust's *Swann's Way*, section of *Remembrance Of Things Past: Volume I*. In a passage that Strasberg often explained to his classes, Proust brilliantly describes affective memory and illustrates precisely the way in which it can be recalled.[5] The last four pages of the "Overture" section of *Swann's Way* describe affective memory and how it is linked to specific sensory keys that can unlock forgotten past feelings. A student does not start to remember emotions; he starts by remembering the place, the taste and smell of something, the touch of something, the sight of something, the sound of something. The student concentrates on remembering as simply and clearly as he can. Strasberg also often quoted Wordsworth's "emotion recollected in tranquility" and pointed out that affective memory is present in all the arts—musical, literary, visual—but usually functions unconsciously. An actor must learn to use affective memory consciously.

The psychologist Michael Schulman wrote a description of Lee Strasberg's method of teaching acting, plus an explanation of the scientific control of behavior, in *Psychology Today*.[6] After describing sense memory, Schulman explained affective memory:

> In a more complex exercise called affective memory, the actor re-creates the stimuli that were present during an emotional experience in his own life. This form of emotional memory, like hypnotic age regression, involves response to imaginary stimuli. The actor tries to re-experience the specific stimuli of the past event instead of simply recalling the event or remembering the emotion. He seeks to recapture the specific sights, smells, sounds, and tactual sensations that provoked the emotion he wishes to express. The actor uses affective memory to evoke the most powerful emotions, and frequently this exercise leads him to recall forgotten incidents of great intensity. Psychotherapists might find this technique useful. There is evidence that the internal work produces corresponding physiological changes in addition to

affecting the actor's subjective experience.[7] [For more details, see appendix C.]

Affective memory exercises train the actor to consciously create and control a desired emotion. For realistic, believable acting external imitation of an emotion is never effective. The basic value of affective memory is to produce honest emotion that is appropriate for a character's needs at a given moment and that can be repeated at will.

The actor is advised to choose an experience calculated to produce emotion similar to that needed in the scene. What stimulates one person may not stimulate another. A parallel experience works best, but, as Strasberg stated, "It does not matter what an actor remembers, so long as it stirs the proper degree of belief and the proper stimulus to make him behave as he would under the conditions in the play."[8] The actor ultimately fuses his recall with the lines of the play (see exercise 4 below). Strasberg reemphasized the use of memory as "essential to understanding the entire process that goes into acting." He added, "This, by the way, is what is new . . . because otherwise experiencing on the stage cannot be done night after night . . . without an inner technique, which previously was left up in the air when an actor did not stimulate the emotion."[9]

Two actresses[10] once cried fourteen times on cue for fourteen retakes of a particular scene in the film *Aloha, Bobbie and Rose.* The characters Rose and her mother were saying good-bye to each other and were able to give the director what he wanted each time. They are Strasberg-trained Method actresses. Another example of effective use of affective memory in repeated performance took place in my class after a student, Anita Noble, worked on an event leading to shock and hysteria in several affective memory exercises. She then relived the scene six times for the camera to give a film director what he wanted. The actress had the inner technique to stimulate an affective memory. Her real emotion was fused with the character's emotion and event of the scene while she was saying the lines of the script. She kept the emotion going for as long as necessary through the lines and then finally controlled the stopping of the emotion when the scene had ended.

How to Find Affective Memories

Beginning acting students are discouraged from doing affective memory exercises too soon. The exercise works more fully after the student has learned to relax, concentrate and become proficient in sensory exercises.

The student just beginning to do affective memory exercises should choose an unusual event in his or her past—but not too dramatic an event. Although traumatic events are not specifically asked for, the incidents chosen often are. The experience need not have been traumatic for the exercise to be useful.

The final outcome of the affective memory may turn out to have little obvious relation to the original occurrence; the result may be far different from what was expected. The actor may laugh when he originally cried or vice versa. This may be because the actor's original response was repressed or because his or her attitude toward the original incident has changed over the years. Once an actor has found through the affective memory how he now responds to a previous incident, he can file the exercise in his repertoire of exercises to use when needed in a scene.

The student is encouraged to think through his entire life to find experiences that took place in the past and that still move him. As affective memory exercise work progresses, the student will find that some memories seemed important and potent when they occurred but mean nothing in the present, whereas others, almost forgotten, may evoke powerful emotional recall. Thus, an actor must experiment with various past experiences to determine which experiences produce which results. He can then begin to build a repertoire of affective memories.

Actors are advised to go back at least seven years to find appropriate experiences. More recent experiences are harder to control, both during and after the exercise, and may so disturb the actor that he or she is unable to terminate the emotions when desired. A well-trained actor may choose an event less than seven years old, but he should be positive that the reexperiencing will not be a traumatic experience that persists. (For example, if you wish to produce a feeling of rage and frustration by reliving a recent experience in which you wanted to kill someone, you might rekindle your desire to kill that person.) An additional reason for choosing an experience seven years old or older is that the actor's response to it, as evoked in the exercise, is more apt to be the same time after time. A newer experience is less reliable and reactions could change each time. As Strasberg told his students, "The further back the memory goes for affective memory, the better. The emotion is dormant and able to be controlled . . . childhood experiences are often the most vivid."[11]

Affective memory is not only memory. Because it is memory that involves the actor personally, deeply ingrained emotional feelings begin to resurface. This awakens the actor's instrument and he then is capable of the kind of living onstage or before the camera which produces a sense of spontaneous reality. The original emotion can be anger, joy, fear or any other emotion. It can involve love, trepidation, frustration, terror or hate. The memory can be anything the actor uncovers when he searches for an unusual, traumatic or exciting situation in his past. If the student's mind does not immediately go to such an experience when searching for an affective memory, this reluctance could be a sign that such an experience is "built into the unconscious mechanism and doesn't like to be remembered."[12] Such repression happens all the time, especially in the young. Traumatic experiences in fact condition our subsequent behavior through the rest of life. If a student claims he doesn't remember or nothing has happened to him, it is possible the student has unconsciously put such recollections aside. "These experiences and memories," concluded Strasberg, "are often stored up in secret. But the actor must learn to face them, because it is only through himself that he can experience on the stage."[13]

An actor may experiment with more than a hundred affective memories and find only five to eight that work fully. Others may work partially. Experiences that turn out to mean nothing should be discarded. By building a repertoire of affective memories in this way, the actor can develop an inner technique to use the proper stimuli for the desired emotional experience demanded by a particular role.

Oftentimes the same affective memory can be used for more than one role. Indeed, many of the same affective memories and other exercises done as homework and and class work can be employed directly for various roles. When discussing the training in the Group Theatre, Strasberg wrote, "The characterization that Luther Adler did in *Golden Boy* was based on the characterization that we did in *Success Story*. So a lot of things were already worked out, and the people [Group Theatre actors] had learned to use themselves."[14]

All emotions experienced in life can be re-created onstage with all or part of their original depth of feeling. The intensity of the emotion will be slightly different each time, as it is in life when the power of an experience affects us in different degrees. The one big difference is that while the emotion may have been uncontrollable in life, a properly trained actor will completely control his reexperienced emotions.

In December 1976 Strasberg summed up his concept of "remembered emotion":

> "Remembered emotion" is not just personal. . . . But I believe that it is a fact that there is such a thing as emotional memory. Let's say that you come into a room in which something has happened; the thing isn't happening now, but you suddenly remember not just what has happened, but you relive it. I think every human being has experienced that. The only thing is that we are much more cognizant of mental and muscular memory than of emotional memory. It is emotion that recurs without the presence of the object of the moment. In order to repeat a performance, you have to have emotional memory. If you don't, then you repeat only the externals of it, and that's why so many performances vary, actually.[15]

Affective Memory Exercises

After fifty years of experimentation Strasberg concluded that emotions occur more easily and consistently when the actor recreates the sensations associated with the original emotional event. Beginning with sense memory works more fully and consistently, whereas working directly for the emotion, if at all successful, produces variable and inconsistent results.

My student Anita, in an affective memory exercise, reexperienced what she was wearing and the feel of the material against her body; what she tasted, smelled and touched; what people or objects were seen and details of how they looked and what was heard. She relived the sensory elements as if they were happening right then in class. Since she remembered a situation of frying meat, the touch, smell, taste, sight and sound were vivid. Her former husband entered the exercise and she relived all sensory aspects connected with him, finally concluding with what he said and her answers—all being said through her intense emotion. As a result, the emotion was fully relived.[16]

Anita had been in my classes for three years and had done this particular affective memory at least four or five times under my guidance. Through her increasing skill she was able to make use of the exercise when working on a movie location. The role was that of an Oriental girl who becomes hysterical and commits suicide by jumping into a river. When Anita did the affective memory in class, another teacher passing by rushed into the room, suggesting that I stop her, as she believed the actress had lost control and was completely hysterical. When I told Anita to stop the exercise, she was able to do so immediately because she was in control.

The affective memory exercise should be supervised initially by a trained teacher or director who guides the actor to relax as well as to focus on the sensory elements, not directly on the emotion. On a rare occasion, the actor may lose control physically or emotionally. For instance, when an actor in my class started to bend the leg of a chair, I ended the exercise by commanding, "Put the chair down and come forward to talk to me." I looked him directly in the eye and we quietly talked about his exercise. I next guided him to focus his concentration on something new. Concentrating on a new area is effective in escaping affective memory emotions. The instructor will at times be gentle and at other times speak in an authoritative, commanding voice, depending on the situation. If a student appears out of control, I stop the exercise and speak to him in an authoritative tone while remaining calm and in command of the situation. I have never had any problems, but at one time a male student became so angry at Strasberg that two husky class members came to each side of Lee as if to protect him. Strasberg handled the situation by quietly talking to the student and calming him. At other times Strasberg has been tough and almost abrasive during the exercise, depending on how he wanted to reach the student.

Emotion should never be consciously remembered. If the actor is fully relaxed and concentrating, the sensory steps will lead to emotion, thus making a craft out of affective memory work. Only seldom does an actor fail to experience at least a partial affective memory if he is completely relaxed and concentrating. Incomplete effectiveness is usually a result of tension.

The following exercises should be done under supervision until the actor is correctly trained. About three years of instruction or experience are commonly needed to produce consistent results. The affective memory exercise is not an easy exercise. If an untrained student tries to do it alone, the exercise may work only to a small degree or the person may not be able to maintain control. A qualified instructor or director should observe the actor frequently in order to determine whether exercises are being done properly. An experienced person guiding can also clarify and explain any unexpected results. Training time varies according to the actor's commitment to diligent practice and according to his or her natural sensitivity. Initially, the affective memory takes longer to work, but as the actor practices the sensory steps at home, in class, at rehearsal and in early performances, the procedure takes less and less time until the actor discovers that a word, image or sensation can set off the emotion.

Exercise 1

First, the actor should relax, as described in chapter 1 as preparation for all exercises, scene work and performance. With practice and experience the time required to achieve relaxation will decrease. Beginners may require an hour or more; those trained two or three years, approximately twenty minutes; highly experienced actors can often achieve relaxation within two or three minutes.

Next, the actor should concentrate on experiencing his five senses in the particular situation. The best approach is to recall one sense at a time, adding one after the other until all five are working simultaneously. The concentration can begin with what happened three to five minutes before the actual event, but the time needed to do the exercise may take from ten minutes to two hours. Strasberg advised the student not to relax too long or work too long, except for those who had experienced difficulty in the early stages of learning affective memory work.[17]

What the actor is experiencing is then verbalized to the instructor and class or to the director. Verbalization by the actor is initially imperative so that the director or instructor can be sure that the actor is concentrating only on the sensory aspects of the situation.[18] The actor answers such questions: "What do you feel against your body?" "What things do you touch?" "What do you feel kinetically?" "Any taste?" "What odors?" "What do you see?" "What do you hear?" "What time of day is it?" Answers should be specific. Beginners are constantly reminded, "That answer is too general." Specific, probing questions may be asked: "Where are you hot?" "What specific areas?" "What is the temperature?" "What kind of heat—muggy, sticky, dry, sunshine, shower?" The actor should remember exactly what makes him want to relate "I am hot." Recalling such specific sense memories leads to the reliving of emotion.

The exercise reaches its climax when the actor has recalled all possible sensations, physical and then emotional. The student should do the exercise again as soon as reasonably possible and under the guidance of the instructor or director. Before repeating it, however, the actor should determine if any elements of the five senses were missing and should work to include them in the next attempt. The emotion should not be anticipated when repeating the exercise. If the student pushes too forcefully to remember and relive the experience, tension can block the emotion. If that happens, the actor can be asked to sit down, take more time to relax and then go through the sensory aspects of the affective memory without worrying about the results. The exercise will then usually work again.

Many fine actors have unconscious sensations or emotions that function without training in sensory work. Such actors subconsciously use past experiences by working from their own lives and their own truths. The only problem is that the untrained usually lack the consistency needed for several takes or performances. A repertoire of sensory and affective memories generally ensures that capacity. Henry Fonda confided in me that Jane once told him: "You are a Method actor but you don't realize it. You can do unconsciously what others train to do consciously."[19]

Exercise 2 (optional at teacher or director's discretion)

After the student or actor has had enough satisfactory experience with exercise 1 (usually after several class sessions), he or she then proceeds to perform the same sensory steps without verbalizing them. As before, the actor must clear his mind of everything but the sensory aspects of the affective memory. When it appears that the actor has all aspects of sense memory working, the teacher asks him to continue concentrating while performing some simple sensory physical task, such as dusting an object.[20] The actor continues to do the exercise with inner concentration without describing what he or she is doing. The emotion generated will usually affect the imaginary physical task, so it is done differently (for instance, the actor could sweep a floor or make a bed in a faster, angrier manner than normal or with starts and stops according to the affective

Henry Fonda confiding to the author: "Jane tells me I'm a Method actor and don't realize it." In the center is Rosella Snyder.

memory emotion). The actor should continue until the exercise is stopped by the instructor or director.

Exercise 3 (optional at director or teacher's discretion)

Follow the procedure for exercise 1. After the emotion is created, the actor speaks out, using his or her own words, not those of a memorized text. A physical task can be incorporated into the improvisation or not. This improvisation can be a situation from a scene or monologue the actor is working on, or it can be an appropriate original improvisation chosen by the actor alone or jointly with his instructor. Some teachers ask students to speak out the words of a familiar song in order to become accustomed to speaking through the emotion.

Exercise 4

When the actor has worked properly carrying out exercise 1 to achieve good emotional recall, he or she is then ready to repeat the exercise silently, recalling the sensory circumstances of the affective memory and then proceeding to add appropriate lines of dialogue. Before adding lines, however, the instructor or director may check the effectiveness of the recall by asking the actor to verbalize what he is experiencing. The instructor may also ask the actor if he is ready to add dialogue or he may simply instruct him to begin adding dialogue. If the affective memory is working well, checking sensory aspects by verbalization may be omitted. The actor will be guided according to the judgment of the individual director or teacher.

The actor can add dialogue, a few lines at a time, after the exercise begins to work. When the emotion is full, the actor should try to fuse both, slowly speaking the lines through the emotion. If an emotional climax is reached before beginning the dialogue, the actor nevertheless keeps the exercise going, fusing emotion and lines. The actor should never be conscious of how he sounds, nor should he anticipate the result or try to show emotion through words. He should just let whatever happens happen. Occasionally, concentration is lost. If this occurs, the actor returns to what he is experiencing sensorily. He should never stop. As the exercise progresses, the actor adds more and more lines of dialogue, keeping the past experience going at the same time as the dialogue is spoken. Dialogue or sense memories may be lost occasionally, but the actor should respond by relaxing, concentrating on whatever has been lost and trying to fuse both together slowly. *The lines come out of the emotion, as in real life.*

After the exercise the actor is encouraged to continue practicing by himself (or with guidance if needed), repeating the same exercise as soon as possible. Practice continues as more and more lines of dialogue are added. The actor keeps concentrating on the exercise while he speaks lines from the script. He should be able to do this just as he does in life, when he talks to someone and at the same time entertains thoughts. Since an actor is trained to concentrate on many objects at once through the sensory exercises, training in the sensory work leads up to affective memory work. Indeed, all the sensory and affective memory training leads to the actor's ability to accomplish more than one objective while performing. After an actor masters one focus of concentration, he adds another, then another, similar to the way a juggler adds balls.

Exercise 5

Exercise 5—unsupervised affective memory work—allows the actor to work individually after he has had adequate experience with exercises 1 or 4. The self-guided exercise can also be an alternative way to work. Strasberg suggested this method to student directors and advanced acting students: "If you cannot rehearse the affective memory on a scene, rehearse it in life [when getting up in the morning, in the shower, getting dressed, making breakfast, on the subway, on a train, in a sauna or sitting around waiting], anytime during the day, so it [the experience] is flexible."[21]

The actor proceeds as in exercise 1 or 4. He or she should choose a specific event, perhaps one with a moment when something dramatic happened to incite the event. The actor begins the exercise by reliving the sensory aspects during the three to five minutes before the prime moment occurred. Whether the actor relives silently or verbalizes the sensory aspects or fuses dialogue with the emotion created is optional.

After the exercise is completed, the emotions of the exercise may linger during the day—especially in its initial stages. In such cases Strasberg advised the student to then switch to a different exercise as a post-script—an exercise like sunshine—to create a pleasant experience.[22] Students also can simply concentrate on something new.

An exercise rehearsed at various times during the day will become flexible as the actor learns control and ways of doing the exercise. At first the emotion may not be easy to control, but practice will soon give the actor that power. If the actor practices every day, by the end of a week or two he should be able to do the affective memory in one minute.

Teacher and Director Guidance

The actor must be led to re-create the physical aspects of the place where the experience occurred. The instructor or director may ask: Where are you? What is touching you? What do you feel against your skin? Can you feel where your bra (or belt) is fastened? Is it elastic? What material are your shorts or panties? Can you feel the material against your skin? Can you feel the elastic at the waist? The thighs? What kind of shirt material is against your body? Smooth? Rough? Heavy? Light? (Note the two different sensations: where the fabric touches your skin and where it does not.) Do you have any sense of material from your trousers? Any tightness? What are your feet touching? What kind of carpet? Where is your foot touching on the carpet? What kind of feeling does the carpet create on your foot? (If an actor says that he can't feel something, such as the carpet or cement floor under his feet, he is instructed, "Try to.") Where, specifically, do you feel warm? Forehead? Where else? What do you taste? Smell? Feel kinetically? Is there light? Where is it coming from? Can you see any pattern that it throws on the wall? Describe specifically what you see—the color of the wall, forms, woodwork, furniture. What particular objects do you see in the room—size, shape, color? Anything else happening sensorily? Try to recall and re-create the sensory objects and realities for yourself. Don't tell me a story or list the characters in the incident. Try to re-create the place in which you stood. Anything else? The last question can be asked periodically to prompt actors to relive other specific details of the event.

If the affective memory took place out of doors, the actor should try to remember the feeling of the air, rain, wind, snow or sun against his body. He should be led to be aware of temperature outside or inside and re-create it. If he says "I'm cold," he's asked, "Where? Arms? Legs? Get the cold."

When describing a person, the actor must be led to describe the person specifically: clothes worn, color of hair, where he is and what he is doing.

If there is pain in the affective memory, such as a broken bone or accident, the actor should describe its exact location and any changes in intensity (for example, from dull to sharp and vice versa).

I usually ask actors to describe the voices or sounds heard last, but instructors and directors can ask questions about the five senses in varying order. The actor describes the sensory reaction to the words first—children's high voices, women's voices, men's voices, a mixture. By this time the emotion is usually working; the next step is to rehear the words spoken. At this point the emotion invariably works full force.

Actors must be reminded not to explain, editorialize or state an emotional reaction.[23] The actor's concentration will wander too far from the sensory aspects of the event if he tries to narrate a story or give extraneous comments. He must also be cautioned not to give a mere factual account, such as "It is dawn." There has to be more than just an intellectual remembering that it was beginning to be daylight. Actors must be forced to be specific (remember how all aspects of the particular place look in the dawn light, remember the physical dimensions of an important object such as a ship). When the actor verbalizes the experiences of his five senses, he must relive the event as though it were happening in the present.

If the actor complains that he can't remember or can't see what was there, the instructor tells him not to worry but to go on to the next object. One student finally remembered even the kind of anklets and shoes she had worn in a childhood incident. She was surprised later at the details she had re-created but had not consciously remembered before starting the exercise.

If an actor is unsure of a specific ("It's blue or I think it's blue. I'm not sure") he is told, "Whatever you think, that's it. Now keep going— and relax." The teacher or director constantly watches for tenseness, especially in the face, and whenever necessary cautions the actor to relax, such as "Relax your chin, your mouth, watch your eyes."

When the emotion appears to be working as fully as possible, exercise 1 is ended. Exercises 2, 3, 4 and 5 continue as described.

Each affective memory exercise should be practiced and repeated for the instructor or director until the sequence of sensory steps becomes logical and orderly and each circumstance recreated leads to the desired results. If nothing emotional occurs, the actor should not become frustrated or agonize over the lack of feeling. He or she should continue experimenting with new choices of affective memories.

After an affective memory does work, the actor should be careful not to anticipate the emotion or reaction in subsequent rehearsals (trembling from fear or happiness, tears, anger). By setting himself up for the reaction or looking for it, he may lose his concentration on sense memories and in that way fail to evoke the emotion. Finally, the actor is cautioned to remember that when an emotion does happen, it will never be exactly the same as in previous exercises. Each re-creation will be slightly different.

Affective Memory in Preparation, Scene Work and Performance

Sometimes actors utilize an affective memory for preparation work to propel them into a scene. Shelley Winters stated, "I always use an affective memory before I enter. It's the most valuable tool Lee ever taught me."[24] Robert Lewis succinctly explains this use as well as affective memory pitfalls:

> The emotional memory exercises that we [the Group Theatre] used mostly before we started a scene, before we came on the stage to "rev up" our motors, very often tended to place the actor in a psychological grip. Unless used correctly, what can happen is that the emotion that you get from the exercises, if you do get it, feels marvelous—as you know if you're an actor. You've got that thing going in you. You come on now. You're on the stage and you've got this feeling. It somehow blinds you and deafens you so that you don't really see, you don't really hear, you don't really play the action of the moment, but you hang on because it is a marvelous feeling. You don't want to let that feeling go. But you are using emotion for its own sake, and that is no better than using characterization for its own sake. That is one of the dangers that came from the work. The trick was to release yourself from the exercise as you came in and play whatever the situation was, so that the feeling that you had in you went up and down normally the way the emotion does in life, depending on what is happening as you play out the moment. Somebody says something to you that makes you a little more upset, or they say something else, which absolutely pulls you off because you can't imagine why they should say that or whatever. In other words, emotion is not a thing that stays on one line. It is something that is flexible according to what is happening moment by moment. That is what should happen with whatever feeling you get. You should bring it on to use because it is simply a fuel emotion. It is not the emotion but the scene that you play.[25]

Affective memories are also employed during a scene. When an actor has found an affective memory that works for the desired emotion in a scene, he fuses this affective memory emotion with the character and event he is portraying.[26] The actor always listens to his scene partner or the other characters in the play or film and answers naturally, but at the same time when necessary he concentrates on his own affective memory to fuse his emotion with the writer's lines. When more than one affective memory is needed, explained Strasberg, the actor trained in this technique can continue going with his first affective memory and approximately "one and a half minutes before the second one is needed start the second one as he also continues the first. [When properly trained the actor can push the right buttons.] In production I will prepare with two emotional memories and tell the director to decide which one he wants when we come to it, so it will be fresh."[27]

Strasberg recognized that moments of shock are very difficult for the actor. The truthful portrayal of shock can require the use of an affective memory, which can be started during the dialogue preceding the moment of shock. Strasberg demonstrated in an interview with Richard Schechner how he could continue the conversation but at the same time do an affective memory:

> The great actor [creates emotion] spontaneously but not every night. Even the great actor cannot do it every night. And that's where Gordon Craig's challenge is right. If the actor can't do it every night, where is the art? If he has the capacity to do it and yet is not able to, obviously he has no craft. This is exactly the area, therefore, where the training of the imagination and the emotions is essential. Every actor should be able to do it and repeat it. The only way of doing it, if you want a guarantee, is by means of affective memory. It is not separate from the play. A lot of actors say, "How is it possible to be in the play and yet think of this?" This is an erroneous idea of what Stanislavski stands for. I stress very much the fact that the actor works on various levels of his being all the time. He remembers his cues, and if he sees something happening, he corrects it, and so forth. All this is part of the actor's reality on stage.[28]

This point became graphically clear to me when I directed *The Zoo Story*. The actor playing Jerry always cried at approximately the same time when he told the story of the dog. He always seemed to be working well, with the tears spontaneously flowing. One night he tried to push the emotion at the crucial time, became tense and the emotion was gone. He had anticipated the end result without previously following the sensory steps in affective memory.[29] We later experimented with affective memory exercises to find one that worked. I guided him in the sensory steps to re-create the place and event, to concentrate on the senses with which they were connected and to recapture sensorily the circumstances that led to the end result. He was able to develop an inner technique. We followed this procedure for repeated performances of *The Zoo Story* as well as when I directed him as Tevye in *Fiddler on the Roof* and as John Adams in *1776*. In each instance he was able to repeat the affective memory consistently. With practice the memory process requires not more than one or two minutes.

The Group Theatre gave themselves one minute onstage to create the

Discussing affective memory with Shelley Winters outside the Actors Studio.

desired results, thus the famous direction, "Take a minute."[30] Strasberg expounded:

> By the way, if you watch the Olympics, you will see [the athletes] take a minute. It is concentrating. The only thing is that in our case it was concentrating on a definite thing, and it literally was a minute. . . . We did it even in the give and take of a performance. Let's say that you're going to say something a minute from now to which I respond with an unusual outburst. That means that while we are talking I start preparing for the other moment, so that by the time you tell me that line, I'm ready for the burst. That's what is difficult for the actor. And literally we would time the cue for the emotion, because that was the only way we could get it. After a while . . . what happens is [that] it becomes a conditioned reflex.[31]

When some actors become aware of the reality created through affective memories by others in a cast, they have asked me to aid them, too, to work on affective memories. Lee Strasberg told of directing Sanford Meisner in *All the Living*. Meisner was aware of other cast members' using affective memories. When Meisner was not achieving the high emotional moment Lee wanted, Lee let him continue to work in his own way without pushing him. Finally, Meisner asked Strasberg, "What do you want me to do? I'm not getting that moment of burst you want." Strasberg replied, "I only know one thing to do—emotional memory." Strasberg later commented, "It was the only way I could get from him that moment of living through. It must have been very painful for him, because he didn't like to work that way and he did not want to deal with certain things in himself."[32] Nevertheless, Meisner did an affective memory, and Strasberg commented to a class, "It was the best acting Sandy's ever done, and I think he would probably agree with that."[33] At another time Strasberg wrote about reluctance to relive past emotional experiences:

> In every human being there are reasons for [not wanting to do emotional memories]. Nobody likes to remember certain things. But unfortunately when artists like Dostoevski create, they write about their diseases, and they write about their fits . . . They use [emotional memory] in their work, you see. In acting it's true that it's a much more difficult process because [life experiences] have to be used physically. . . . Now you can then say, "I don't want to do it," which is fine. Then you are left without total emotion. If you want to settle for that, that's fine. But if you insist, or if you believe

that the actor is capable of creating reality on the stage with a certain kind of totality (and that I believe because I've seen it done on the stage by great actors), then those of us who may be lesser actors should be able to do [create that reality] as well as the great ones . . .[34]

Thus, if an actor delves deep within himself, sympathetic emotional experiences in the actor's life similar to his character's may be called up. Often this process is painful for the actor, but Strasberg stressed that learning to use the pain is an important element in the development of a fine actor.

Affective Memories with the Untrained

I have directed many untrained actors in affective memory work. Most of them had a natural sensitivity and a developed concentration from participation in theatre. A director especially needs to work closely with the untrained actor in individual affective memory sessions so there will be a foundation of sensory work and so the actor will not anticipate the results.

A young girl playing Chava in *Fiddler on the Roof* asked me to help her motivate the feeling of anguish. She was aware that the father used an affective memory for his role in the scene. After individual work with "Chava" where we explored several events, we finally found one that fully worked for the scene. This affective memory led to tears. Each night, when she told her father good-bye onstage, they both sobbed with tears streaming down their faces, and the audience wept with them. During her homework she had to be carefully guided to concentrate on the sensory circumstances of the affective memory in order to reexperience them.[35]

Once an actor finds an affective memory that works, careful guidance is also necessary to ensure that the actor recalls the same event each time. When I guided an actress playing Lady in *Orpheus Descending*, the actress chose an event that led to agitation and frustration. The fourth time she did the exercise she silently worked on reexperiencing the scene sensorily, but the exercise was not working. When I asked her to verbalize what was happening sensorily, I learned that she was altering the circumstances of the last part of the event. She was recalling another day similar to the original. When she was guided to go back to the original circumstances, recalling and reliving the sensory steps involved, the exercise once again worked as fully as before.[36] She learned that if she desired consistency she could not change the circumstances of a specific event.

Strasberg agreed with his mentor Vakhtangov that the idea of affective memory is the central experience with which the actor works. Strasberg claimed, "Stanislavski and I both believe that only remembered emotion can be relied on during a scene, not literal [current] emotion."[37]

Strasberg also explained how he could use affective memory for shock moments with any actor:

> Usually, we interpret [affective memory] only as the emotional memory, but it is not meant to be only that. That's a device very useful for high moments on the stage, shock moments. For these, the affective memory is the only thing that I know of that will work, and I can make any actor work with that. I don't care whether he is a Frenchman or anyone.[38]

When Affective Memories Don't Work

Strasberg told Actors Studio people that "once an affective memory has worked, it is theoretically capable of working always."[39] If an affective memory appears to wear out, it usually is because the actor is anticipating the result or focusing on what he thinks should happen during the exercise. Such an actor is guided to relax, begin again and work properly with full concentration. Verbalization usually enhances concentration because it can help the actor to avoid getting off track.

There are times when an affective memory will not work, even if the actor does the exercise correctly. The emotional value of the experience could have changed, or as Lee explained, "A counter-conditioning has somehow taken place, and the original experience has lost some of its emotional force."[40] An actor could end up laughing when he thinks he'll cry or vice versa. The exercise need not be discarded as it can be used at another time for the emotion it currently evokes. As the actor experiments he or she finds what works for each particular emotion. By doing many affective memories the actor's stock of memories becomes permanent and consistent—as well as easier to create. The more the actor uses specific affective memories, the easier they become until they be-come *golden keys* to the desired response.[41] "If an actor works system-atically," Strasberg advised, "at the end of three or four years he will have ten or twelve emotional [keys] and he'll know when to use them."[42]

As the actor trains and practices, he is gradually able to bring his own experience to and substitute his own reality in scenes where he needs strong emotional expression. Eventually, the actor becomes so condi-tioned that he can command himself to experience almost any emotion. He has developed new conditioned reflexes for himself. After rehearsing the sensory steps, a good actor can even eventually have unconscious sensations functioning and unconscious emotions functioning, so what is needed for the role becomes second nature. The actor has learned to stimulate and control his physical, mental, sensory and emotional be-havior.

Once Shelley Winters asked Lee Strasberg if the term was *affective* memory or *effective* memory?[43] When Lee explained the word *affective,* the amazed Shelley exclaimed, "I've always thought it was effective memory because it is so effective."

6 Other Exercises

Other Exercises and Theatre Games for Youth Classes and Play Casts

Except for the first half of exercise one, Strasberg never actually taught the first section of seventeen exercises listed in this chapter, but they do incorporate some of his concepts and those of many other teachers I have known throughout the years. Incorporating from many sources, as well as evolving some myself, I have utilized these exercises especially for teaching youth. They are intended to foster observation, concentration and sensory awareness. The gibberish and object exercises, however, derive from Strasberg, as does the "Song and Dance," his special invention.

Lines Have a Meaning

An actor's preparation for a scene is as important as the actual lines. Careful attention must be given to what has happened immediately before a scene begins. This exercise aims to demonstrate the above points and to show the student how the same lines can convey different meanings in different situations according to the actor's intent.

A simple script that can be quickly memorized is prepared:

A: Hi.
B: Hello, how are you?
A: I'm fine.
B: Well, what happened today?
A: Nothing much.

This script is given to two students, who are told to memorize the dialogue without regard to the situation in which it takes place. Then each student is instructed to enact this little scene assuming a specific experience just preceding it. One partner, for example, may be told that he has just (a) lost his job, (b) won $500,000 in a lottery, (c) wrecked his partner's car, (d) learned that his partner has wrecked his car, (e) been falsely accused of stealing or (f) got a big part in a new movie.

The students are given time to prepare themselves for the scene, and as soon as they are ready, the skit is enacted, often followed by a short improvisation to discuss "What happened today." After the scene is finished, the class may participate in a critique and may ask the actors how they prepared for it.

A variation of this exercise uses a script like the following:

A: Hi.
B: Hello.
A: Want a lemon drop?
B: Thanks. Don't mind if I do.
A: You're looking well.
B: Think so? I can't say the same for you.
A: Want another?
B: No, thank you.
A: Strange, isn't it, you here and me, this place and all the rest of it.[1]

After learning these lines, the students are told to prepare and perform the scene as if in one of the following situations: (a) guiding a canoe through rapids, (b) practicing walking a tightrope, (c) waiting outside a dentist's office, (d) waiting outside a principal's office to be reprimanded, (e) B trying to sleep while A teases, (f) in a bomb shelter, (g) in a haunted house, (h) hearing a possible prowler downstairs or (i) seeing an old friend for the first time in several years.

This type of exercise is useful not only to the students who perform but also to the entire class. It shows that the actor's preparation and use of his instrument can convey meaning to the audience even when he is saying lines that have little meaning in themselves. I have used these exercises in my Teachers/Directors/Writers/Actors class to illustrate that words derive their meaning from the actor's intention, from his actions and from the circumstances behind the lines.

Moment-to-Moment

This is a good "get acquainted" theatre game for casts and classes. I explain that there are objects of concentration in acting; in the Moment-to-Moment exercise partners concentrate on each other while they play moment-to-moment, that is, follow their inclinations. The two people are asked to have physical contact in some way (hands, feet or legs touching or one hand on the other person's arm or shoulder). Each actor is to have complete eye contact with his partner throughout the exercise while each says whatever he feels like saying or asks questions. If there is time, the actors are rotated, so class or cast members become better acquainted. This theatre game can be repeated with new partners many times in one session or at various intervals in several sessions.

Some directors use Moment-to-Moment as a rehearsal technique. Two actors play Moment-to-Moment as described but repeat lines from the script rather than speaking their own thoughts. The exercise heightens the awareness of the partner as the character and sometimes new elements or concepts surface.

One-, Two- or Three-word Circle Theatre Games

The actors stand in circles of approximately five persons each. Each actor says one word contributing to a sentence. Eventually several sentences create a story, as if one person were relating the incident. The individual saying the word that ends the sentence can say "Period" so that the next person is aware that he is beginning a new sentence. The same theatre game can be played with each participant contributing two or three words each time. The group must concentrate completely, listen well and respond spontaneously and imaginatively in order for the story to unfold as if one person were talking. This is considered an excellent exercise for ensemble playing.

There are many variations of the circle theatre game. A favorite is Peter Brook's exercise for casts in which each of ten actors repeats one word of Shakespeare's "To be or not to be, that is the question." When the sentence finally flows around the circle, the cast or class realizes they are playing as a group, just as they would form in an ensemble unit. If an actor does something unexpected "but true," the others can go with it as if it had been intended. Variations of this exercise occur when other verbs are substituted for *be* (for example, fear, go, jump, hear, swim, run or see). The teacher can also call out sensory work or moods for the group: create when you are sad, exhilarated, angry, in pain, hot or cold. Each actor can try to create sensory reality, substitute or personalize (see part 2, chapter 8) on the spot for the appropriate physical or inner feeling.

The above theatre games, along with individual sensory exercises and a scene, were done in my class when Shelley Winters brought her twelve-year-old goddaughter to the class. Shelley later asked her what she had learned in her first class. Heather reviewed her experience, "I learned about sense memory, playing moment-to-moment, improvisation and ensemble playing." The talented Shelley nodded approval when the young lady mused, "I always thought acting was feeling things, but I'm beginning to think it's also thinking things." "She was absolutely right," noted Shelley, who is famous for her intelligent approach to a role: "Actors have to be intelligent." Miss Winters shared this incident with my students in 1981. [2]

Lights Out

When the lights are turned out, each student is asked to run, scream and throw himself around in order to lose his inhibitions, release tensions and "let it all hang out." When the lights come on, the student freezes in whatever position he is caught. He does not decide the pose beforehand. He is then asked to use his creativity to decide who he is, where he is and what he is doing in that particular position. He can use real or invented circumstances, tapping his imagination to justify what might appear to be an uncomfortable or senseless pose. Each student relates his situation to the instructor. Without changing his position, his body (external) and his thinking (internal) assume the truth of his invention. The actor has now justified what was originally only a physical attitude. When finished verbalizing, he continues being the character in this particular place, occasionally walking all around the room until fellow classmates speak and are "unfrozen." Sometimes two actors may be told they can interrelate. I terminate the exercise at my discretion. The exercise may be repeated by each student's reassuming his original "frozen" position but directed to choose a new set of circumstances: where? who? and why? The exercise may be repeated several times utilizing the same position or it may be repeated with numerous Lights Out with a new pose each time.

A variation of this exercise involves four distinct poses portrayed in order. The student runs through the four positions twice to learn the sequence. Then, while the student rehearses the positions again, the instructor (or the student) creates a logical progression of events to explain the changes of position. In the next run-through the instructor or another student may call out new circumstances to justify the progression of events. Positions may be altered slightly to accommodate business, but the idea is *not* to alter movements to suit the story. Rather, by studying the muscles, the actor creates a story justifying the movements.

Freeze

Two students act an improvisation until the instructor or another student calls "Freeze." Both actors stay "frozen" in their positions until a third student replaces one of them. The replacement creates a new situation that begins in the same position. The replacement speaks first to begin the new improvisation and to indicate the setting.

Are We All———?

Students walk about the room while concentrating on relaxing. The exercise is done as if each person were in the room alone. One student calls out, "Are we all———?" The object called can be live or inanimate (a tree, rock, animal, baby or whatever). The classmates answer, "Yes, we are all———." Each student then becomes the object, involved in his own concentration even though he might wander around the room near others.

Becoming Inanimate Objects

Students take turns becoming inanimate objects (a spoon, statue, chair, vacuum cleaner or food blender, for instance) and classmates guess what the object is. This game often inspires creativity and imagination, and innovative concepts are often portrayed.

Becoming a Machine

One student begins the game by becoming a part of a machine, moving appropriately. A second student connects to the first by touching some part of the first student's body while moving as his own cog in the machine. Other students connect wherever they wish to become cogs in the machine. The principal part (the first student) sets the pace for the movement. Sometimes I ask for slow motion, accelerated pace or other appropriate alterations. The entire class cooperates by being aware of the leader and "playing together."

Moving to Various Rhythms

Students are told, "You will be walking to all kinds of rhythms, tempos and accents. Concentrate on your own walking, as if you are in the room alone. I, or a student under my direction, will beat a drum starting with a slow 4/4 beat, then varying the pace by hitting the drum faster and then slower. Walk or run to the various tempos heard." Different rhythms and accents can be explored by directing the class to keep going but accent (with a stamp on the floor) a different beat in each bar: for example, **1**, 2, 3, 4; 1, **2**, 3, 4; 1, 2, **3**, 4; 1, 2, 3, **4**. Various changes are possible, such as accenting only a particular bar of a four-bar sequence and walking to the other three bars without an accent, accenting a different count in each bar of the four, or accenting a different count in the first of every four-bar sequence. The time can be changed to 2/4, 3/4 or 5/4, and the tempo can be altered every four bars.

A variation of the above exercise is to play music on a record or tape while the students move to the music. The students can also imagine where they are as they move and explore that place.

Listening for Sounds

All actors relax while they listen for specific sounds in the classroom, hall, building and outdoors. After the first student relates sounds that he heard, others add to it, one at a time, until all sounds are identified. Students are not allowed to repeat noises already labeled. This is an excellent exercise for youth groups if the members become too hyper.

Partners Concentrating on Making Sounds

Two partners sit in chairs facing each other. One closes his eyes while the other makes three sounds—with his mouth, his body or an available object. The student with closed eyes repeats the sounds. Next, the soundmaker repeats his previous sounds, adding one more each time. The partner repeats each time, but if he cannot figure out how a particular sound is made, he is told to open his eyes and the procedure is repeated. He then watches before doing the sounds himself. Not only is this a concentration exercise (for each player must remember and repeat every sound) but it develops a heightened sense of hearing. The game continues as long as one of the participants can remember the order and makeup of the sounds. Some students create twenty or more sounds before switching to the other partner to make the sounds or discontinuing the game.

Other Hearing Exercises
(see also part 2, chapter 4, "Sound")

The student plays a simple song on a phonograph or tape cassette. At the beginning a piece with a single voice or instrument is preferable. After listening, the student rehears the music imaginarily several times. His homework is to go back and forth between the real song and a sensorial re-creation. Then in class, after relaxing, he creates the song imaginarily. At times the instructor asks the student to hum or sing what he imaginarily hears. This exercise can progress to more complicated combinations of instruments (a rock group or a symphony orchestra). The student can experiment with music in varying moods.

Sight Exercises
(see also part 2, chapter 4, "Sight")

Using complete concentration the student studies a poster or picture that does not have too much detail. He or she then turns to a blank wall and resees the poster or picture on the wall. The student goes back and forth between the real object and the wall, checking on details that he or she left out. At times another student or the teacher listens to the student describe what he or she sees on the blank wall. When the verbalization is completed, the observer notes what was left out.

As a variation the student studies the scene outside a window, then resees that scene on the blank wall. The student then follows the same procedure described above for a poster or picture.

Touch Exercise—Leading the Blind

Students work in teams of two. One student closes his eyes while the other takes his hand and leads him around—in the classroom, into other rooms, down hallways and outdoors, if feasible. The "blind" student must trust his partner not to let him stumble on stairs or run into anything. The leader must be aware and considerate of his "blind partner" at all times, so the trust is earned. The leader guides his "blind partner" to a large object or hands him a small one. The "blind" student completely explores the feel of the object, textures, weight and all its properties while his leader verbalizes all these sensorial aspects. The procedure is repeated with more objects investigated. One student becomes sensorily aware of the touch of the objects explored while the other one carefully observes and relates all details connected with sight. The partners decide when to switch roles, so each can be "blind" during the exercise.

Taste and Smell Exercises (see part 2, chapter 4)

I like to assign improvisations using these senses.

Changing Three Things

Two people stand approximately three feet apart facing each other. One partner takes a minute to observe the other completely. He then turns his back and the observed person changes three things about himself. The changes can be in apparel or in the body (for example, hair, blouse or collar in a new position). The first partner turns back and guesses the three changes. He may need to ask for clues. This exercise, like the Making Sounds exercise, can be continued indefinitely as the partner making the changes adds new alterations, one at a time, accumulating four, five, six and several more changes. The exercise continues as long as the changes are continued and remembered or until the imagination has been exhausted.

A variation of this exercise is for the observer to study his partner for one minute, then (with the partner behind him) he specifically describes the partner and his clothing from top to bottom. After the exercise is completed, the class notes any details missed.

Orientation Sensory Theatre Games for Youth

Numerous other theatre games and exercises are described in Viola Spolin's *Improvisation for the Theatre*[3] and Robert Lewis's *Advice to the Players*.[4] I especially like to orient beginning youth to complete concentration and sensory awareness by teaching some of the theatre games and exercises described in this chapter. Other fine exercises are Spolin's "Three Changes," the "Mirror Exercises," "Taste and Smell," "Seeing a Sport," and "Space Substance" as well as Lewis's "Giving Names or Words to the Next Person," "Mirror Exercise Variations," "Counting by Eights," "Two People Telling a Story with Variations" and exercises developing imaginative use of props or articles of costume. Lewis's "Justification" exercises are also beneficial.

The Outrageous Assumption and Lay It on the Other Actor

If there is a short time left at the end of the class period, the group can do one or more of the many theatre games listed in this book. The favorites of my youth classes are "Group Improvisations" (see part 2, chapter 7), the "Three- or One-word Improvisations" (see part 2, chapter 7), "Lights Out" or short improvisations for two entitled "The Outrageous Assumption" and "Lay It on the Other Actor." In the Outrageous Assumption one partner makes a statement about the other actor's body. This statement is accepted as true and must be portrayed (examples: "I'm sorry you are blind" or "have a twitch in your left eye" or "broke your leg"). In Lay It on the Other Actor one partner relates an event or feeling about the other actor (examples: "So you were married today" or "I hear your operation is tomorrow" or "I know you are angry about what I did"). The partner must assume the condition(s) to be true and both actors improvise the situation. Actors are cautioned to make statements rather than ask questions. The actors must listen closely and respond spontaneously. All acting should be as if the scene were happening for the first time.

Object Exercise

Through my years of teaching I have discovered numerous methods of using Vakhtangov's object exercise. This exercise is often useful for young people just beginning acting training or for adults having difficulty doing sensory work with imaginary objects. It may be used either with individuals or with a group of five to ten students seated in a circle.

In the individual exercise a real object (a hat, paper cup, sweater or book, for example) is placed on a table. The student is asked to look at it carefully, observing aspects such as size, shape and color, in order to suggest the sensory qualities of an object to be imagined. The choice of the imaginary object should derive from and be an extension of the actual object: a small paper cup could become a telescope or a camera but would be theatrically illogical as a big shovel. The imaginary object must be different from the actual object. The student then picks up the real object, treating it exactly like the object he is imagining (handling a pencil as if it were a diamond bracelet or baton, or a sweater as if it were a pizza). A student is cautioned not to merely pantomime the idea of the imagined object but to sensorily create all features of it. Finally, the student places the object back on the table, still sensorily treating it as the imagined object. I advise the instructor to comment on the student's sensory work during and after the exercise, just as the teacher guides during any other sensory exercise.

The student may also re-create a small animal instead of an inanimate object (beginners usually find an inanimate object simpler to create). Initially, the student is asked to look at the actual object as if it were a small animal (such as a cat, dog, mouse, rabbit, hamster or whatever), re-creating the animal visually imaginarily while using the actual elements of the object. The student then handles the real object, treating it like the animal he is imagining, playing with it, looking at it, petting it and sensorily creating all aspects of the animal.

When performed by a group, this exercise demands careful observation of all players as well as good sensory work. An object is again placed on a table or handed to a student. He or she is asked to go through the same process described above, handling the object sensorily as if it were an inanimate object (or an animal). But instead of replacing the object on the table, the student passes it to the next student in the circle without telling him or her what imaginary item is being passed. This second student is expected to create sensorily the same imaginary object set by the first student and to keep the same anatomical orientation. If one side of the hat or one end of the sweater has been established as the animal's head, the instructor should not let a subsequent student treat it as the tail. Each student must make an effort to create the reality and to adjust to the characteristics of the imagined object set by the preceding student. The exercise continues without interruption until the circle is completed. Each student continues to sensorily create the object after handing it to the next person, and until the exercise is completed. The instructor comments and questions during the process, according to the needs of each student.

At the end of the exercise young people especially enjoy having each student (starting with the *last one*) describe what object was handed to him and what he created about that object. The student continues the sensory creation while describing his work. Students in this way become aware of who are the best observers, who does the best job of sensory creation and why these two capabilities are so important.

Many variations of this exercise are possible. The first student in the circle may simply be handed an object and told to re-create something specific and then pass it on. Or the first student to be handed an object may himself decide what to create; he may then hand it to the next student, either telling him what it is or not. If the instructor or first student does not announce the nature of the imaginary object, then of course it is always interesting to see if the "object" changes as it goes around the circle. Even though the instructions usually specify re-creating the same object as the person before did, an unaware student may inadvertently change the object. Another variation is for the instructor to hand an object to a student and tell him to examine it closely, then stand in front of the class or in the middle of the circle with the item and improvise a short moment using the object as anything except what it really is. The actor must believe in his object and what he is doing.

Children particularly like to handle objects and pretend they are something else. A good theatre game has fellow students guessing what the imagined object is while the player continues sensorily until someone guesses correctly. The sensorial training of re-creating and retaining all characteristics of an object is one technique of introducing sensory awareness to children.

The variations for adults depend on individual student or group needs. Sometimes the students doing this exercise will pass the object around the circle three times. Other times, the nature of the object can be varied (try a food, another inanimate object or an animal). This exercise can also be useful for an adult with a concentration problem. Dealing with a real object can give the student a hook into sensory work. The real object provides a focus for concentration.

This exercise, like most, is flexible. Instructors often get ideas for variations right in class.

Gibberish Exercises

Gibberish is meaningless or unintelligible talk.[5] In this exercise students use nonsense sounds in place of understandable speech. This forces them to communicate by means other than speech, such as carriage, tone of voice, gestures and body movement. As the participants speak their nonsense lines, however, they must think of the meaning behind the sounds.

For young people and inexperienced actors I sometimes ask a student to give a short talk or demonstrate a product using gibberish while another student translates into words what is being communicated. Young people love this exercise, and it not only aids the person doing the gibberish but also helps the translator (and the rest of the class) learn to observe the performer closely and listen to his tone of voice.

Gibberish is most often employed, as Strasberg used it, in scene work, where it serves to break up verbal patterns and habitual responses, opening the way to true expression. Here two actors are given a scene to play in which they are to portray a given mood or intention or are given a specific objective to achieve. The scene may be an actual one from a play, often a play they are actively rehearsing. Then they are instructed to use only mixed up, crazy words and sounds while communicating with and responding to each other.

Gibberish exercises only produce understanding in a general way. Nevertheless, the actors are instructed to proceed with the scene as if

At a reception with Princess Grace during a directors workshop in Monaco.

they understood each other fully. But if one actor fails totally to understand the other, he or she may respond in a noncommittal way (such as, "Uh-huh"), forcing the first actor to make clearer what he is communicating. Thus, the first actor must make the second understand in spite of the gibberish. Each actor must listen freshly and closely.

Even though what the actors are really saying to each other may be hazy, somehow voices become more expressive and the thought gets into the tone. Often students who have previously been tied to the verbal and punctuation pattern of lines can become fluent, flexible and colorful when doing the scene in gibberish. These more expressive and colorful qualities are portable and can be carried over to become part of the character when the actor returns to the script.

Strasberg learned gibberish exercises from Richard Boleslavsky and Maria Ouspenskaya. He believed that such exercises train the student to "expedite the sense of expression in the words and draw out dramatic results when other exercises have failed."[6] He insisted that each actor be able to make the other understand, even though they were using gibberish, and he warned that each must pay close attention to the other. In Strasberg's words, "Each must hold the other to strict account . . ." The exercise, argued Strasberg, "calls for more convincing acting without the lines than the actors would give with them."[7]

Strasberg used gibberish in the Group Theatre for a specialized purpose:

> I found it most helpful in dealing with actors who had an emotional problem in that they could feel, but expressing the feeling was difficult. In one play I had great problems with an actress, but also with my backers, who wanted the show to be finished so they could see what was going to be done. However, because of my difficulty with this actress, I didn't wish to finish the production. There were scenes in which she had to cut loose emotionally, but there was no real life. They were cloaked in conventionality. I wanted her constantly free and improvising in the hope that what we were working for would break through. Fortunately in the last week the breakthrough came, and it came through gibberish. She had to keep doing these emotional things and talking about them in gibberish, and in using sounds and words that broke away from her conventional and habitual tightness, she exploded.[8]

Strasberg also used gibberish exercises with the Group Theatre when actors were having difficulty communicating on a literal level. When a scene is acted in gibberish, the participants think real thoughts and listen to and respond to other actors. Gibberish demands great concentration and innovativeness to transmit and receive ideas, intentions, feelings and thoughts without the use of words. The exercise draws the actor away from his habitual manner of saying lines and forces him to communicate intentions more clearly.

Strasberg always fought against the cliché in acting—the habitual response or, as he sometimes called it, "the verbal line." Such clichéd work, in Strasberg's estimation, meant that "the primary impulse to creation is lost and work on a scene goes into unconscious patterns."[9] The gibberish exercise, through its unidentifiable combinations of unrelated consonants and vowels, broke up verbal patterns and habitual responses so that the actor was forced to be more expressive.

Regardless, Strasberg cautioned his faculty that gibberish is to be used only at a certain point in the training or a certain point in production. "Use it when you are dealing with actors who have difficulty and are stuck in a verbal pattern. Earlier in the training use improvisation, speaking out or singing the words."[10]

Gibberish can aid actors to listen, respond and relate to one another. I found this true even when actors did not speak the same language. While teaching acting workshops at the Monaco International Theatre Conference and World Play Festival, I encountered actors from all over the world. Even though my instructions were translated into French, many participants could not understand one another. So I assigned gibberish improvisations, giving each student a place to create and an objective. Particularly memorable was the improvisation between a man from Yugoslavia and a young lady from Finland. The scene was at a bar and his objective was to get her to leave the bar with him; her objective was to stay at the bar. Their gibberish was expressive, fluent and colorful, and all of those watching understood them well. Frustrated, the man finally picked the girl up bodily and carried her away. I stopped the exercise as they were going out of sight. Later, the girl asked me, "Why did you stop us? I wanted to find out what would happen next. Perhaps we can continue the scene by ourselves." I have often wondered how that exercise finally turned out.

Song and Dance Exercise

Certain types of theatre, such as opera, operetta and musical comedy, require that the performer be both an accomplished singer and actor. Strasberg invented the Song and Dance exercise when he was teaching acting to singers. Music has its own pace and rhythm, and singers spend many years learning to follow these musical patterns. Such patterns can become habitual, and when singers turn to acting they tend to carry these patterns into their speech and movement onstage.

Strasberg reasoned that it was important to interrupt this habitual connection between music and the verbal pattern, between rhythm and movement. To accomplish this he began to experiment with exercises separating the sounds in a simple song. He reduced the music to rhythm-less, single sustained tones (preferably with the same count for each tone) and prescribed spontaneous and sometimes explosive movements following no preconceived plan. Strasberg soon discovered that such exercises produced "extraordinary results" when used to deal with all manner of acting problems. Not only did the Song and Dance exercise release inhibitions but it also inspired new modes of expression for "strong responses which have not been inhibited but simply not expressed."[11] "Often," Strasberg explained, "by channeling the sensation, and then, at the moment of feeling or impulse, permitting the actor to do things he's never done before, without knowing in advance what he's going to do, you help him break away from his set pattern [of movement, behavior and words]."[12]

Description

The student stands relaxed in the middle of the stage, his weight on the balls of his feet. When completely relaxed, he starts the exercise by standing absolutely still, his hands at his sides, vocalizing a simple song, such as "Happy Birthday," or a nursery rhyme/song.[13] The song is done in a monosyllabic fashion, each syllable usually having approximately equal time and emphasis. The song may follow the melody or be done in a monotone. Although equal time is not mandatory, the student should strive for an even, resonant, sustained tone created with a relaxed throat and maximum chest vibration. Each sound should be stopped while full and committed; the breath should not be allowed to be exhausted.

After the song has been completed the student executes a spontaneous movement. The movement should be larger than life and should involve the whole body, if possible, although the feet usually remain still. The relaxed arms will naturally follow the body movement. The movement may be explosive. The first movement lasts only a few seconds, but the student then repeats it five to eight times. During this repetition the actor vocalizes syllables of the song fully in an irregular, explosive monotone, letting the sound erupt occasionally through the movement. The student is instructed: "Let the sound (not the word) explode whenever you feel like it, but keep the rhythm of the movement going. Don't let the words decide the rhythm or vice versa." The teacher may direct the sound to erupt one, two, three or more times, depending on how full the sound is each time.

After several repetitions of the original movement and a full, explosive sound has been produced, the student initiates a new movement, which can involve the feet moving (jumping, marching, skipping in place or whatever). At first the teacher tells the student when to start a new movement (by calling "change"), usually after approximately three attempts at exploding the sound. As the student becomes more experienced with the exercise, he is encouraged to decide when he has made a full sound and then when to begin a second, third or fourth movement. The new motion is repeated five to eight times as the first movement was, the student continuing to erupt the sound as before. The exercise continues in this manner until at least three different movements have been executed separately.

At the appropriate time the instructor terminates the exercise and asks the student to stand still in the same position as at the beginning of the exercise. Next, the instructor asks the student to relax, to think about what he is *now* feeling, to take his time with his thoughts and feelings and to make contact with them. Finally, he or she tells the student to share with the class what he is thinking and feeling. The teacher may ask: "How do you feel now? Happy? Frustrated? Afraid?" "What do you feel like doing? Shouting? Crying? Laughing?" "How did you feel during the exercise?" "How did you feel about the audience?" "Was it hostile or friendly?" "Do you want to embrace them?" Such questions often encourage the student to examine his own feelings, to become aware of what is happening within and to talk about that awareness. A flood of feeling and expression connected with the student's own life will sometimes gush forth. The thoughts articulated at such a time are often astounding. Frequently, a rather personal dialogue develops between teacher and student leading to considerable mutual understanding. Consequently, the exercise not only tends to release inhibitions and eliminate habits of voice and movement but it also can provide a pathway for the student actor to become more aware of himself.

As a Solution to Actors Problems

Strasberg repeatedly insisted, "Anyone who can do the Song and Dance exercise can do anything onstage." He found that this exercise enabled the instructor to understand an individual student better and diagnose his or her acting problems (those connected with the actor's will and ability to express himself or herself). The exercise turned out to be an "X-ray into the problem of will and the relation of will to consummation,"[14] that is, the ability of an actor to carry through what he is trying to perform. The student actor displays this ability by breaking the song into single tones and changing the rhythm or movement at command in the dance. The student is instructed to follow his own or the instructor's command freely and flexibly without knowing in advance how he will do it.

This following of a command should not be practiced and habitual. If the student cannot follow his impulses in the production of the tone or by freely changing his movement, the exercise reveals someone who clings to habits. Since the exercise forces the actor to make sounds and movements counter to habit, it and the instructor can make the person aware that he often is not doing what he thinks he is doing. The instructor can point out these instances of distracting, unconscious mannerisms and automatic behavior. One student learned from Strasberg: "You thought you were not doing things with your hands, but you were. That shows in all your work. [But] often you are not doing what you *think* you are doing, and the exercise makes you aware of it."[15]

Even after a student actor learns to relax, concentrate and believe in the logic and reality of what he is doing, his expression of these qualities may still be weak. He can come onstage with habits of nonexpression. What is going on inside the actor may not come out. Emotions may not come through. The actor may want to laugh or cry but be unable to break through strong conditioning that blocks the expression of such emotion. As Strasberg explained, the actor "may not be able to uncurl muscles to let tears flow."[16]

Strasberg experimented with the whole problem of hidden emotions. An extreme example of blocked impulses and expression of emotion occurred during the song portion of the exercise when a student complained, "I'm going to faint." Strasberg handled this problem as follows:

> Put your head down. Take your time to get up. Too quickly will make you feel dizzy again. Feeling dizzy means something emotional is happening. Stop the song and tell me, "Can you put a word to what is happening?" [The answer was "Panic."] Take time to acknowledge what is happening. Too many things are happening that you are not acknowledging. Dizziness is comparable to people panicking at a door when there is a fire. What is happening to you is the same thing . . . a lot of impulses are trying to get through, so you block up and get dizzy. Oxygen is needed. Take it easy, take your time and acknowledge what is happening or you'll get panicky again. Continue the song. See? When she tries to commit herself in the tone [after two more syllables] other things come through. Her instrument is more alive. . . . [During the movement portion of the exercise Strasberg instructed:] Dance with the body. Not so much with your hands. The hands will naturally follow. Hold your head straight and do what you are doing. Fine, otherwise you'll get dizzy. Don't move your head.[17]

An important purpose of the Song and Dance exercise is to make the actor aware of the nature of his impulses and emotions. The actor silently asks himself any of the following or similar questions: What is happening? What kind of sensation is this? What sort of an experience is this? Am I angry? Do I feel shy? Am I embarrassed? Am I afraid? What is causing my fear? Is it one type of reaction or another? The instructor may ask such questions aloud if it is necessary to make the student become aware of the answers. Again and again students are urged, "Make contact with what is happening in you and let it come through the tone." While the student is standing still (during the song part of the exercise), the instructor should be alert to see whether the student's impulses and emotions are expressed through his voice. During the dance portion, the instructor watches to see if impulses and emotions come out in movement or in the sound exploding through the movement. The instructor observes too if the student moves or jerks parts of the body in involuntary, nervous expression (an indication of the conflict between spontaneity and repression). If this is evident, the teacher can urge the student not to hold back impulses. The teacher encourages the student to let his or her impulses and emotion come out through the sound and movement. The goal is for the actor to make contact with himself, allowing impulse and awarenesss to connect and become externalized (vocally and/or physically).

Role of the Instructor for Song Phase

The role of the instructor is paramount in this exercise. The teacher sometimes must substitute his will for the actor's in order for the actor to profit from the exercise.

The instructor's first task is to assess relaxation. Standing alone in front of the class often causes tension in the student, so the instructor should be alert for twitching fingers, strained muscles or any other evidence of tension. Prior to the song the usual tests of relaxation can be employed. The instructor may lift the student's arms to check relaxation or he may monitor head, neck, legs and other parts of the body in the same manner as for the sitting relaxation position. He may also tap the student's back or chest while the student makes sounds to determine relaxation or to ascertain if sounds are vibrating fully from the chest. Occasionally the teacher just watches and comments.

The student may at first involuntarily shake his hands and fingers after being instructed to stand upright and still, his hands at his sides. At times this arises out of nervousness, but it can also be a relaxation technique. Strasberg sometimes pulled fingers apart or asked the student to move the thumbs or fingers slightly. The student may be told, "Let tension flow out through the fingertips. Watch various muscles through the body that are shaking and just relax them." Sometimes the student will bend a knee or sway or lean forward; then he is asked to assume a position (with his legs straight yet relaxed) in which he is comfortable, for he is not to move his feet or bend his knees once he is in position.

Students will often assume awkward positions, their feet too far apart or too close together. The choice of an uncomfortable position may indicate that the student is doing what he thinks is wanted rather than what is comfortable for him. Adopting a military stance, for example, can be a clue that the actor is more concerned with doing the right thing than with his own feelings and comfort. That kind of stance can suggest that the individual is not used to making his own choices but responds to being ordered. At times a student will brace himself, as if about to be hit. If he stands with his feet wide apart, he appears to be bracing for a fight—the so-called Atlas stance in which the individual stands ready to take on the world. The point is this: the instructor should not specify the position of the feet. The actor is given the option of standing with the feet apart comfortably. The burden falls on the instructor to be aware if there is nothing to perceive or to recognize and understand the student's impulses, habits and conditioning and help him to free himself if necessary.

When relaxation and a comfortable stance are achieved, the student is told to put his hands at his sides and stop moving. The song is then begun as described earlier. At this point there is often some twitching of fingers or other involuntary nervous reactions (such as the body swaying, arms moving, chest or shoulders heaving or the body trembling). There may also be conditioned movement of the head. The instructor informs the student of such problems and urges him to keep still or to use his mind to relax. The student is not to move any twitching area.[18]

Even though the teacher tells the student not to shuffle his feet or move, the exercise is flexible. The instructor determines whether movement is detrimental or incidental. If the instructor feels that the student is really trying to follow directions and do the exercise properly, then the student may be told to return his feet to their original position and continue. If the instructor decides that the student is not committed to doing the exercise properly, it is terminated and the student is told to return to his seat.

During the exercise the instructor monitors the student's control of voice and body. He may also have to warn the actor not to try to "sell" the song, even though the student has contact with the audience. The student is instructed to take a full breath of air and to sing one syllable at a time. The effort is not so much on the letters of the syllable as it is on good, open-throated, resonant, full sounds made with strong commitment. The student is instructed to stand still and not worry about the words; if he forgets the words, he should proceed with the sounds. The student should not fall into the rhythm of the song or the meter of the music; he may need to be instructed, "Let there be a longer vibration of the tone until you feel it's right. We want you to control the sound, so it does what *you* want it to do."

The instructor may sometimes ask a student to sing the song through once, either before or after the exercise, in order to find out if the student knows the melody. This makes it easier for the instructor to evaluate the student's execution of the exercise. A mistake in the melody, for instance, from an individual who has shown that he knows the tune might reveal a very habit-dominated person who loses control when not allowed to sing in his customary way.

If the actor is having difficulty producing the sound itself (a tight throat, a tense mouth whose position is blocking sound from coming through or the voice and chest not vibrating), the instructor may urge the actor to stand still for a few syllables and produce a full, committed sound vibrating from the chest. Melody is unimportant. The sound should come from an open throat and pour forth freely. Some actors produce the entire song in monotone. Ordinarily, however, it is preferable for the student to follow the melody. Accurate pitch shows that the student can control voice placement.

The actor is encouraged to keep the song going, for stopping and starting indicate habitual blockage. Nor should the sound be allowed to fade. Each note should be maintained fully until the student moves on to the next. The instructor may ask the student to stop the sound periodically, at will, showing the extent to which the actor is in control of himself and the extent to which he is willing to express himself. The instructor may have to encourage an insecure, inhibited student: "Don't be frightened of the next tone if it's high. Keep going with the same kind of energy."

The song exercise demands a break with the actor's habitual attack. The instructor should be able to assess the attitude of the actor toward the audience, the actor's mannerisms and his ability to express himself openly. For example, the actor may slide his voice into a sound—almost sneak into it. Even though there is no right or wrong approach, this mode of singing can reveal someone who is tentative about his own choices, who may not trust his own action or commit himself initially but try to slide into things half committed, which will show in his acting. Another actor may reveal a wonderful commitment. If sound is distorted, the actor may be trying too hard. Many, many things can be revealed.

If the instructor feels the student is trying to retreat from the audience, he will direct the student to look at the people while singing the song. Some instructors instruct the student to establish eye contact with the audience in order to see what will happen. If the student glances over the class or looks at class members with a kind of glazed look, the instructor may ask him to make individual contact by looking at particular people to precipitate real communication. Students are guided not to look at the ceiling, at the floor or off to the side but to make contact with the people in the room.

The instructor may find that deep down the actor suspects that people are judging him as he stands up there. The way to deal with a negative attitude is to have the student repeat the exercise a number of times to show him that he is not being judged, that the audience is not hostile and that he can make contact, can put energy or impulse into the sound.

Strasberg's original intention in this exercise was to break an actor's habits by requiring him to give each syllable of the song approximately equal value. But sometimes in the course of the exercise, perhaps in some cases because of the relaxed standing position, strong impulses arise, some emotional in nature. When the instructor perceives such a situation, he may ask the actor to make a conscious effort to make contact with the impulse, to discover whether it is sorrow, fear, anger, embarrassment or another emotion. At this point, giving equal value to the sustained tones is unimportant, particularly if the student becomes aware of his emotional impulses and himself. The instructor may ask, "What is happening?" "What kind of experience is this?" "What do you feel like doing? Laughing? Crying? Screaming? Hitting?" "Do you want to punch somebody? Kick? Choke?" "All these things can be done without actually touching somebody. You can take your fist and punch it into the air. Or you can kick your leg without actually kicking a person." The instructor may notice tears, in which case he can stop the song to discuss that impulse or talk about impulses of tears and laughter as the student continues the tones. Strasberg theorized, "Whenever actual impulses cannot be expressed, we either laugh or cry, as these two basic expressions become representative of many things that cannot be represented."[19]

The instructor thus guides the actor to make contact with his impulses, identify them and express them vocally through the sounds of the song. The instructor should remember that the immobility of the student's body does not mean the actor stands rigid or tense, thereby holding in an impulse. Staying relaxed channels all energy through the voice. Impulses thus have no place to go but out through the sound.

The exercise proceeds for an indeterminate period. Sometimes an instructor may have one student do only four or five syllables; other students may go through the song and start over again. The teacher has the students continue as long as necessary for the instructor to evaluate the exercise. The instructor may discuss the exercise with the student immediately after the song half or wait until both song and dance are completed.

Commentary during the exercise varies according to the student, his or her problems and the value of the comments to others in the class. Typical comments include: "Relax your throat. It is tight. You are not getting the lungs into the exercise so there is no vibration. Relax, don't rush. Take a breath and start again. Do each syllable separately. As soon as you finish the syllable you finish the sound." After one student produced an exceptionally long sound, however, Strasberg inquired, "Why did you make that sound so long? There's an element of compulsion in you. You'd like to tell people off? [The answer was "Yah."] Okay, that's a good response. Otherwise, it's blocked."[20]

When a teacher talks during the exercise, the student sometimes just stops and listens and at other times continues. Many students have a tendency to slide syllable by syllable, because they can follow the melody that way by habit. The instructor may then say, "Wait, pause, breathe. Just breathe." Such an interruption can also be made when the student is getting tense or when he or she has fallen into the rhythm of the song. After the pause, the student has to recapture the tune without reference to the preceding note. The point is to disrupt the student's habit and see if he or she can regain control of the count or the tune.

The student's will, state of relaxation, concentration and expression are obviously all involved in this exercise, making it a useful tool for diagnosing problems (for example, tension, hesitation, tight vocal cords, stopping) the actor should recognize. Because the exercise involves an abstract series of syllables or tones, the actor can concentrate on what he is commanding himself to do and go with the impulses that arise. During the song he should try to channel his immediate feelings, resulting from the investigation of himself and the people before him, into the sound he is producing. Some actors have an easy time doing the exercise; others may lack the conviction to follow their own instincts.

This simple exercise with its simple sounds can conquer the problem of expression. Strasberg told a class, "This [exercise] has nothing to do with the song. Because we use a song, we call it the song part. Likewise, the dance part has nothing to do with dance. It is the movement part of the exercise."

Role of the Instructor for Dance Phase

The student is instructed to make an unpremeditated, single movement that involves the entire body. The student then repeats this movement, attempting to remember what he did spontaneously and reproduce it accurately. He then repeats the movement again and again as accurately as possible. In this process the student should establish a fluid, connected rhythm. Generally such a connected movement will originate in the center of the body and the limbs will follow. The student is instructed, "Get the whole body into the exercise. Don't tighten your arms. They'll come after you." The movement can be circular, as the student throws his arms wide, moving his entire body from the waist but keeping his feet still for the first movement. For subsequent movements he can swing the torso up and down or from side to side, throw arms and feet wide, jump high, make large marching steps in place, move the entire body to jazz rhythms, change directions or combine movements.

The role of the instructor is to guide the student to retain control of his movements and to develop an awareness of the various parts of the body so that he can reproduce a spontaneous movement easily and accurately. The instructor may have to tell the student to stand in one spot, and then to shimmy all over the body or to use jazzlike movements, to slow down or take it easy. Sometimes he should keep his feet still, especially, if his movements have been too random, such as trotting aimlessly around the stage or jumping in general. Keeping the feet still limits the field of action and focuses concentration. Strasberg frequently admonished students, "There's no excuse for not taking your body and making it do what you want it to do."

Unless the student is advanced and knows when to change the movement himself, he will be asked to keep the same movement going until the instructor tells him to change. Usually, the instructor will call for a change of movement after a full sound has erupted. The instructor may also tell the student when to produce a sound or to let the sound erupt through the movement occasionally. Having the instructor give commands helps develop spontaneity, especially in beginning students.

The instructor often has to urge the student to make larger than life movements in order to get away from small, habitual movements. Then the student is guided to stand up straight and try to recall what he just did spontaneously and do it again exactly, deliberately, consciously. What was once spontaneous is now deliberate. This in fact is the whole acting problem: "To deliberately appear to be spontaneous." The student then pulls himself back up straight, repeats the movement again and continues this procedure. The instructor may talk to the student as he is making the movement. He may point to different areas of the body: "Let the arms follow more." "Try to find a way to let the movement originate from the central parts of the body—the torso and the trunk of the body." "Let the head and limbs follow the movement." "Don't deliberately move the arms or head. They'll come after." "Make a more connected or fluid movement, not so controlled, or mechanical, like a tin man." "Don't think. Continue the rhythm of the movement."

Even though there are no prescribed movements, the instructor may suggest changes. If a student does something similar to a former movement, the teacher may ask for a different type, such as, "Do something wiggly." He might suggest a jazz or shimmy move if the center of the body is too tight or if the arms movements are too planned rather than flowing out of some movement coming from the trunk. The idea is to get the actor to move with uncensored commitment.

If a person is moving in a way that is too muscular, with a tremendous amount of energy, the instructor may ask him to move in a way that's more "like jelly." For the actor who approaches movement as if he were trying to contract his muscles, this jelly instruction can be so contrary that an interesting change may occur. When movement is slow and easy the instructor should observe whether the sound, when added, is properly explosive or whether it is passive like the movement. Passivity can suggest a lack of awareness or unbroken habits.

If the student's movement is too small or if he is not committing himself enough, the instructor may tell the student to engage in a bold movement, like jumping for the ceiling or jumping as high as possible.

After a continuous, connected rhythm is established a syllable from the song is occasionally thrown in after a warning from the instructor not to let the throat become tight or the sound turn into a scream. But the sound is of no value if done easily. It should be done fully, with support, and the student should strive for chest vibration. The sound should not be tied to the muscles or the movement, as in a pattern, but should consist of short bursts of explosive sounds erupting occasionally through the movement.

If the actor has difficulty making the sound freely, it may mean he has difficulty with expression. If the vocal cords are not relaxed, the student will not be able to respond to the dictates of his impulse. The teacher may speak to the student about making the sound fuller, supported, more explosive or more resonant; he should not do too much from the throat but instead relax it. Students typically try to prolong the sound too much in this portion of the exercise.

If the movement and sound follow too much of a pattern or the sound is accompanying the movement, the instructor can tell the student to breathe and continue the movement; the instructor then tells the student when to throw in another syllable or sound, letting it out full from the lungs. If the student continues to have trouble exploding the sound while doing the movement, the teacher can ask him to stand still and make an explosive sound, letting it resonate in the chest, just to illustrate to the student how the sound is produced.

When additional movements are executed, the instructor guides the actor to create a different kind of movement and insert it without thinking. The new movement is then repeated, as described for the first movement. The instructor usually asks the student not to throw in a sound until he has established a rhythm. If the student fails to reproduce the exact movement, he or she is advised of the problem and not allowed to proceed to the sound until the movement is established, based on the first unpremeditated movement switch.

There is no set formula for optimum movement, for investigation and individual effort are important aspects of this exercise. Since the entire exercise is so flexible and is done in a variety of ways, analysis and changes primarily depend on the instructor's ability to perceive what is happening.

Since the movement is unpremeditated, there is no way to practice at home. But occasionally the instructor must make allowances for an extraordinarily insecure student who may be told to go home and practice movements or simply moving so that he or she has some movement available when it is needed.

The Actor's Will and Spontaneity

The purpose of the Song and Dance exercise is for the student to become more spontaneous, to concentrate better, to be aware of and avoid habits or mannerisms and to activate his will and energy in order to let himself use himself and do things he has never done before. While sensory concentration exercises and other exercises deal with the creation of impulses, the Song and Dance permits impulses to take their own course. Strasberg explained that this exercise thus trained the actor's "peculiar ability to be free and yet to will the freedom. [The actor] gives himself a definite act, deed, or object. He is aware of what he is doing while he is doing it. Thus, the impulse pours, is permitted to come out in expression." In the Song and Dance actors sometimes cry, laugh or react in unusual ways. Sometimes the actor does not know why and discussion at the end of the exercise often reveals the reasons. The actor is thus "induced to be a more expressive instrument, like a piano which does not censor the pianist."[21] When a pianist strikes a key, the piano responds with that note. When a person hits a note, however, an entire process of conditioning can interfere with his expression. One of Strasberg's greatest concepts is that the conditioned, fixed instrument of the actor has to be retrained or reconditioned so that the instrument will do what the actor wants it to do.

Habits often deflect an actor's intentions. Mannerisms and unconscious behavior can impede the actor's work. The Song and Dance exercise helps make the actor aware of such problems at the time they occur.

Strasberg believed that this awareness constitutes the difference between life and acting. In life a person can be unaware of what is happening, but in acting the actor knows what he is doing while he is doing it. Stanislavski called this split awareness "the feeling for truth." Strasberg argued that this awareness "must develop as kind of a sixth sense, and yet it cannot do so at the expense of the actor's belief, his concentration, his involvement in what he is doing."[22]

A human being can be aware and involved at the same time. Strasberg stressed this concept: "One of the most serious misunderstandings of actors is to assume that to act truly and believably [is] to forget what you are doing. But that's hysteria—in life as well as in acting. When a person forgets, it means that he has gone beyond the point where he is willfully doing something."[23] Art is willful creation, even though it can have results the artist has not predicted. Moreover, in order to repeat—as an actor must—there has to be awareness. Awareness does not preclude the actor's giving himself fully to the role. According to Strasberg, "The awareness is essential if [the actor] is to accomplish that fusion and involvement."[24]

The Song and Dance deals with the essential problem in acting: how to create, re-create and maintain spontaneity. The actor must know what he is going to do when he goes before the camera or on the stage, but at the same time he has to let himself do it as if he were doing it for the first time. So just as the actor is confronted by the element of repetition in the work situation (onstage or before the camera), so he is confronted by the element of repetition in the Song and Dance exercise, *but* with the voice, body and every facet of expression following the natural changes in impulse. The presence or lack of spontaneity in the impulse can be discerned by movement and tone of voice. The strength of the impulses may even change from performance to performance. When the actor can do this exercise successfully, the results are clearly visible in his scene work.

7 Improvisation

Improvisation is the act of performing without previous preparation; it is the spur-of-the-moment attempt to deal with a given situation or "solve" a given problem. The essential element is spontaneity. While the given situation or problem may be a familiar one, its "development" must be unrehearsed.

For the actor, improvisation means assuming a particular character (sometimes the actor's own) in a given situation. The actor creates his own dialogue and movements as he goes along—acting without a script. Improvisation is often overlooked or even deprecated by actors and directors, especially by inexperienced ones, but the technique has great value in actor training, casting, rehearsal and performance. It can even aid the playwright.

The relationship of improvisational technique to most normal human activities is obvious. Most of daily life is planned only in a very general way. We may choose where we will be—at home, at work, at lunch, at play—and perhaps who will be with us. But we rarely plan, rehearse and memorize exactly what we are going to do and say. Most human interactions and activities therefore have an extemporaneous quality about them, a spontaneity the actor must preserve onstage.

Of course, some activities are planned and carried out in a ritualistic fashion. Church services are an example, as are fraternal initiations, inaugurations, weddings and other functions in which the words are memorized or read from a text and the movements of the participants planned and rehearsed. We often describe such events as stiff, formal or artificial. Naturally, when we portray such events onstage, we want them to look just like that: formal, contrived, ritualistic. But the majority of situations that occur in a play are just the opposite. They represent the spontaneous interaction of characters encountering one another in their daily lives. If we present these interactions in such a way that the audience feels the words are memorized and the actions rehearsed, then all sense of reality is gone. The next day the critics will call the performance stiff, contrived and artificial—and they will be right.

Strasberg always proclaimed that acting should appear to be happening for the first time. This means the actor must create the illusion of spontaneity. The audience knows the script has been written, that the actors have planned and rehearsed it and committed it to memory. Yet the members of the audience must be induced to believe they are witnessing an event from real life—a unique occurrence taking place for the first and last time. This is the Great Illusion of the theatre, Stanislavski's "sense of truth."

We all know that the way to achieve excellence is through practice. If we wish to achieve spontaneity in acting, we must practice being spontaneous.[1] Improvisation is probably the best way to develop that skill. To improvise is to be spontaneous.

Improvisation exercises also work toward the solution of some typical actor problems: not listening or relating to other characters, speaking lines as if memorized by rote, habitual verbal patterns, lack of concentration, inability to develop a train of thought as the character or create behavior for the character, inhibition and blocks.

Improvisation in Casting

The traditional method of casting is to have actors read parts from the script individually and with other actors being considered for roles. The chief difficulty with this method is that many fine actors are poor "readers" while others who read exceptionally well do not do nearly so well in performance. In cinema casting the screen test solves some of these problems. But it is expensive and time-consuming. Even then, it is still difficult to determine whether an actor really "has the role in him," whether he is capable of achieving the level of performance desired by the director. Quite clearly, any technique the director can use in making good casting decisions is useful—especially when he is confronted with several talented prospects with seemingly equal ability.

Improvisation as a casting technique can be very helpful to the director. He may simply discuss with the prospective actors a given scene from the play, the nature of the characters in the scene and the general direction of the action and then ask the actors to improvise a scene instead of reading it. Or the director may have the actors improvise a scene that is not in the play but is designed to show a particular quality or emotion he is looking for. Obviously, a director may also simply ask the actor to read his scene over in a new way, that is, with new feelings, choices or interpretation. Such improvisational techniques can show the director whether an actor can take direction and can demonstrate the actor's ability and versatility. Improvision provides the director with an additional method of finding out what is "inside" the prospective actor. And sometimes it may give the exact information needed for a crucial casting decision.

Improvisation in Rehearsal

The director should consider using improvisational techniques at any stage of rehearsal to help solve actor problems or to use as a tool whenever a scene is not developing the way the director wants. Sometimes in this situation the director may not know why the scene is not working, and improvisation may help him discover the reason.

It is the actor, however, who profits most from the use of improvisation during the rehearsal period. Improvisation teaches the actor to speak naturally rather than to read lines. A sense of talking can develop that can later be applied to the written script. Improvisations allow the actor to investigate a scene by trying to create for himself a sense of who he is and what has happened before the script begins, what has happened prior to a particular scene, what his individual characteristics should be, what his relationship is to the other characters. The director may make one suggestion for an improvisation and then let the exercise develop freely. He then notes the actor's choices, actions, staging and impulses with the idea of keeping what is good for the final product. Much spontaneity so developed can later be incorporated into the play.

Improvisation in all phases of rehearsal must have a specific aim. The theme or purpose should be properly defined. A problem to be solved should be similarly addressed. Is the improvisation utilized for an actor or director to deal with a psychological problem, to develop behavior to make a characterization more believable, to develop a better sense of the character's physical life, to develop some aspect of the character not evident in the actor's work on the role, to understand a character better, to execute an intention set by the actor or director, to check how one character feels toward another and how well this feeling will work, or simply to note what instincts actors follow in staging a particular scene?

The point to remember is that all improvisation should be done for a reason, and *the director must know the reason.*

Probably the most common way of using improvisation in rehearsal is for the actors to execute a scene from the script using their own words, behavior, and movements instead of those in the script. Improvisation can indeed begin during reading rehearsals. Careful attention should be given to what each character was doing prior to entering the scene and what the character is trying to accomplish during the scene. The actors should be prevented from interrupting the improvisation for self-criticism or other reasons until the director stops the action. The improvisation may then be discussed and good things that developed can be incorporated into the role(s).

Another valuable technique is for the actor to improvise what happened to the character immediately before his or her entrance or just before the scene begins. If this produces the appropriate state of mind and emotional level, then the actor can use the same improvisation idea in preparing for the scene during a performance.

When directing "The Dirty Old Man" (Lewis John Carlino) for a professional theatre in Los Angeles, I took two young actors to the Hollywood hills to improvise what happened just before their first entrance in the play. I hoped to establish in them the sensory experience of squinting into the sun as they trudged up a steep hill with the wind in their faces. I strived not only to aid them in sensorily creating the outdoors but also to help them discover the behavior of a boy who is trying to "make" a girl while she attempts to avoid this. Since all of this happened before the two characters' actual entrance in the play, the improvisation colored their behavior in the scene itself. The young woman's intention during the improvisation and on her entrance to the scene was to avoid intercourse. The actress motivated her feeling of apprehension and justified nervously, insisting on moving from spot to spot rather than staying in one place. In this way she rejected the boy's advances. Our planning of the improvisation had included substitution decisions (of a frustrating situation) for each character. Both actors motivated and justified feeling frustrated and angry through the given circumstances in the play itself along with the addition of substitution. During the improv they met another couple coming down the cliff who stopped to warn, "Don't go to the top. There's an old bearded weirdo up there talking to trees." The weirdo was the "dirty old man" from our play doing his

own preparation for rehearsal. He was improvising the given circumstances for his character by going to an isolated, familiar spot day after
day in order to be able to create onstage the sense of aloneness in a
specific place. It is beneficial to improvise not only what happened immediately prior to the scene but also any other given circumstances pertinent to the script.

Sometimes when the director wishes an actor to achieve a special
intensity of expression during a scene—perhaps involving such qualities
as anger, disgust, secretiveness or apprehension—he may introduce an
improvisational situation that does not actually occur in the play but that
encourages the actor to develop the quality desired. The actor explores
the improvisation to find a behavior that is truer and more expressive of
what the scene demands. If nothing much happens, the actor knows he
has not found the kind of mood or behavior from which this kind of
character and this kind of event can emerge, so he goes on exploring
with more improvisational work. At this point the director can also ask
the actors to do an improvisation of the scene itself as if the words had
not been written. The improvisation could be for any number of actors'
problems listed earlier, such as finding behavior and activity or to discover the relationship between two people. Sometimes a director or
teacher may divide a scene into units and have the actor improvise each
unit according to his own inner action or goal. Each unit may be improvised separately, or the improvisations may be strung together in a series.
During the latter procedure the director may call out individual inner
actions when necessary.

Students are cautioned not to set a problem and then act what they
think *should* take place. The goal is to be aware of themselves in the
situation as human beings. There should be an inner logic and an outer
logic to the actor's exploration of character. An example of creating an
outer and inner logic is a scene in which the actor must throw a cup of
coffee. Improvisation frees him from the script to discover the logic of
a real incident. If he doesn't feel like throwing the cup, he doesn't throw
it. He tries another improvisation to try to create the reality. Reality can
then be re-created by including all the improvisational steps when the
actor does the scene with the playwright's lines. Of course, an improvisation can get too far afield to be incorporated into the scene, but
nevertheless certain truths discovered in the improvisation can be incorporated into the role. If the actor does stray from his character or if

an improvisation becomes too ridiculous or illogical, the director or instructor will generally call a halt.

Perhaps the most valuable use of improvisation is at that critical time in rehearsal when actors go "off book," that is, when they cease reading their parts and start to give lines from memory. From this point on in rehearsals, when actors forget lines during a run-through, they can be forbidden to seek prompting or to stop the action in order to find the proper words. Instead, the director can insist that members of the cast continue the scene by improvisation until they are back "on track" or until the director stops the improvisation as being no longer profitable. This technique is extremely valuable, especially with inexperienced performers. It makes the actors so accustomed to covering line drops and staying in character that a break during performance is practically impossible. During rehearsals, of course, either the director or the actor has the option of returning to the troublesome section to review and repeat it with scripts or prompting after the improvisation has stopped. Thus, the actor rehearses the scene or unit at subsequent run-throughs during the same rehearsal period through improvisation, prompting or using the book.

Improvisation forces the actor to think, to speak naturally, to listen, to create behavior, to find the relationship between two people and to discover the significance and objective of a scene. It compels the actor to work creatively rather than to rely on a skillful mechanical repetition. Strasberg asserted: "Improvisation is the only means that helps the actor to break the grip of the cliché—the conventional and mechanical form of expression that still rules the stage today and must always be fought."[2]

Improvisation in Performance

No matter how much improvisation may be used in preparing a role or in rehearsing a scene, there comes a time near the end of rehearsals when most directors direct actors to return to the author's lines. Actors may also be urged to concentrate on motivating and justifying their roles as conceived by the playwright. At this point it would seem that the time for improvisation is over. Not so.

In cinema production a scene may not develop as the director has expected. In the effort to alter the scene so that it has the quality he wants, the director may find improvisation of movement and timing helpful. Tampering with the written script is even more common in movie production than on the stage; indeed, at times, even improvisation of lines and special scenes may be useful. Many fine film directors, such as Roberto Rossellini and John Cassavetes, are noted for their improvisations of special scenes, which often became the final cuts or were repeated to become the final cuts. Actors, too, often like the spontaneity of their film acting when allowed to improvise. Dustin Hoffman relates about improvising during filming:

> We improved a lot in [*Kramer vs. Kramer*], and at one point I had a good emotional thing going. The judge said, "Why should you have the child?" I said, "Because I'm his *mother.*" And I didn't know I said it and I couldn't get . . . to use it [the word *mother*] in the cut. . . . In *The Graduate,* some of the most wonderful moments were accidents. The same is true in *Midnight Cowboy, Tootsie, Kramer.* . . . Of the films that I've done, by and large, people point to the same moments all the time, and they don't remember the rest of the film. They just remember these moments. And a lot of them were improvised, a lot of them were accidents. Banging on the taxi in *Midnight Cowboy,* "I'm walking here," that was an accident. That was a hidden camera, and it was a cab that almost ran us over. Schlesinger left it in, but many directors wouldn't have.[3]

When discussing improvisation for the film *Wild River,* Lee Remick too reminisced: "We [Remick and Montgomery Clift] would do much improvisation. The script was very sparse, but we would flush it out guided by [Elia] Kazan [the director]."[4]

Robert Duval told of improvising "a little bit" in the film *True Confessions.* He expressed his opinion of the technique:

> If [improvision is] done in a good way it can be okay; you have to free yourself in order to make the written text work or add to the written text without indulging. It's got to be within the form.

> There's a scene in *Tender Mercies* where I teach the kid in the kitchen—the first half was script, the second half just went so we used that. It became life almost in that we weren't pressured by a script. The script and the improvisation combined together to make the scene. I think in certain cases you can learn by doing improvisation as part of the rehearsal process.[5]

Improvisation can be very useful during stage performances. As noted, improvisation *must* be used during performance whenever something unexpected occurs, such as a line drop, the failure of a doorbell or telephone to ring or a late entrance by another character. The actor (thinking and responding as the character) acts as if whatever happens onstage were in the script. Anyone who has ever acted has stories to tell about necessary improvisations in performance. While appearing in summer stock, my tight velvet lounging pajamas split completely down the rear. Since the scene was with my stage husband, I intimately confided, as if it were part of the play, what had happened, cooing, "I'll go to the bedroom to change into a robe before the children or servants come in. Do come with me." Laughing in character, I used the unexpected tear to improvise seductive words of endearment in order to fulfill the action of the scene, which was to subdue his anger, to cause him to succumb to my desire and finally to persuade him to submit to my demands.

At another time, while doing my first scene in Strasberg's New York class, a large overhead stage light fell just in front of me, barely missing me and almost causing serious injury. Since the setting was in a kitchen, I improvised, "The bloomin' burner has fallen off the old stove [imaginary] again." "Bloomin'" was exclaimed rather than a stronger expletive, for I was playing Cora in *The Dark at the Top of the Stairs* by William Inge. I imagined the burner had been pushed off because of the rumbling boiling of the big pan behind it; with a pot holder I lifted the "burner" back onto the imaginary stove. Strasberg commented that I had responded as the character would have and was complimentary about my spur-of-the-moment improvisation.

Actors often use improvisation as a means of preparing for a scene. When the actor discovers during rehearsals an improvisation that is successful in preparing him, he is wise to continue using that or a similar improvisation to prepare for the scene during performance.

And there is another use for improvisation onstage. Plays generally run for multiple performances, sometimes for months or years. To keep a portrayal looking fresh and real the actor should vary his or her performance from time to time rather than simply repeat everything the same way. The changes introduced can be slight and subtle—and they probably should be. The actor can make new choices—can choose new objects of concentration—that will not change the basic nature of the scene. Simple changes in the character's train of thought, slight changes of behavior or in reaction to fellow actors or slight changes in business, pace and timing—all to be approved by the director, of course—can revitalize a tired moment. For example, the framework of a play may call for a character to begin to be attracted to another character. Knowing that this should occur and having to arrive at this point night after night may lead to the common acting sin of anticipation. To overcome this tendency, the actor might try each night to look for something different in his partner to serve as a spur to his attraction, such as captivating eyes, hair, skin, smile or profile. By using a slightly different approach each night, a spontaneity and sense of reality is achieved via what is essentially an improvisational technique.

Some of an actor's suggested changes may upset the director, and he may quite properly insist that they not be attempted at critical points in the play. But the director does well to permit, even encourage, his actors to take improvisational liberties in other situations.

One final point deserves emphasis. Every good actor who has done a serious play through a number of performances discovers that his understanding of the character he portrays grows considerably during the run. This growth of understanding is naturally expressed by a gradual change in the actor's approach to the role. Knowledge and experience in the art of improvisation stands the actor in good stead as he seeks to expand his interpretation of such a part.

Improvisation as an Aid to the Writer

We don't often think of improvisation as being helpful to playwrights. But in a sense almost everything the playwright writes is his own improvisation. Plays written by two authors are especially interesting. From the accounts we have of the working methods of some of these writing teams, we see that the authors frequently develop dialogue by using improvisational techniques on each other.

Improvisations used during rehearsal often influence the playwright or screenwriter. A talented actor, improvising on a scene originally structured by the writer, will often produce bits of dialogue or new ideas the writer will want to incorporate into the script. We all know that when we write a letter to a friend, we do not use the same sentence structure or even the same words we use when we talk to that same friend in person. Similarly, the dialogue generated during improvisation has a freshness and spontaneity that the writer may have difficulty in finding when working alone.

In the Group Theatre much of the writing of plays emerged through improvisation. During *Men in White* rehearsals, the playwright Sidney Kingsley observed improvisations and incorporated many excellent lines into the play, particularly for the boardroom scene. This type of collaboration between author and actors has also been prevalent at the Actors Studio, as best exemplified by *A Hatful of Rain*. Lee J. Cobb told of the extensive improvisation work he did with Elia Kazan during preparation of *Death of a Salesman*. We do not know exactly how much of these improvisations ended up in the final edition of this magnificent play, but it seems likely the work of so talented a pair as Kazan and Cobb had some significant influence.[6]

I often teach simultaneous workshops for actors, directors, teachers and writers in which we experiment with original scripts through several of the improvisational techniques described in this book. Some writers prefer to work with several different directors or actors, and some are comfortable only with one student director and/or a specific cast. Others direct their own works, casting the actors enrolled in the workshops.

I encourage writers to bring cassette tape recorders to class to tape improvisations based on their works. Sometimes various actors repeat the same scene, using the script first and then doing improvisations. The writer can note different interpretations and choices. Oftentimes writers have asked actors, "May I change my dialogue to your words? They're better than what I wrote." This kind of class improvisational work has enriched many movies, plays and television scripts that were eventually produced.

It is always exciting to see how much creative energy is generated in writers as they follow improvisations based on their own works. In such an atmosphere the inexperienced writer quickly begins to see how valuable the assistance of actors and directors can be to him in his work. Indeed, class writers' original scripts often offer a wealth of material for the development and creative growth of the actors, directors and writers.

Improvisation in Actor Training

Improvisation is clearly an important part of the art of the theatre— important to writers, to directors and most of all to actors.

Improvisation has always played a prominent part in the Method. Reputedly, its use in actor training was suggested to Stanislavski by the writer Maxim Gorky, and the technique was employed very early in the First Studio of the Moscow Art Theatre under the direction of Leopold Sulerzhitski. Stanislavski eventually came to place great emphasis on improvisation in the training of young actors, and many of his techniques are still in use.

Some of the exercises I use with students involve improvisation (see also part 2, chapter 6). Individual class sensory work can be periodically incorporated into an improvisation, even though there is not time to do this every class period. This beneficial acting training technique can be utilized especially when there is no scene work for a particular class session. Improvisations are performed after a mid-class break or immediately after sensory work (the student continues the sensory exercise in an improvisation with a partner). The improv can be assigned spontaneously or before the sensory exercises begin, with the planning limited to where the actors are, who they are and their relationship to each other. Planning may also be more extensive, involving a beginning, middle and end or steps of the event. The situation of the improvisation may be assigned by the instructor or decided by the participants. Regardless, the instructor warns the students not to insist on telling a story or acting a sequence or plan of what he wants to happen, but rather to be aware of and listen to his partner. Whatever the arrangement, the sensory exercise continues during planning and while the student watches other improvisations. Improvisations of this nature can also be utilized to apply the sensory work to an improvisation of a specific character or scene on which the actor is working.

Improvisations are assigned according to the student's level of development, but even beginning students are encouraged to participate. The beginning actor is often an inhibited actor with a mechanical form of expression. If such an actor merely memorized a script and then performed, he would probably continue his mechanical problems of inexpressiveness.

In guiding the student in classroom improvisational and scene work, the instructor can ask: "Did you create the place, the environment?" That question would probably be followed by specific questions connected with the environment. "Did you concentrate on your physical task, other objects, your partner?" "Did you create specific thoughts for your character in this situation?" The questions depend on the student's assignment and level of training. In a directing class the student director guides in the choice of an action and after the improvisation is asked to determine if the actor carried out the action or objective intended. Did the actors give him the desired result?

It is important in any improvisational work to teach the student to be completely involved as the character through his objects of concentration, his awareness of his partner and his listening to his partner. New students, in particular, must be cautioned not to try to amuse or perform for other members of the class. It is much better for the student to be fully involved as the character, not saying anything at all, than to try to think of entertaining things to say or do. A student quickly becomes aware of the difference between "doing too much" as an actor and creating a reality. He knows when he is thinking and behaving as the *actor looking at the character* rather than as the character. When the actor acts the effect or indicates behavior, he is thinking of the audience and is not totally involved in the character.

Because an actor uses the improvisation to explore, advanced students can focus on a problem, theme, objective or action answering the question "What does the character want?" At the beginning of improvisational work, however, the technique can be used more simply to develop concentration on a place, the other actor, simple physical tasks or a sensory experience. A theme or attitude can be assigned later in the training in conjunction with a place. When an actor begins to work with more than one object of concentration, the prior circumstances and relationships of the characters begin to be factors in the improvisation. As the actor explores the situation, he may continue any or all of the objects of concentration, but he should play moment-to-moment, leaving most of the storyline open, going with whatever happens. By making whatever happens logical and real for himself, the actor is playing spontaneously and going with the sequence of reality rather than the sequence of the scene. Once the actor decides the inner action of the character (what the character wants—also involving "Why am I here?"), then the actor who has had improvisational training should be able to improvise in various ways: for the intent behind the situation, character aspects of the role, behavior, props and circumstances of the scene. The more experienced student is able to concentrate on a larger number of objects.

At times the instructor or student director will give one actor an objective or action without telling the other actor what the objective is. That objective or action is often directly opposed to the partner's—in fact, the partner becomes the obstacle. One actor might be given the objective of staying on a park bench, no matter what, with sometimes the added action of wanting to read an absorbing book; the partner may be instructed to get the other person off the bench and get him to do what he wants him to do. While teaching the workshops in Monaco some time ago I assigned opposing objectives to the man from Yugoslavia and the girl from Finland. His objective was to entice the girl, a waitress in a bar, to leave the bar and come up to his room with him; her objective was to stay at the bar—to become his obstacle. Neither knew the other's objective. Despite the lack of intelligible words being spoken in this gibberish improvisation, the thread of the action was easily followed, and the other workshop participants were delighted with the scene. When the frustrated man finally picked up the girl bodily and started to carry her offstage, it was to the applause of the audience. The girl's desire to find out what would happen next and to continue the scene gives evidence of her complete involvement in the improvised scene and illustrates how this involvement made the improvisation an effective piece of acting.

Because there are so many improvisation ideas that could be part of class exercise work, this discussion will be limited to some of those I have actually used. Beginning acting or directing students can start with improvisations having one main object of concentration or one physical task. Most of the exercises described below can be done in either type of class, but the student directors or the teachers decide the object of concentration and objectives in a directing class and the actor himself or the instructor decides the object of concentration and objectives in an acting class.

The teacher or director in a teachers/directors class has the opportunity of working with a variety of actors at different times. The directors learn to work with all kinds of actors and the actors learn to work with many directors. Improvisations in acting or directing classes can be based on a scene or project and the needs of an actor or director for that work. How well actors fulfill the objects of concentration and/or the director's intention are paramount in evaluating how well the actors worked. In a teachers/directors class the director of an improvisation can give his actors one objective or one action. The assignment might be to look at a window from a street. In planning the improvisation the director helps the actor decide "What is behind the window? What do I want? Why am I here?" The improvisation is successful if the actors concentrate fully and give the director what he wants. Sometimes the director gives the actors an obstacle (as described earlier). At times improvisations are done with each director using the same furniture. Since improvisation involves exploring a role, an actor must never worry about what to say. He or she must take time, keep concentrating and improvise on the theme. Instructors and student directors often need to force students not to stop but to keep their improvisation going.

My Understanding of the Method, basic acting and youth classes sometimes use time near the end of the session for improvisations that just create a specific place. The beginning actors, portraying themselves, re-create a place they know, such as a bus stop, room, street or park. All the sensory aspects of the place are created (colors of the sky; the park bench—sight, touch, etc.; the smells; what is seen from the park bench—grass, flowers, trees, streets; sounds heard—children, adults, traffic, birds, animals; the weather—sunshine, cloudy, temperature, breeze, etc.; or a bus stop—with concentration on objects and sensations similar to those in the park, with the addition of a city street and occasional glances down the street to try to see the bus arriving). One student will explicitly create the place and when the other students realize what the place is they will join in the improvisation for a group improvisation. The group improvisation is allowed to continue as long as the actors work sensorily on creating the place and listen and relate to one another. If the improv becomes too busy or too much of a performance, it is stopped. Sometimes I will call directions from the sidelines, such as, "The camera is on Jay and Mary." Jay and Mary continue their conversation while all other characters silently continue the scene, always staying in character.

While improvisational work for beginning actors is still on physical objects, a scene at a picnic or eating at home or in a restaurant can be improvised. Concentration in these exercises is entirely on handling the objects and passing food around. Assignment of improvisations varies according to the actor's progress and according to his or her needs.

The next step in improvisational work can be to choose simple situations that call for the actor's creating a simple reality and his relationship to the situation. The picnic or restaurant improvisation can involve being hungry, bored, anxious to finish the meal or disgusted by the food.

Another type of improvisation deals with characterization. Each actor chooses one characteristic to define his character, such as shyness, suspiciousness, aggressiveness, illness or even a physical handicap. The actors can portray students, business people, farmers, soldiers, factory workers or clubmen or women. But the situation should remain simple. The exercise can include simple adjustment to the other people—being aware of who they are, what they are doing, what they mean to the actor.

Eventually the actors will be assigned an improvisation that is more dramatic but has no planned ending. The situation might focus on an explosion in a specific place, a stuck elevator, a robbery or an argument. Each student should create for himself who he is, what has happened to him previously and what his relationship is to the situation and the other characters. As in all acting, the student should not anticipate the outcome.

Another improvisation can be chosen by class members themselves. The group selects the locale and then each person discusses his own character's mental, emotional and physical state of being, why he is in that place, his occupation, his relationships, creating as much of a biography as possible. The first to describe their characters begin preparation and are the first to enter the scene. The last to discuss their characters with the instructor and group enter the scene later in order to have adequate preparation time.

The actor's concentration (in improvisation work in acting training) thus evolves from one or two simple objects to more complicated objects of character, situation and event, to creating a life for a character.

Sometimes a student is assigned a private moment in conjunction with an improvisation closely related to his own nature. The exercise begins with the private moment. When the actor's concentration, expression and impulses have achieved a sense of truth, then the improvisation begins. The student tries to maintain the freedom of expression created with the private moment. Here the guidance of an experienced instructor is important. An astute instructor can observe the moments in a student's work when the student displays a reluctance to translate what he is beginning to feel into words or action. That is when a student ordinarily wants to stop and when an instructor must force the student to continue.

Sometimes the actor does the opposite of what he should do, stopping laughter or tears or words. If the instructor observes the student stifling or holding back his impulses, going on to something else or delaying lines rather than speaking them when appropriate, the teacher can guide the actor to unlock himself, to do what he wants to do. If the actor believes in himself, he can hope to inspire belief in an audience. This kind of improvisational work, guided carefully by the instructor, can encourage the student to create by himself.

The one-word improvisation teaches the student spontaneity in acting. Here the student is told that he will be given a word in response to which he must stand up at once and react to the word with action, speech or both. The reaction may be silent or verbal, so long as it is brief, impulsive and unplanned. The word should be a noun: perhaps the name of a country or a word with broad implications such as "religion" or "politics." The instructor may supply the words used, or each student who responds may give a word to the next student. This exercise helps the actor follow his impulses to achieve a feeling of true spontaneity that can be applied to a script.

The two- or three-noun improvisation is also a useful device. Two partners improvise with three unrelated nouns as a basis. The partners determine the situation, locale and their characters. The three nouns may be included in the dialogue or implied through props, the place or situation. The partners may also plan a beginning, middle and an end to the improv, with the understanding that these may have to be altered as the scene progresses. If the actors spontaneously improvise (perhaps because only one partner has an idea of how to incorporate the three nouns), the planning may be minimal. Regardless, the improv should have a general form. The partners can plan the sections of the improvisation similar to when they set for themselves sections of one based on a written scene.

A variant of the two- or three-noun improvisation is to give partners a news headline as a basis for their improvisation. A basic situation can be decided by using the words in an unusual, interesting, even unexpected way as integral parts of the scene. Or the words need not be used at all; instead they suggest an idea for a situation. This exercise is most effective when the headline is used in the most imaginative manner possible, the words becoming a springboard for unusual meanings and situations. Planning a beginning, middle and end or a few sections provides a skeleton for the actors to follow, but neither knows exactly what will happen. Strasberg explained the importance of improvisation as follows:

> The whole point is to learn to see behind words, to learn not to think of words as a safeguard, but always to look for imaginative comprehension which will extend the actor's own avenue of thinking. The improvisation trains the actor's willingness to act without knowing the end result and at the same time to permit fantasy. The actor's imagination is trained to perceive possibilities of thought and meaning.[7]

Entire books could be devoted to various improvisation ideas for class participation. The above suggestions are those I have found most beneficial to students.

8   Preparing and Learning a Role

Preparing the Role

Before and during rehearsals the actor should read the play or script[1] several times for increased understanding of the script as a whole and his part in particular. He asks questions such as: What is the theme of the play? (What is the play about?) Does his character have a main action (spine) or driving force? How might a character's main action be expressed in each of the character's scenes? Some teachers and directors, if an actor is lucky, help the actor find his character's main action or spine by leading him to think in terms of active verbs.[2] The spine of the character can be what the character wants (also referred to as the inner action, intention or objective of the character). After this is determined, the actor can decide why he has this particular desire and what the character does to satisfy that desire (see part 3 and glossary for definitions of spine, inner action, objective, intention and choices). For instance, James Tyrone in Eugene O'Neill's *Long Day's Journey into Night* wants to maintain his self-image as an actor, husband and father—his spine. He has to defend himself to hold onto his self-respect and the people and possessions he loves. In his attempts to do this, he comes into conflict with his sons. The pain the father suffers is somehow transmitted to other members of the family. Mary Tyrone's spine is to find peace of mind. She seeks this through drugs. She wants to find her lost faith, a "home" and a center to her being.[3] The spine for Edmund, the younger son and playwright, is to examine himself and his immediate family; understanding may lead to Edmund's finding forgiveness, a catharsis and a realization of love. The older son's spine is to find freedom from guilt. In the process Jamie tries to devastate anyone who gets in the way.[4]

As an actor works on a character he should investigate and explore the role thoroughly in terms of the following questions. The answers may be decided much later as character work progresses.

Lorrie Hull holding a plaque won in an American Theatre Association competition. The judges, shown above, were Henry Fonda, Michael Langham and William Glover.

Initial Questions

Who Am I?

The actor may find it useful to reconstruct some of the character's life prior to the play's beginning. Some directors and teachers in fact advise actors to prepare written biographies, utilizing the imagination to fill in what the playwright or history has not provided. The actor should feed on every bit of information the author reveals about the character, including what other characters say about the individual. The actor might also ask whether the character's education, occupation, income or religion affects the way he sees things and behaves. What are his likes and dislikes? His habits? How might age, weight, height, health or physical handicaps influence his behavior and outlook? What are some of his behavioral characteristics? How might his attitudes be determined by his family life, the customs and habits of the era in which he lives or the society in which he moves?

What Is the Present Situation?

What did the character come here to do? What is his physical condition: tired, hungry, cold, ill? What is his mental condition: aware, confused, angry, calm, drunk? What stimuli are affecting the character? What is the character's relationship to the other people in the scene? The actor must also query preceding events in order to answer these questions. What happened just before? What did the character do just prior to the scene?

Where Am I?

This question refers to the *place* where the action occurs—the setting of the scene. Here the actor considers the environment as a force: era, year, season, time of day, temperature, humidity, weather. Whether the locale is indoors or outdoors, the actor should create all the objects that surround him. Preferably the actor specifically creates a place he knows in order to stimulate sensorial reality for the role. In his imagination he may create his own bedroom, living room or whatever. He may visit the actual spot where the action occurs or a similar place. When I was directing *The Zoo Story* for national competition, one of the actors actually spent some time at the exact spot in New York's Central Park where the action takes place. The other actor could not visit New York, so he sensorily created a park that he knew. The actors re-created these locales both prior to and during performances. Henry Fonda, one of the judges, stressed in his critique that the actors were so convincing in creating the place that he himself felt as if he were in the park with them.

What Is My Emotional Condition?

The actor must be aware of the physical stimuli affecting him, but he should also investigate the emotional stimuli operating. Such knowledge tells him if homework on a substitution or on an affective memory will be needed. If so, the actor then proceeds with experimentation to make the proper choice. Homework to practice the sequence of sensory steps is advised until one word, image or sensation will set off the affective memory. Students should follow the guidance of their instructor for affective memory work in order to learn the proper steps (see part 2, chapter 5).

What Is My Relationship to Other People in the Scene?

A complete analysis of relationships and attitudes toward everyone the character knows—mother, father, sister, brother, aunt, uncle, lover, stranger, victim, hero, villain—precedes the scene analysis. Then the actor asks himself: Is the scene logical? Are the responses logical? These and other questions usually form after work has begun with the other characters and inner actions are determined.

What Do I Want?

This question, according to some directors, leads to the actor's most important decision.[5] The answer determines the overall character objective or action. When the actor answers "What do I want" along with "Why am I here?" he has the information to explore his character. Determining what the individual basically wants or strives for and what he will do to get it leads to a discovery of his behavior throughout the course of the play. When the actor, as the character, pursues this overall goal in each of the scenes, real behavior (the "how") will spring to life of itself. What the character does to get what he wants is the motivating force leading to the script's action.

Another question related to "What do I want?" is "What is in my way?" or "What is the obstacle?" Sometimes the obstacle is physical (for instance, Susie in *Wait until Dark* is blind), but in most cases the obstacle that causes conflict in the play is psychological. The character may not be able to execute his desires because of family, moral or social constraints.

How Do I Research My Role?

An actor should research his role by visiting the locales in the script or similar locales. He should research geographic, historic and social factors as well as read pertinent literature. One of the most valuable ways to approach an unfamiliar role is to use observation. If the actor is playing an individual with an obvious profession (like a doctor, judge, waitress or librarian) he or she should spend some time watching these people in their occupations to see how they behave, how they handle their equipment, how they relate to others. The actor can then become accustomed to behaving like the professional being portrayed.

When I directed the prison play *The Cage* by Rick Cluchey for a national contest, I had the cast members locked in the county jail so that the feeling of confinement and restriction became real to them. This almost backfired when one rather emotional cast member became nauseated during the experience. Several years later I learned that Montgomery Clift stayed overnight in San Quentin's death house to research his role for the film *A Place in the Sun*.[6]

Before filming *Raging Bull* Robert De Niro spent almost a year training with Jake La Motta. He wanted to be in shape and to look and act like a fighter. He took a job as a taxi driver before filming *Taxi Driver* and became a cyclist for *The Gang That Couldn't Shoot Straight*. "I did all that," he reasoned, "so it would not look like I didn't know what I was doing, so it would become second nature. Still, I did not want to overdo it or become obsessed with one thing, like learning to play a saxophone for *New York, New York*."[7]

Louis Gossett, Jr., Academy Award winner for *An Officer and a Gentleman*, went through ten days of basic training at Camp Pendleton, the Marine Corps base near San Diego, for his role as a drill sergeant,[8] and Dustin Hoffman spent three months backstage at television's "General Hospital" while researching his role in *Tootsie*. This may be why Hoffman did such a convincing job imitating television soaps imitating life.[9]

How Do I Justify and Motivate Myself to Fulfill the Requirements of the Script or Director?

This question, as well as the questions listed above, is usually explored as rehearsals progress. One of the most difficult problems in advanced acting training is for the actor to think and behave in ways that are not normal or natural for him while at the same time bring some part of himself to the role. He must learn to respond to situations as the character he is portraying would respond and find that response within himself. Robert Duvall explained this paradox:

> If I play a Pope I try to find what's spiritual in me—so it's still me doing it from within or a certain side of me. . . . I think every individual has to express his individuality. I always wanted to be an actor who could play himself plus different characters. . . . I wanted to find some facet of myself operating under the character and do as many different characters as I can. There's obviously a limitation but I want to see how many I can do.[10]

An actor must justify his character elements by making inner choices that bring alive the particular character he is playing. Lee claimed, "What would motivate me [the actor] to do it [to behave] that way is the 'principle of justification.' "[11] If necessary, the director will have to suggest motivation and justification choices for his actors (see part 3, "Directing").

If in spite of preliminary research and homework the actor still feels uncomfortable in a scene, it is his job to seek proper motivation and justification through use of his imagination. The "Salome" incident described in the "Learning the Role" section of this chapter is an example of this technique. The actor can say to himself, "It is as if . . ." to help him develop a belief and faith in what he must do. Another technique is for the actor to place himself in imaginary circumstances in order to justify what is required. For instance, if the director wants the actor to rush through a scene, the actor can imagine that he is late for an important appointment (even though this situation is not in the script). Innovative demands on the actor's thinking can produce creative choices that not only justify the character's behavior but also lead to a variety of "colors" and hence a more interesting performance.

All the above questions are not meant to be "answered" as though in response to an exam. The purpose of these questions is to help stimulate the actor to an alive and meaningful portrayal.

Learning the Role

Learning a role, whether for class or for the stage, takes a lot more than just memory work. I suggest the following method (see also appendix G, "Advice to Actors") as one way of working that has been successful with many of my students and with many actors I have coached or directed.

The actor's first reading of a script and his first impression of the role can inspire his imagination as much as any work done later. The actor should be aware of this initial stimulation of his imagination so that he or she can recapture these responses as the character develops. Initial work on a part involves following instincts and impulses.

Speaking the Lines

I suggest that actors never memorize lines by rote when learning a role.[12] As Stanislavski said, "An actor never reads lines, he speaks them."[13] Actors are encouraged to study lines silently as well as by reading them *aloud* over and over until the dialogue begins to come naturally and spontaneously with a sense of talking. It is helpful to have someone (preferably the scene partner) read the lines of the other parts. If necessary, the actor himself may silently read the lines of the other characters in the scene. His own lines, read aloud, should be repeated simply at first; later the actor can concern himself with projection, emotion, sensory and other elements of the character. Strasberg always advised the actor to stay relaxed and emphasize naturalness and a sense of talking early in rehearsals. Giving more energy and projection can be worked on later after an inner line has been developed for the character.

When the script is guided by a director, the actors often sit around a table for initial reading rehearsals, talking, listening and responding to the other actors. Strasberg suggested that reading rehearsals be held for five days (see part 3, "Stages of Rehearsal"). On the first day the actors should just "talk" the part, without any dramatic interpretation.[14] Certainly this is the best technique for inexperienced actors to follow. Experienced actors, however, often must learn roles in a limited time (new lines each day for a television series or rewrite changes for a film). At such times Strasberg suggested learning the lines by rote but in a monotone, without inflection and without any interpretation of the script or character. In this way the actor learns the lines quickly but does not try to produce a quick "result," which, as I have stressed, is harmful. Then, when the actor actually says the lines during performance, they usually have a spontaneous quality they could otherwise lack. When required to memorize quickly, the actor can fill in colors and other specific elements close to or during performance.

Improvisation

Stanislavski, as director, is known to have started rehearsals without benefit of scripts. The actors improvised their roles in the play. Then, when lines were added, the characters spoke with reality and behaved as the character would, so the words fit naturally. This technique is similar to some of the improvisation procedures described above in part 2, chapter 7.

A suggestion for learning a role in rehearsal is to alternate between using the script and improvising the scene. Improvisation forces the actor to know what the lines and situations mean; he must listen and think as the character, feel and behave as the character. Improvisation helps the actor create the role and also gives him the assurance to remain in character even when things go wrong in performance. As long as the actor knows the meaning of the lines, and thinks as the character, he can go on when a line is not there; as long as he understands and thinks as his character, he can improvise when necessary to cover an unexpected problem onstage or before the camera. The actor goes with whatever happens as if it were supposed to happen.

Once the script is put aside and the scene is "off book," it is essential that the actor stay in character and keep going, even when lines are forgotten. When lines are dropped, the well-trained actor will remain in character and improvise until the performers are back on track with the script. Only then can the cast stop the rehearsal and go back to correct whatever was forgotten, using the script or a prompter. Adherence to this practice gives the actor a confidence in performance that cannot be achieved in any other way.

Substitution and Personalization

I always encourage actors to be specific in their work. When the objects and people specified by the playwright are vague and abstract to the actor, he or she can substitute objects or persons that have personal meaning. Substitution or personalization might be used for a character spoken about in the script or seen offstage. (When the stage manager in *Our Town* talks about the sites in Grovers Corners, for instance, he can point to actual spots offstage as he substitutes images of specific places he knows.) If the director wants the actor to feel or care for those buildings or landmarks, then the actor must choose an image—such as buildings, streets, mountains or canyons—for which he has that particular feeling.[15] Persons can be—and often are—substituted (personalized) in the same manner, especially in love scenes. As an actor learns to personalize and substitute he begins to make the role his own.

Strasberg's work with a young actress[16] illustrates how personalization is incorporated into acting. Strasberg walked the student through the scene from *Our Town* in which Emily dies and returns from the grave to see her childhood family. "Remember someone you really want to see and visualize that person," directed Strasberg, obviously intending her to re-create a person in her own life. Afterward he declared with approval, "That's the way to work. You are working specifically. Tell me, who were you thinking of?" Serious, wide-eyed and naive, the actress sighed, "Paul Newman." Amidst the roar of the class, Strasberg raised his eyebrows in his characteristic surprised way and exclaimed, "Oh . . . I'll tell Paul about this. I'm seeing him next week on the Coast."

Personalization can be utilized to replace a coactor, a model the actor is talking or thinking about or an imaginary person offstage.[17] Occasionally the actor even substitutes another person for the character he is portraying. The individual personalized should be real to the actor. The actor should be specific as far as details of appearance and manner are concerned. This leads to belief in what the actor does. When Shelley Winters appeared in the play *The Gingerbread Lady,* for instance, she at times looked at the girl in the play and saw her own daughter. This technique can be employed for specific moments. But Shelley warned, "There is a danger if the actor doesn't relate to what happens in the play. He must do both [personalize when needed and relate to the other actor]. Call on personalization if the thing isn't going on strong enough, but the most important thing is to use the other actor."[18]

Substitution can also involve particularization. Here the actor recalls an incident or occasion in his own life. If the writer has a character refer to an incident that evokes certain feelings, the actor can choose a particular event from his own life that evokes similar feelings. He uses the words of the writer, but with those words he describes his own secret, personal memory. If the playwright refers to a holiday, the actor can choose a specific holiday, such as July 4. To particularize he can select a particular July 4 or even another occasion that has a special meaning for him.

For substitution Strasberg used the example of various actresses playing Salome and substituting an imaginary object for the bloody head of John the Baptist. In the scene Salome, rejected in her passion for John the Baptist, contrives to have him executed and his head delivered on a tray. One actress, attempting to communicate Salome's madness, contorted her face and body, shrieked, laughed hysterically and mauled or

Lee Strasberg guiding Dianne Hull in a scene from *Our Town*.

caressed the head—but she completely failed to be convincing. She was trying to "play" insane. Strasberg asked her to repeat the scene but to create a puppy: "Imagine that sitting on the tray is the cutest puppy you have ever seen. Treat the head as you would a puppy." The second performance was startlingly different. When the actress saw the head on the tray, she responded with childlike delight. Her movements were excited and gleeful, conveying a sense of anticipation and joy. She lifted the head lovingly and delicately, giving it several short loving kisses. As she petted and fondled the bloody object as she would have handled a puppy, her actions conveyed a frightening picture of insanity.

Another time Strasberg asked an actress to substitute her dead dog for the head of John the Baptist. Her portrayal was personal—the dog had been precious to her. There was passion, yet she was dealing with a dead object. Strasberg had asked her to see and hold the bloody dead dog, and when she visualized the poor creature, the result was heartrending. Strasberg explained substitution further: "I always warn people to try to see [specific] things [they know personally]. . . . [But] a substitution or personalization (which can also be a substitution) does not always relate to the object or the thing that seems to be needed in the play."[19] This last point is important, for the same object does not always work for different actors. The actor must be prepared in rehearsals to explore more than one substitution object if necessary to achieve the desired effect.

Costumes and Props

Movement of the character—his stance, the way he walks or sits, his behavior—should become second nature to the actor. Consequently, real costumes and props or a close imitation should be used in rehearsals as soon as possible so they can be used naturally. If the real costume is not available, the actor is advised to use pieces of cloth or substitute costumes and props to simulate the real costume elements, especially in period pieces for which the actor may need to become accustomed to a robe dragging on the floor, a ruff at the neck, tights, a skirt with a bustle, a hat atop an elaborate hairdo, a sword, unusual shoes or boots. Some actors wear the costume or a facsimile at home in order to feel at ease with the stance or walking and sitting. Improvisations of events (not necessarily in the script) in the characters' lives with costumes and props are also beneficial.

Total Acting

The movement and behavior of the character are sometimes referred to as external characteristics while the thoughts and emotions of the character are deemed internal characteristics. Whatever the terminology, total acting, integrating the outside and the inside so that all characteristics become second nature, must be achieved. Robert De Niro was asked if he begins by working on external or internal characteristics. De Niro responded, "I don't feel movement and behavior are external. I do things so they become part of the character and truthful. If I do something enough, it can be second nature. If it's like life, it will be simple."[20]

The inseparability of the external and internal is apparent when one is neglected. Once an actor loses his concentration (worrying about lines, or anticipating what is going to happen next), his sensitivity, feeling and conviction leave.[21]

Many variations of the above suggestions may be used by skilled actors in the course of their development. A professional, through experimentation, finds the rehearsal techniques that work best for him or her. Shelley Winters, for instance, writes out her part and writes specific thoughts (subject to change) for her character in the margins of the script. "I wrote *Virginia Wolfe* two times," Shelley noted.[22] She advised students:

> . . . in *Hatful of Rain* . . . we improvised and worked on scenes . . . the last thing we did was lines. I memorize with thought connections. On each beat [unit] I have to find something personal for me. I separate the play into beats and use the most powerful emotions I've known for affective memories. But first I read the script and in twenty words or less decide what it's about—what did the writer want to tell the audience? Why did the playwright put my character in and why am I there?[23]

Robert De Niro too confided to students: "I like to work slow, sit around a table and read and read to get a sense of [the script]—not hurrying—in a play, especially, when dialogue is clear. I don't worry about memorizing lines, but they eventually come and I stand up when I feel like it, or when the time is right to get up I will get up, or that's when a director I trust says, 'Let's go.' "[24]

As in all Method training, each actor must find the parts of the Method that work for him; he follows his own "path of discovery."

Identifying Units, Beats or a Sequence:
Choices, Intentions, Actions

Some directors and teachers prefer to guide actors in the identification of units or reserve such work until the student reaches an advanced stage of scene work. After a director or actor discovers the play's spine (see part 3), he has found the moving thread that weaves itself into each unit of the script and ties together all elements of the production. A unit (also called a beat or sequence by teachers and directors) starts when an immediate intention (also called objective or action) begins. The unit is complete when the intention has succeeded or failed and a new one begins. When something happens that makes the character move in a new direction or start doing something different, a new beat or unit begins.

A unit may take the actor briefly away from his main objective, but the work throughout the scene, when directed carefully, is usually affected by the actor's effort to accomplish his main inner action.

After the script is broken into units, the actor can determine the character's smaller intentions or actions in each unit and make a statement about each intention for himself. The intention is what is going on inside the actor at any given moment, whether he is speaking or silent. This is his reason for being in the scene, and the reason can be completely at odds with the dialogue. Some actors write their thoughts and intentions at the side of their scripts, although the train of thought can change from performance to performance. A useful technique is to express the intentions or inner actions through active verbs. Within a unit or scene there can be a general intention or action going on for that section along with the character's smaller inner actions or intentions. The relationship between these intentions can be diagramed as a tree trunk with branches emerging from it, smaller branches emerging from larger ones. The actor's determination of his main inner action as well as his related smaller inner actions put him on the track of both his character and feeling. If the actor understands his character's attitudes and feelings, then he is able to make inner choices to assist him in developing the role. The way the actor states the inner action to himself depends on aspects of the character. How the actor chooses his inner actions or intentions and the specific way he thinks of them (even at times drawing from his own life through substitutions and affective memories) can determine the quality of his performance. Good actors make imaginative or strong choices and are able to translate them into actions. Indeed, fine actors are distinguished by their creative choices.

By performance time all choices and planning of inner actions should be absorbed into the characterization. These unconsciously become an integral part of the lines and behavior. Strasberg clarified this integration: "An actor can actually learn to 'turn on,' to stimulate himself, to share fully with the character a totality of sensation, of experience, of belief, of conviction and of behavior of a kind which transcends the mere imitation of that same act, which many actors do and do very well [imitate the same act in subsequent performances]."[25] By involving himself in activities, thought and sensations that help him to live on the stage, the actor is capable of sharing or participating in the thoughts, feelings and emotions of the character. Working this way, the actor will not merely imitate what he has done before. "John and Lionel Barrymore developed a whole series of stencils," criticized Strasberg. "They weren't themselves anymore—just an imitation of themselves."[26] At a Los Angeles Actor's Studio session shortly after Alfred Lunt's death, Strasberg praised Lunt as a great actor with strong inner motivation. But Strasberg characterized Lynn Fontanne, Lunt's wife, merely as a highly skilled, trained, technical actress.

Further Development of the Role

When an actor starts work on a role in beginning training, he is likely to ask Stanislavski's question, "What would I do if I were the character in this situation?" As the actor develops an inner technique, he works toward fusing himself with all aspects of the role. His senses, emotions, and impulses are beginning to respond. By the time an actor has trained for some time—in acting classes, in rehearsals or through experience— he should be able to ask himself, according to Vakhtangov's formulation, "How do I motivate myself or what would have to motivate me to behave as the character behaves?" By helping to find workable answers to these questions, instructors and directors can guide actors to come up to the level of the character rather than allowing the character to come down to the level of the actor.

An actor can also watch others to incorporate observed behavior and

attitudes into his characterization. De Niro confessed how he lets observed behavior become part of the character:

> An actor can find something his character is noted for—like Jake always
> goes like that a lot [makes a sound with his nose as La Motta does], so I
> did it a few times. When working on *Raging Bull* or any movie, I'm always
> thinking about what the character is doing or some behavioral thing, always
> aware, but almost unconscious. I may not even know where I picked it up,
> as long as I didn't pick it up from something done before. I can be watching
> someone or something that's right for the character, so I behave in a certain
> way.[27]

An important character element is the character's particular way of
seeing things (attitude). Improvisation of activities that occur during a
character's normal day often help an actor discover and absorb his character's behavior and attitudes. Even if the activities are not in the script,
the actor's imagination is an excellent source to draw from. Justification
of logical choices can lead to a truthful performance. An actor has to
justify and set objects of concentration for himself that are direct out-
growths of the logic of a particular script. These objects may or may not
produce the results a director wants. If not, the actor may try any of the
techniques, or a combination of techniques, described in this book.
Sometimes the other characters or the situations in the script stimulate
adequate responses and arouse all the feeling an actor needs. Personalization, substitution, affective memories, strong inner actions and the
other techniques discussed are for use where their help is needed to
evoke the desired feeling. Another possibility is to combine various acting techniques, for instance, an inner action and an affective memory.
In this way the actor fuses the role with his own emotional recall.

Even though character can be developed by playing the inner action
or intention, an actor should be warned that playing an intention too
strongly could bottle him up sensorily and emotionally. The sensory
reality must always be an integral part of acting. But sensory and affective memory work should be done in homework, rehearsals and preparation. In performance the re-creating of such homework and
preparation should be there naturally. They should not interfere with
the actor's awareness, his or her interaction with other actors or the
fulfilling of the writer's intent. Onstage the actor should listen to and
look at other actors, maintain verbal energy and guard against antici-

pation. Shelley Winters expressed it well: "Once you've done all that [sensory and affective memory work], forget it so it is habit and is so ingrained it comes naturally whenever you are in a scene. You have to watch other actors onstage or film, as that's really what's interesting. The camera photos your soul."[28]

No matter what the actor discovers works for him, he or she must remember that the logic of the play cannot be ignored. The actor's imagination should deal with that, sometimes through one or more techniques as just described or, if needed, through a director's guidance. The director and actor can work together in discovering the logic of prior circumstances, of the character, of the situation, of basic sensory work and of a particular unit. Strasberg cautioned that the logic must be real rather than mechanical:

> If the answer to every actor's problem began with the play, there would be no difficulty. What actor ever thinks of anything but the play? What director ever starts work without saying, "This is my interpretation"? If we think mechanically, we suppose that an approach that concentrates on the play should lead invariably to creative, sound, worthwhile, excellent work. It doesn't—not because it can't or shouldn't. The difficulty comes from misunderstanding the relation of actor's work to the scene . . .
>
> Mrs. Siddons left a brilliant descriptive interpretation of Lady Macbeth—totally different from the Lady Macbeth she really played. Creation does not come merely from what the actor intends to do. The sources of creation lie in whatever it is that stirs the unconscious and the conscious powers of his imagination. That is the real logic of the actor's creative life.[29]

Strasberg continued this guidance by talking of the logic of the character, referring both to an awareness of the character's qualities and to the degree of experience needed to produce those qualities. Later in his work with the actors he guided them to realize the "logic of essential sensory objects," stressing that certain things not emphasized by the author are still part of the environment of a particular event and should be created imaginatively by the actors in order to play the scene. He used the example of a scene from *Three-day Blow* by Hemingway in which the actors omitted a crucial object in their re-creation of the scene: the storm. The actors did not create the difference between outside and inside the cabin. Because they did not sensorily create the storm for themselves, they left out what was necessary for the scene.

A word of caution: it is possible to become so preoccupied with one or another Method concept (in a trance, as it were) to the point that an actor lacks his normal easy contact with reality, the other actors, the present, the lines. His relationship with the other actors in the scene becomes strained and labored, "under water." He seems removed, like a patient in a mental institution. There could be a tension about him. There can be so much going on inside that the actor's external awareness stalls. There can be enormous internal energy but the appearance of nothing on the outside. When an actor finds himself in this bind, he should be willing to consciously let go of the Method concepts and have faith that they will carry over into his performance on an unconscious level. He should make every effort to relate to the other actors with clear, aware eyes and good solid verbal energy. *Awareness* and *energy* are the key words.

Preparation before a Performance

An actor should never go onstage or before the camera "cold." Like the athlete before a tournament, the actor must warm up. This preparation is more effective if it relates to the scene that is coming. As early as possible in the course of rehearsals the actor should experiment with preparation techniques. These can involve relaxation, creating the place, overall sensations, other sense memories, concentration on objects, emotional work (if needed), a private moment, characterization, developing specific thoughts, a train of thought, and speaking out as the character, not necessarily in that order. Some actors improvise what happened before the scene. If the actor chooses the prior events, he can often establish the emotional meaning the scene has for him. The instructor or director initially may guide the actor in the use of any of these techniques, but the actor should eventually be trained to use them himself.

Some directors take an active role in rehearsal and pre-performance warm-ups. A technique used by Elia Kazan in rehearsal preparation is that of making up something new that happened just before the actor entered or telling the actor something that happened yesterday. To encourage further experimentation he will sometimes change the circumstances under which the scene is played.

Problems in preparation are not limited to the amateur. Strasberg related how the great Mrs. Siddons had difficulty getting herself in the mood and starting herself in a play. When playing Constance in *King John*, for example, she would either stand in the wings and listen to the plot developing against her stage son or keep her dressing room door open to involve herself in the action. The famous Salvini, playing Othello, recognized the need for preparation. He would come to the theatre early, walk around inside, put on a little makeup, walk around some more, all the while thinking about the role. Macready chopped wood in the wings before entering as Macbeth and cursed and violently shook a ladder before his third act entrance as Shylock, all so he could feel imaginative grief and rage at his daughter's flight. All of these pre-Method actors were aware of the need to stimulate emotion before an entrance.

Modern actors too find effective preparation techniques. Shelley Winters says lines that happen before the play, "creating a life." "When I was younger," explained Shelley, "I started to play the character at three in the afternoon."[30] At another time Shelley confided, "Sometimes before filming I play music to shut out crews and become more fully concentrated. They usually become quiet, as they think I'm doing some strange Method preparation."[31]

According to fellow actor Rudy Bond, Marlon Brando used to answer the phone as Stanley before going to the theatre to play in *A Streetcar Named Desire*. When he arrived at the theatre, he imagined everyone as part of Stanley's factory job: Kazan was the foreman; ushers were guards; the doorman, the factory gatekeeper; and actors, fellow factory workers.[32]

Ellen Burstyn once worked on the role of Medea at the Actors Studio by going through a preparation process that included an improvisation Strasberg himself termed extraordinary. Trying to depict a primitive woman, she deliberately gnawed at a large bone and finished by throwing it down on the ground. Strasberg could see the growing behavioral effect of this investigation. Burstyn then personalized a chair as a child. Robert De Niro, when he's alone and sometimes when he is with people, likes to behave as the character would. He does this during his daily activities at home as homework as well as before a performance, behaving the way the character would. He admonished, "I watch myself and sometimes realize this is the way *I* am doing it, but not as *he* [the character] would do it. So it has to be as he would do it, and not as I would. It's

Hull with Ellen Burstyn at Actors Studio West. Photo © Demetrios
Demetropoulos.

good, because then you are in a situation that allows you to be spontaneous and react the way a character would react. I've spent a lot of
time alone by myself doing that."[33] Strasberg himself told how he prepared all day subconsciously for the role of Hyman Roth[34] in
Godfather II, to the point that his wife did not want to come near him
on those days because his personality was more like Roth's.

Strasberg claimed that in order to develop in preparation, a creative
mood or moment, when "something begins to happen," the actor relaxes
and stimulates the kind of subconscious answer "that brings him alive,
feeds him, makes his imagination work, makes him feel 'I can now get
up and act. I would like to act. Things are working for me now.'" Strasberg cautioned that he did not mean that the actor did not know what
he was doing.

Beginning preparation with a private moment is another way De Niro
works. This technique is often invaluable because it stirs the actor's inner
reality so that his concentration, expression and impulse become full.
He begins the scene by trying to maintain the fullness of concentration
and freedom of expression created in the private moment.

Preparation can also involve a conscious concentration on objects as well as sensory work to inspire the actor's imagination. The actor's concentration should be strong enough to carry over into the scene's beginning. Preparation gives the actor a sense of feeling, thought and behavior that he cannot get from words alone. A sequence for the character is developed. The actor's belief in himself is aroused while at the same time a continuity of behavior for a living being is formed.

A new student should take a long time for his preperformance preparation. As he gains experience, less and less time is needed to prepare. Conscious preparation is particularly important if an actor has to enter feeling high emotion. But if the actor has done his work in homework and rehearsals, he will know how to use an affective memory or other techniques to excite his imagination quickly and will have no problem walking onto the stage ready to go.

While lecturing about preparation at the Actors Studio, Strasberg advised:

> Actually the less time employed, the fresher and more spontaneous the response . . .

> The technique should actually be so quickly and skillfully used that no matter what the scene the actor needs no more than five minutes—and actually should be able to start the preparation two minutes or even a minute before curtain time. However, the actor may unconsciously start the preparation when he enters the theatre and starts to put on his makeup. Thus, a new conditioning is gradually built up quite apart from the conscious technique.[35]

This advice can work well for trained, accomplished actors. But most young actors, particularly those who have not trained for long, need more time for preparation than two or five minutes.

A final word of caution: the actor should take care that in preparation and in performance he does not anticipate what is going to happen. Rather he should make the scene possible by doing those things that propel him into it. Strasberg frequently encouraged actors to take adequate time in their preparation work. He encouraged his students to prepare on the stage, in front of the class or Actors Studio members, and not to start the scene until they felt they were ready.

Preparation choices are critical because they affect the way the scene turns out. If a concept used in preparation brings the actor down or defeats his general energy, then he must get his energy back up before going onstage. He tells himself, "I must get my motor going again." A different sensory or emotional exercise may be needed, such as a new private moment preparation, or something very simple may work. A little dance to some familiar, favorite tune with a good crisp rhythm may be just the thing. Such a dance can actually be done very quietly in a chair or standing in a corner, moving the toes, the hands, even the whole body, to this very specific song and rhythm but at the same time being willing to relate to others. Children do this all the time. Ultimately, however, the actor must stop all this type of preparation and go act.

Quite clearly the actor must know what preparation is appropriate for his role. This is equally applicable to movies and television. Walter Matthau cleverly compared the three mediums, saying, "Television acting is marbles, screen acting is ping-pong, and stage acting is tennis. Stage acting needs more preparation."[36] (For more information about preparing and learning a role, see chapter 9, "Class Scene Studies.")

The Trained Actor

Imagination must be utilized at each stage of training, rehearsal and performance. The actor should be able to create anything that has to be created, whether an object, thought or sensation, in much the same way as a musician creates any tone that is needed in his work. When an actor can create what is needed, he may be called technically trained, and he will be able to hit many notes in a performance.

The technique of a trained actor involves controlling his personal resources and repeating what has worked. Effort, discipline and will are needed in order for an actor to lead himself into a creative mood. Developing will involves self-awareness. This will expand an actor's consciousness of how his organism functions unconsciously: "What impulses rise under what conditions, what happens when he tries to feed these impulses into expression?"[37]

An actor should realize that everything he does is not necessarily difficult. The actor uses the exercises as tools when needed. Some scenes are simple and should be performed simply without recourse to unnecessary techniques, such as too much sensory or affective memory work. Strasberg acknowledged this problem, counseling the actor to learn when to work and when not to work. The actor "must have sufficient faith and confidence in himself to realize that certain things are simple. Only when what he has to do becomes difficult should he become concerned with helping himself. Otherwise, he often gets in his own way."[38] Thus, the crux of some actor's problems is to know when to work and when to get out of the way.

At another time Strasberg stressed, "There is a confusion about people acting naturally, so it's just casual and dull. If a role should be intense and it is played only naturally, it comes over casual. Conversely, too many people try to work all the time. All they need do is make something specific, definite and concrete. All work is for one purpose—to make you [the actor] real and my [the audience's] reaction to you real."[39]

Sensory reality and specific emotion can also be generated from events operating on the set or stage. De Niro was asked what he was working on in the *Taxi Driver* scene (with Peter Boyle outside of the cab) when he conveyed great confusion.

> We did a lot that was written in the script, but in that scene I did not stick too much to the dialogue. There was a feeling of trying to get out. I did not worry about adhering to the dialogue per se. I was worried that I wasn't doing enough. One has an image of how one wants to do something, and then when I do it, I say, "I wish I could have done more, could have been fuller." All that I felt, but I knew instinctively I didn't want to overdo anything. I just wanted to put my focus on Boyle. At that very moment I tried to think of something in my own life I could use—that would make me relate to him—something common between us. I'd use things of that sort, and then I used the fact that I was personally confused and did not know what I wanted to do with the scene.[40]

De Niro went with the reality of his real-life confusion, which worked, just as Marlon Brando used his own feelings, both sensory and emotional, in filming the last ten minutes of *On the Waterfront*. Terry Malloy, Brando's character, had been severely beaten by union thugs, and then he had to somehow drag himself to an intimidated group of dockworkers. On the day of the shooting, delays and retakes resulting from technical problems and bad weather forced Brando to wait almost twelve hours in rain and wind. By the end of the day he was wet, cold, hungry, tired and irritable, so he let those sensory and emotional feelings flow through his words and actions. His true feelings worked for the character and led to a brilliant performance.

Specific emotion can also be generated from what happens in the scene. Affective memory for the emotional reality of a character is used only when the actor has a problem and affective memory is needed. Some scenes require the actor to determine an objective or inner action before (or instead of) doing emotional memory work. Even though some scenes do not require affective memory work, a trained actor always has a sensory life present. An astute trained actor discerns whether affective memory, an inner action, both or something else is needed for the scene.

After an actor explores his role thoroughly, an instructor may ask him to repeat a scene by doing it a different way and trying new choices. Sometimes this request is for the growth of an actor. Al Pacino once did two monologues for Strasberg: Hickey from O'Neill's *The Iceman Cometh* and Hamlet from Shakespeare's play. When he had finished, Strasberg said, "Now do Hamlet as Hickey and Hickey as Hamlet." Pacino explained the value of such training at the studio:

> I first did monologues at the studio because I was too shy to ask anyone to

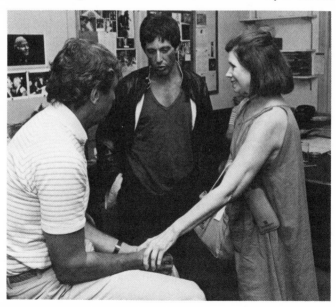

Mark Rydell, Al Pacino and Lorrie Hull discussing monologues at the Actors Studio. Photo © Demetrios Demetropoulos.

be my scene partner. I knew what Lee was getting at when he asked me to do Hamlet as Hickey and Hickey as Hamlet. These monologues broke the ice for me to work at the Studio. The Actors Studio was like a repertory company for me where I did everything leading to my finally working in theatre.[41]

Asked why he had assigned this change of choices, Strasberg explained that he wanted Pacino to be as real as Hamlet as he was as Hickey and to bring to the part of Hickey the same kind of intensity that he had brought to Hamlet. Pacino had been willing to give Hamlet this intensity because "Hamlet was a great character,"[42] but he had failed to realize that Hamlet could be portrayed as being as real as Hickey and that Hickey could be portrayed as having the same intensity of emotion as Hamlet.

The language of Shakespeare's *Hamlet* is so brilliant and powerful that an actor tends to spontaneously bring great intensity to the role, but he often tends to lack reality. O'Neill, however, necessarily portrayed Hickey with more restrained language, so it is easier for an actor to make Hickey seem real but harder to achieve great emotional intensity in the part.

9 Class Scene Studies

Classes in Method acting usually meet four hours per week, and approximately half this time is devoted to scene studies. Since most classes are continuous, students can enter at any time and there is no definite termination date. Consequently, new students observe scenes performed by students who have been in the class for a longer period. Beginning students focus on relaxation and sensory exercises, but they are encouraged to do a scene as soon as they are ready and express a desire to do so. This should take place approximately at the end of three months of training but may be scheduled as early as one month.

I prepare handouts for my classes describing the type of scene to be used, explaining how it should be prepared and listing a number of appropriate scenes to choose from. Sample handouts are reproduced in appendix G. In both beginning and advanced work the scenes have only two principal characters and are five to fifteen minutes long. All scenes performed are selected under the guidance and with the approval of the instructor.

Two-character Scenes

Beginning students are advised to choose a scene of proven value with logical physical tasks. Then if the scene is not going well, the instructor knows the problem lies with the student and not the material.[1] Students may occasionally choose material from short stories and great novels. As Strasberg said, "There are novels with marvelous parts and scenes. Some have been made into movies but others will never be bought for the movies. New material from short stories can show students off in fresh, new ways."[2] Scenes that are infrequently performed often have special value because they do not invite comparison with the way others have done the same roles. Of course, the most advanced students are encouraged to investigate and perform the classic dramas of the Greeks and Shakespeare.

After a scene has been selected, the student is required to read the *entire* script of the play, film or literary work. The scene is then prepared in the manner described in chapter 8, "Preparing and Learning the Role." I prefer to guide each stage of rehearsal, beginning with a first reading in class. The actors sit across from each other so they can see their partner clearly. They are encouraged to connect, really talking and listening. This initial class reading is a rehearsal procedure, so I ask the actors to talk simply and easily without worrying about picking up cues. They pause when necessary to experiment with looking at the partner or with an inner action or intention, always realizing that final choices will come later as rehearsals progress. If some situation in the script moves the actor, he or she is encouraged to let it happen. The idea is not to hold back emotion but to avoid forcing emotion before the actor is ready. After this first reading, discussion focuses on the character and on possible physical activities and sensory work. I may also suggest improvisational rehearsal procedures to be explored in class or for homework. Some of the preparation may be done in class, but most of it is done as homework, preferably with the partner. When the students feel rehearsals have gone as far as possible, they schedule the scene for presentation to the class.

After the scene is presented, I question each actor, ask the class members for comments and then finish with my own critique. I begin by asking each actor what he "worked for," what specifically he wanted to achieve in the scene. Here, I find out whether the actor is clear or vague about his intentions, whether he is simply repeating the plot or whether he has chosen specific productive tasks (as discussed in chapter 8 as well as later in this chapter).

The class is then asked to comment on the scene *based on what the actor has tried to do*—whether or not he succeeded and to what degree. I guide this discussion so that the comments are not personal or directorial (avoid "I would do the scene such-and-such a way"). I ask the class to comment before I do so that no one will feel obligated to agree or disagree with me. Also, quite frankly, it is not unusual for a class member to make a particularly astute observation that had escaped me.

While I save most of my comments for last, I freely disagree with the critiques wherever necessary and promptly disagree if a suggestion is made which would not benefit those acting in the scene. Finally, I make my own comments as to how well the actor achieved what he set out to do, and I outline how he can approach the role and what further work he can do (for instance: create a place, circumstances behind the dialogue, physical activities, sensory or emotional work, an action or goal, relationship to other characters, more specific work, the use of personalization or substitution). Strasberg explained his approach to the critique: "In criticizing acting always criticize positively, so the actor can build on what is there." He added, "As a teacher-critic I pick out one thing that is good to build on and then suggest different ways of doing it—always in a way that people can do something about."[3]

Not only do I usually question the actor to determine if he or she has chosen specific tasks but I probe to discover if the actor knows the difference between the plot and the situation (the event or circumstances behind the written words). The scene is the verbal framework that springs from the plot. The situation will become clear through the creativity of the actor and director, and the resultant behavior makes the scene more than just words, words, words (see also part 3, "Directing"). If the actor does not know what lies behind the dialogue, he cannot really understand the scene.

If a scene is particularly well done, or if time presses, my critique concludes the study. If further immediate work will be useful and time permits, I work with the actor(s) on the scene, suggesting personalization, substitution, relating more to other characters, new actions or choices or sensory homework. I also may guide other methods, such as improvisation, gibberish, discussion, affective memories or "speaking out."

"Speaking out" is a learning technique that can be used in two ways: as an inner monologue or as a narrative monologue. When the actor speaks out his *own* feelings during a scene or exercise, he is employing an inner monologue. When the actor speaks out the thoughts of the character he is portraying, this is a narrative monologue; it may be spoken either between or in place of the lines of dialogue as well as when the other character is speaking. The teacher or director may ask the actor to use one of these techniques, or the actor may sometimes speak out spontaneously. Speaking out is clearly different from improvising, but sometimes an actor is not clear in his own mind as to which one he is doing. In such a case, I stop the scene and make sure the actor knows what he or she is doing.[4]

The inner monologue, involving the actor's speaking out what he or she is experiencing, can help the instructor or director understand why the student is not performing as he or she should. The instructor can thus guide the actor in overcoming problems. The inner monologue at times leads to the narrative monologue, which enables an actor to develop a life and train of thought appropriate to the character he is portraying. The reverse process may also be used or the two techniques may be combined.

If I feel a student is not working well in a scene, possibly because of some personal reason (fatigue, frustration, personal conflicts or a professional block), I sometimes call for an inner monologue to discover the reason. If I feel a student is weak or stymied because he is not thinking or responding as the character or does not understand the character, I will ask for a narrative monologue.

When I work with a scene I demonstrate how a director can work with actors and how actors can work by themselves. I try to pinpoint what is good in a scene or what could be changed for a better or different result. Most scenes are worked on and repeated one or more times in subsequent classes.

The scene selected must be suitable for the student's level of development yet facilitate that development as the scene is repeated. In beginning scene work the scene should be simple and the character close to the actor's nature so he can identify with the role (see appendix G). Hollywood calls this typecasting. A simple scene has a clear, uncomplicated line of physical behavior with a conversational type of dialogue. The scene should not demand any characterization or extreme emotion. Avoid scenes involving the death of a loved one, contemplation of suicide, a mental breakdown, heavy characterizations, such as aged persons or individuals with foreign accents, or psychologically abnormal persons.

Simplicity in a scene does not mean dull material; it means uncomplicated material. This first level of acting demonstrates the degree to which the actor can use himself simply yet with reality. This level also permits the instructor to note how the actor carries out the dictates of his own will. The instructor can also determine what has to be worked on immediately and what can be addressed in later classes.

Choosing a scene that suits the actor's psyche or personality is appropriate for the beginner. Ordinary physical actions from the actor's everyday life are readily observable and therefore more easily created in scene work. Moreover, the student can compare his activities during the scene presentation with familiar activities in his personal life. If what he does in a scene is not true, the actor can sense the difference between his stage work and his living reality.

Natural Behavior

Strasberg was never concerned with interpretation in early scene work. Rather, he focused on making the objects of concentration alive and real. I too concentrate on the actor's ability to use daily physical activities for the scene by doing real things connected with the script; on his ability to behave simply, naturally and believably; and finally on his capacity to "get" what he is working for. One of the central problems of acting is to be able to create a reality that the actor himself believes in. That is the difference between life and acting. In acting spontaneity must be created. In order to create this reality the actor deals with what is immediate in his environment—he begins with what he knows. Indeed, in all scene work (beginning as well as advanced) I encourage the actor to start with himself and his own instincts. If an actor goes to sensory or affective memory work too soon, he could cut off his spontaneity and imagination.

Thus, in beginning scene work I try to get the actor to behave naturally, avoiding planned movements, preoccupation with lines or preplanning of any kind. I look for physical activity, particularly in the student's initial work on a scene. Simple physical tasks can be found in the play, or an actor can select physical tasks not specified in the script, for instance, eating an apple, filing nails, getting dressed, applying makeup, cleaning, setting the table or sweeping. As the actor performs these tasks simply, he often finds that he begins to create other elements of the scene and the behavior of the character. This is especially true when the author has written an interesting sequence of objects on which to concentrate. In "Ludlow Fair" (by Lanford Wilson), for example, Agnes does the following: brushes her hair, eats peanut brittle, files her nails, blows her nose, sets her hair in large rollers, smokes a cigarette, blows her nose again and finally dabs cold cream on her lips. The actor searches for objects (especially physical tasks) that awaken his concentration and contribute to his own belief in the scene. As I observe I note what the actor can do when he behaves as himself and whether he can act simply and logically. My concern is to help the actor solve problems. Eventually scene work will deal with creating physical, sensory and emotional reality as well as overcoming habits and blocks.

Sensory Elements

If an actor has successfully dealt with physical tasks and has not incorporated sensory work into his initial scene work, he next adds the sensory elements to his current scene or to the subsequent one. Strasberg advised that the objects used in this second stage of scene work be imaginary objects (like heat, cold, smells, pain, sights, sounds and the place) (see chapter 8) in order to create a sensory reality. But an actor should guard against superimposing sensory work where it is not needed or not connected with the scene (for example, heat when heat is not called for or when the behavior as a result of heat is not logical for the scene).[5] Sensory work relating to the scene is done not only to create a reality but also so that the actor does not fall into a set sequence or worry about words or cues. He should begin to experience and sensorily "fish in every puddle to see what he will find."[6] This type of scene work enables the actor to apply what he is practicing in his sensory exercises and to perceive how the exercises are useful in preparing a role. Parallel results are achieved in exercise and scene work. Exercises develop the actor's sense of reality, preparing him for times onstage or before a camera when he will have to focus on more than one object of concentration.[7]

If the actor does not make each thing he does real, he may start to indicate (that is, *show* a result or assume a feeling rather than generate a real one). Examples of indicating include pretending to shiver for cold but not really feeling cold; wiping perspiration from the body, indicating heat, but not realy feeling heat; clutching the body, indicating pain, but not really feeling pain; and showing surprise but not really feeling surprise. When the actor indicates, he is generally looking at himself with a third eye and thinking what would look good.

If an actor does not find means to arouse reality in himself, he should not go forward in the role. But if a student actor continues to do the same sensory work and tasks scene after scene, because he or she is comfortable and afraid to take a chance, the instructor must then assign new work. The student must incorporate new tasks and sensory work in his scenes, and the instructor must urge him or her to go on to new levels of development.

The Actor's Tasks

The third stage of scene work aims to awaken a real relationship with other actors and with objects. By this time the actor should have a sense of what is taking place in the scene which will color his work with objects and fellow actors. The actor will have answered the questions "What do I do here?" and "How will I feel?" I encourage students working on scenes to ask the following about their characters: "Who am I? Where am I? What do I want? What will I do and how far will I go to get what I want? What is stopping me? (What are the obstacles?)" The actor should have determined the logic of the event, which derives from the given circumstances of the play,[8] and what he has to do to make that event real and therefore convincing. The actor needs analysis, belief, concentration, spontaneous imagination and an inner technique that allows him to use himself as required. Strasberg claimed, "We [teachers] can only develop in students a sense of logic."[9]

Actors should know what has happened before the scene starts. Recreating these given circumstances just prior to the beginning of the scene steers an actor's thoughts and behavior toward the scene itself. For instance, in William Saroyan's play *Hello Out There,* a character has been hit on the head before the play begins. When the play opens, he must deal with the pain. A poor actor would ignore the injured head. Thus, in preparatory work as well as in the scene an actor can work for a sensation, sensations or an emotion. Mentally thinking of a sensation (for example, a painful head) is usually not enough, so the actor is encouraged to pick something sensorily real to him and to reexperience that sensation. It may be helpful to improvise an event preceding the scene and then follow with the rehearsal of the scene itself.

The actor's understanding of a character may also be enriched if he improvises other given circumstances of what happened before the play begins. Classmates may participate in such improvisations, even though they might not necessarily be in the scene. If class time does not permit such work, the actor can sometimes just work alone to create the prior events. He might, for instance, remember being fired from a job, winning a lottery or having a fight with a good friend and then personalize or substitute to make the remembering truthful. When the actor works alone to create emotionally or sensorily what is needed, he keeps the sensations going during the scene if it is logical to do so.

An actor can create the location before the scene (or as the scene begins) through a private moment or through sensory work for the specific place. If an actor works just in his mind for a specific place, like a room, he might get a feeling or mood from it. But when he works sensorily—using his five senses to create the locale outside of himself, around himself, not only in his head—the result is visible in *behavior.* That is why working for a particular place can be most effective in scene work. Creating the place not only makes something that is imaginary real to the actor but makes it real enough to create a coherent context for behavior. When this behavior is both intimately connected with the actor's own reality and is logical for the scene, the actor weds his own realities to the play.

At an Actors Studio session Strasberg gave one approach to scene work: "I believe in a basic premise when working on a scene . . . ask yourself, what would you be doing here [in this place and situation] if the scene had never been written [if the situation had been specified but not the words]?"[10] Asking the above question, an actor can build a whole behavior and experience, without the playwright's words. This kind of improvising leads to other colors and behavior for the character. The actor concentrates more on the situation and what he feels about the character rather than jumping to the literal meaning of the lines. In this way, Strasberg argued, the actor motivates what he creates so it is an experience instead of a literary phrase. "Think of time in terms of experience and reality . . . ," Strasberg emphasized, encouraging the actor to create the "whole thing" without the words.[11] All the words do is tie together the actor's approach (based on his homework) and his imagination. What did the playwright mean? That is the reality. If reality comes before the words, then words and actions are motivated, which then gives them depth of meaning.

As an actor continues working on scenes, he should explore his characters thoroughly, being particularly aware of areas where his own personality differs from that of the character. An actor who does not naturally have some of the qualities needed for the role will have to work for those qualities since the actor must motivate himself to behave as the character, not as himself. Understanding these differences leads the actor to a better understanding of the task before him. He must enlist superior concentration and imagination to draw from himself the behavior needed to lend truth to the character.

Preparation before a Scene

If the students have not prepared, I suggest preparation choices to rehearse (relaxation, creating the place, appropriate sensory work and given circumstances, any emotional work needed, and thinking specific thoughts as the character). Occasionally, I guide students through their preparation prior to rehearsals. At times I guide preparation work of two students while other students do sensory assignments. At other times, preparation work is guided just before a scene is repeated. If students have not prepared the given circumstances, five minutes or so of guidance before the scene is repeated is helpful. If there is time in class, or in another class, the actor(s) can explore improvisations of events that occurred before the scene began. The partner or other class members can play the parts needed.

Advanced Scene Work

Advanced scene work does not permit the actor merely to use himself as a beginner does, for the advanced actor must often deal with a character whose nature and background is quite different from his own. The actor should explore the life of the character by working with aspects of dress, speech and attitude as well as physical, mental and emotional conditions. Investigation and exploration procedures draw on everything the actor knows about life, whether it is conscious or unconscious. Improvisational work can be based on the script or the given circumstances and should be utilized to explore concrete aspects of the character.

Affective memory, gibberish, singing the words, speaking out, a narrative monologue or an inner monologue are useful rehearsal techniques if the actor falls into conventional stage behavior or conventional stage speaking. Conventional stage behavior involves planned, self-conscious movements in which the actor is gauging his performance only from the lines and has not created a life of his own for the character. He is merely paying lip service to a piece of literature. Conventional stage speaking generally involves speaking loudly and clearly without much sincerity or feeling; the actor is just projecting words. The actor may be vocal, lifeless and nonspontaneous, and there is a sense of a recitation in which the actor's total concentration rests on the words and/or his own voice rather than outside of himself on the other actors or on other elements such as sense memory, affective memory or the inner action.

An advanced actor can usually begin working on a scene by following his own instincts. Often in class scene work he freely speaks out his own thoughts to himself or about himself (an inner monologue) when the scene is not going well. In such a case the actor's partner does not relate or react, except occasionally when the speaking out is about the partner. At other times an actor is stimulated to speak out the subtext (a narrative monologue), the thought behind the words, not just the literal meaning. At these times the actor speaks out the real meaning and diffuses it into the words of the author. Nonetheless, the actor is always encouraged to express the written dialogue of the author between his own words.

Strasberg boasted that Berthold Brecht learned another use of the narrative monologue technique from him. "When I was working on one of his plays, some actors were phony in alienation, trying to do conventional ideas of Epic Theatre, so I told them, 'Brecht wants theatre to be real.' Brecht, who was at rehearsals, nodded his head in agreement. We used the narrative monologue for the actors to describe the scene as the character experienced it."[12]

Even though the actor will progress in scene work enough to motivate himself to behave as the character, he must always remain aware of himself as the actor. In 1976 Strasberg cautioned:

> The actor on the stage does not lose himself in the part. There is no such thing as that. The actor works on a number of levels. Now it is usually assumed that if he is committed, he cannot be aware. That's what I believe to be a wrong psychological idea. Awareness, by the way, only demands a slight fraction of energy. Most of it goes toward the doing. The awareness is only one small part of it. It's always dual. It's not a monomaniac thing, otherwise the actor is crazy. Therefore, the idea that the actor is not aware, and that he loses himself in the part, is a wrong idea of creativity, especially actor's creativity. This duality is part of the actor's training.[13]

For the actor to devote most of his energy "toward the doing," he should make conscious decisions about what the character would do in a particular situation. Sometimes insights into a character's behavior are derived from what other characters say about the character in question. It follows that exploration and investigation of a character are accomplished by reading the entire play. In fact, student actors are never allowed to work on a scene in class unless they have first read and studied the entire script.

The actor can analyze the play as a whole, as well as analyze separate sections of the play, by dividing the script into units or beats (see part 2, chapter 8). When the significance of the unit is established in relation to the chararcter's objective or inner action, the actor's concentration is intensified. Strasberg warned that analysis should not be mere mental exploration:

> Analysis permits you to enter the fold of the role, to study its separate elements, its nature, its inner life, its entire world. Analysis consists in seeking to understand the outer, external elements and experiences insofar as they affect the inner life of the role. But analysis also attempts to find the comparable feelings, emotions, experiences and other elements in one-self by means of which one will get close to the role. In short, analysis finds the material essential for the individual process of creation.[14]

Playing the role of an insane person may be far from an actor's experience, but it is an excellent example of how one can enter the "fold of the role":

> First of all, an insane person behaves very logically in relation to the thing that makes him insane . . .
>
> There is not actually much difference between a sane person that kills and an insane person that kills. Both will give you a very logical reason for the killing, but the sane person's reason is founded on an actual happening. The principle Stanislavski used to approach a great variety of difficult parts should be suggestive. This is the principle of looking for the opposite. Thus, when you play an insane person, you do not look for the insanity. You look for his rational side. You look for the thing that makes him insane, but you do that insane thing with full belief and full reality.[15]

While conducting a scene critique, I often question the actor as to what he understands about his character. We have found that if an actor finds one little thing that he does not understand about the character and discards that little thing as unimportant, he often misses the key to the role. Strasberg explained:

> If the actor cannot find the reason for something that seems to him insig-nificant, invariably that is the key to the character. If you ask the actor, "What does that one line mean?" and he says, "Well that's the one thing I couldn't understand. Everything else makes sense," the explanation of this one line is always the key to the character which the actor has not yet found. In playing an insane person, the actor should be particularly careful to search for the special logic or experience that conditions in this particular person the behavior that we call insane.[16]

After all of the preliminary stages of work (read-throughs, following one's impulses, physical tasks, work with sensory objects to inspire reality and conviction, bringing the imagination alive, involvement with the role's given circumstances, observation, improvisations, speaking out, playing inner actions, characterization and at times gibberish work), the actor then follows his instincts and lets the emotion result. Specific emotion can come out of what happens in the scene, but, if needed, the actor finally concentrates on creating the emotion that the previous work and analysis has disclosed. Strasberg believed that this emotional work leads to a final and comprehensive understanding of the problems of the role:

> This emotional work opens the way to search for the inner meaning or truth of situations and events and given circumstances. This should lead the actor even more deeply than has any previous work into the past both of the character and of himself, so that a final and comprehensive understanding of the problems of the role emerges.[17]

Even when the actor understands the problems of the role, things can go wrong in a scene. If something happens to disrupt the scene, the actor's concentration should be sufficient to allow him to go on with the scene. The instructor sometimes guides an actor in his emotional work while at the same time instructing him to continue the scene. Strasberg advised: "You have to make an effort to get back to the scene. You have to face the technical problems that you have . . . You have to know the steps and sequences to follow to make the thing convincing and believable."[18] Sometimes students speak out their thoughts or the character's thoughts in a troublesome scene, or I may ask questions in order to motivate the student as the character (for example, "Do you hate anybody?"). I generally advise students to follow my directions and stay in character. Strasberg, at such a point, once counseled a student, "Once you put peas in water, don't bother it. That's how it happens, as it comes hotter and alive, it will make pea soup."

Strasberg's questions during the scene often indicated how the advanced actor should work in rehearsal as well as in performance. He once asked an actor, "What are you doing to create hatred for her [your partner]?" The answer (while the scene was in progress) was, "I can use someone in my own life." Strasberg responded, "Are you doing that?" And the answer was, "No, but I can." "Ah, let's see that. Whatever you are going back to, think of it in sensory terms, the whole event—

all five senses should be used—and we will then need to use inprovisation, as the lines might not be there." Strasberg not only guided the experienced actor to try to use affective memory onstage but also showed him what to do in homework so that the affective memory could gradually be fused with the lines from the play (see also part 2, chapter 5).

Strasberg next encouraged the scene partner to think of what she was concerned with to get a motor for the scene: "We are concerned with the reality of the scene and the truth of the play. Keep thinking of the time you were unjustly accused in real life." Using this substitution, the actress became more believable. She created for herself the reality of the scene by letting it become personally real, and then it became more dramatically real.

Sensory and affective memory work can be supplemented with the playing of the character's objective or action. An actor doesn't always need an inner action if an affective memory is used. The affective memory propels the actor and gives him the impetus, which an objective or action could also give him. Actors can work on either the inner action or affective memory, or both simultaneously. The astute actor determines what combination of techniques is needed. Emotional work or affective memory is done only when the actor needs it. Sometimes following one's own instincts, exploration of the play, the inner action or other actors give the actor what he needs, eliminating the immediate need for affective memory. In any case, sensory reality should always be there.

Some actors mentally decide the objective or action early in rehearsals and work just for that. Some can decide "What do I want? Why am I here?" for the action and still bring in all the other necessary work, especially the foundations of sensory life. Others, particularly beginners, find it easier to follow their own instincts: to work gradually for naturalness, then for physical tasks, then for sensory and other objects of concentration, next for characterization and dialogue and finally for the emotion or for the action or objective. Each actor ultimately discovers what works best for him.

What have great actors done in their approach to a role? Strasberg answered thus:

> The approach which has been characterized as that of great acting, not only
> in Shakespeare but in any play, is the approach in which the actor tries to
> add to the lines not only what the lines mean, not only what the character

is feeling and is aware that he is feeling, but also . . . "the emotions or experience of the character, which the character himself is unaware of, but which the actor must be aware of in order correctly to expound what is transpiring." This leads to the true creation of character. It is the approach to a play that all great actors have exemplified. Whether it was Garrick or Kean or Mrs. Siddons, the brilliance of the acting was not founded on the melodic or rhythmic reading of the lines . . .

Those great actors were brilliant in their approach because they created a character, and people seeing their performance came away with a sense that the person in the play was different from the conventional ideal of that character. When Kean played Shylock, the essential element of his performance was a different sense of the character, a sense of Shylock as a young man, a sense of man impelled by motives and events and characteristics and emotions different from those commonly indicated in the playing of that character.[19]

Students are advised not just to prepare a scene but to *build* for themselves the scene and the situation so they can "play the drama." They should prepare the character for "many aspects of his behavior, not just those referred to by the verbalizations."[20] This is one reason why both Strasberg and I encouraged improvisation, particularly when work begins on a scene. In improvisations the actors have to carry out a certain logic of the scene and relate to other characters. Improvisation of scenes helps the actor with simple physical actions and objects and can be valuable in proving to an actor that all he needs to do is think in order to become real.

The instructor should monitor scene work to determine if the actor is able to deal with the tasks he has set for himself. He should not go on to new tasks if he has difficulty in carrying out the old ones. Strasberg used the following analogy to stress the above point:

If a violinist has difficulty playing the notes and you tell him "This has to be played faster," his playing will get worse, not better. It is already difficult for him to play slowly. When you are able to throw one ball up, then two balls, then three balls, then four balls, and to keep them going, that means you are gradually developing the skill. After you have learned the skill, you can do it even if you have other things to do at the same time. . . . When you play a run from a sonata as an exercise, you do not worry about conviction or feeling. You try to play that run as fast and as definitely as you can, so that later you will be able to play it under any conditions. Otherwise—if you try to play it with feeling—you train yourself to do it only that way, and when you have to do the same thing with another feeling, the fingers do not respond.[21]

Sometimes actors use personal problems as an excuse for not being able to create more than one object simultaneously. Personal problems in the individual should not be a problem in the play, scene or exercise. Students can be asked to prepare with a great deal of homework so that they can combine relaxation, objects, inner actions, sensory and emotional work and specific thoughts with full concentration. Professionally, the actor should be prepared and disciplined. Strasberg said it well:

> I frankly don't know what label to put on any actor who would accept it as logical that he can plead his personal comfort [problems] to a director, as if asking for the director's understanding and sympathy in an area where the director can have no understanding and sympathy whatsoever.[22]

Directed Scenes

Directing classes teach directors and actors how to work with each other professionally and harmoniously to inspire creativity. In Strasberg's di-

Directing an audience discussion. Photo by Mark Shahn.

recting classes the students directed scenes. The emphasis was on the director's work with actors. In my Teachers/Directors/Writers/Actors classes the students direct scenes, one-act plays (see appendix G) and original scripts. Beginning directors start with scenes with two characters only.[23]

The scenes approved for a directing class should have a good physical logic so the director can get an idea of blocking, movement and physical activities. The director is guided to create the situation, that is, how the scene takes place and what the actors are doing. If scenes from plays with known values are directed first, the instructor can get a sense of the director's ability to solve problems and deal with physical logic. The director must therefore choose a scene that he understands. The blocking should enable the actors to play the scene easily and securely. Much can be learned if two students in the class direct the same scene.

Following a scene or class project performance the directing student explains what his intentions were—what he was trying to accomplish. I question the director about what actually happened onstage and what the director planned to happen. The director usually states what he thinks the scene is about, background research done on the play, how he worked with actors, what problems he tried to solve and how. Class members sometimes also pose questions. My questions may encourage the director to clarify a particular point or express himself more precisely or fully. The questions can be similar to the following:

What were you working for?

Did you achieve your intention?

What is the author's intent?

Were your choices and intention correct for the play?

How did you work on the play or script? The events?

What does the script call for? Do you need to look at the script to find inner actions or objectives?

Where are affective memories necessary for your actors?

How does the scene fit into the entire play?

How did you work with the actors?

Working with Actors

When I critique a directed scene, I emphasize the director's aims, intentions and ideas. It is imperative that the director and actor agree on
intentions and choices. If there is a conflict, the actor should try to give
the director what he wants. But the director should allow the actor to
show him the actor's choices. The director should be flexible about
changing his opinion if the actor's choice works better. In most instances,
however, the actor must realize that the director is the final authority.[24]

The director's understanding of the script should lead him or her to
guide the actor in motivating and justifying behavior. The actor should
somehow find a *justification* for whatever the character does (see glossary
and chapter 8). Several choices can be explored jointly by the director
and his actor. The good director realizes that he must lead the actor in
such a way as to strengthen the actor's belief and concentration. But
even if an actor must do what he believes to be illogical, he should
approach the task with all the conviction that he would bring to carrying
out logical tasks in life, avoiding the temptation of creating a superficial
imitation of reality.

The director should encourage the actor's sensory life as the basis for
creating a reality. A director may decide that some scenes require the
actor to determine an objective or inner action or to do emotional memory work. An astute director or actor discerns whether justification,
affective memory, an inner action, a combination or something else is
needed for the scene (see chapter 8).

Most directors I know, in order to explore what is needed for a scene,
agree on the value of asking what the character in the scene wants, what
the circumstances are in which he is working to get what he wants, and
why he wants it. The director has to set the conditions under which the
inner action of an actor (what do I want?) can be achieved. Fine directors
find ways not only to make all these elements important to an actor but
also to lead an actor to question his character's relationships with other
characters.

Ultimately, the actor makes the role his own. He explores many av-
enues while remaining creative and free in the part for as long as the
director allows. The director and actor should guard against the role's
becoming set and fixed until the final stages of rehearsal and then only
when a director insists. Indeed, some directors encourage talented actors

never to be set or fixed in a role, especially if an actor's ability enables him to be spontaneous and free while at the same time following the director's and writer's intentions. During the Broadway run of *A Streetcar Named Desire,* Kazan confided to Martin Ritt: "Marlon [Brando] is so good that I never know what he is going to do. He is so relaxed in the part, so full, rich, and creative that something different happens every night, yet Marlon always plays the scene [to the playwright's and director's intent]."[25] Thus, a role grows gradually, the actor and director working together slowly and thoroughly to create a life for a character.

Part 3
Directing

Today's directors, actors and writers must learn to work in various media, moving from one to the other with ease. Although the basic principles of directing (work with actors and handling of the script) are the same for stage, film and television, many of the technical aspects are different. The advice given here is geared chiefly to stage presentation. Film directing requires additional technical training or experience.[1]

Strasberg once commented that while a director needs technical knowledge most good directors have also worked as actors or playwrights. Even by first acting as an assistant director or stage manager, the beginner may observe the methods employed by those already more experienced and successful. In Strasberg's estimation such a background is the best training ground for the young director. This is perhaps the reason why my Teachers/Directors/Writers/Actors workshops have been so effective. The novice director would also do well to read some of the works written by or about outstanding directors (see appendix G, no. 9).[2] Finally, the director's technique matures through experimentation as he directs on his own responsibility.

Preliminary Work

As the director reads a play for the first time, he gets an initial reaction, much as the audience does. This first response is an important one, and the director may want to come back to it later. Some directors write an impression of their first reading of the script.[3]

The director may find it helpful to make early notes on the play's theme and main action or spine (for some directors these latter two terms are interchangeable). Each character's spine will then derive from the play's main action. Notes can be made regarding individual character's spines as well as attitudes and main characteristics of each character (see part 2, chapter 8).

The theme of a play is its central idea—what the play is about—and of course each director has his own point of view as to what this is. There is not just one possibility. This concept can be an individual director's point of view of what the author is trying to teli the audience. Some directors try to capture in a sentence the essential theme of a play or film before beginning work. For instance, one director might express the theme of *Long Day's Journey into Night* by Eugene O'Neill thus: Each person is alone and lonely with his or her own secret guilt. The "long day's journey" denotes probing into one's own dark interior (into night) to find one's true self. A second director might explain the theme as: The pain that befell the father is somehow transmitted to other members of the family.

The theme is a more general idea than the spine, which is the main action pervading the entire play. Some directors call this main action the overall objective. Thus the main action or spine of the script can be considered the overall objective of all the characters: what in general they all want or strive for. The spine of *Long Day's Journey into Night* could be explained as: To search within oneself for what is lost in one's life. Another director might define the spine as: To seek to forgive (one's family) and to try to forget (resentment). In my opinion, the Tyrone family would like to forgive and forget but they cannot, and they do not find their answers.

The individual character's spine is his chief motivating force, conceived from the character's point of view. This is what he as an individual wants or strives for (also referred to as the inner action, intention or objective of the character). (Examples of the individual character's spine or main action can be found in part 2, chapter 8.) Most directors agree on the value of asking what the character wants, why he wants it and what the circumstances are in which the character works to get what he wants. Fine directors find ways to make all these aspects important to an actor and lead him to probe his relationship to other characters. Elia Kazan explained Method concepts in conjunction with an actor or director's finding the character's spine or inner actions:

> He'll inquire into relationships in a way that any alert, intelligent person,

whether he's Method-trained or not, will do. The basic elements of Method really are just horse sense. They humanize acting. You know that you've just been somewhere which makes you come into a scene in a certain way. You know you want something of the people you're playing the scene with. You know that want can be achieved only under certain conditions. So, the director has to set the conditions under which that want can be achieved. Well, if you use these elements, someone asks, "Are you working in Method?" Why ask? Any good director uses them. . . .[4]

By writing down all the above concerns the director begins to see possibilities. A work script can eventually include all these thoughts, plus characters' inner actions for each unit, adjustments, activities and other directorial ideas. Even though I recommend writing a work script for beginning directors, I myself do not always write one. I am also aware that many fine directors do not. But this is a valuable method to help young directors whose goals are vague or unrealized. The goal is for the director to determine early in the directing process his point of view or theme for the play, which leads to the concept and style for the production. If the play was written for another era, I suggest that the director explore parallel examples of the theme in modern society. For Arthur Miller's *The Crucible,* for instance, parallels can be found between the Salem witchcraft trials of the 1600s and the McCarthy trials in the 1950s.[5]

As the director studies the play, he should try to visualize it as a series of events, a sequence of situations. Each of these situations—called a unit or beat—is distinguished by a physical action that has a beginning and end or by an inner action or intention that also has a beginning and end (see part 2, chapter 8). In *The Crucible,* act 2, scene 2 could be one unit. Abigail Williams wants to seduce John Proctor again (wants to make him her man); this is her inner action. This example shows how the unit itself can be made up of smaller units or beats as Abigail tries to play on Proctor's sympathies, tries to charm him, becomes outraged, threatens him and finally refuses to believe he does not want her. A director can break the play into units or beats by drawing lines across the script after each situation. One play may fall into smaller units than another, and one director may work in smaller units than another. Strasberg deemed units equivalent to bars of music: "A unit is more fundamental than blocking, interpretation, reading a line. A unit is the event that is taking place."[6]

The director should decide what is really going on in each unit—not simply the physical action but the underlying desires and motivations of the characters. He is searching for the inner action or intention. Another example, Chayefsky's *The Bachelor Party,* has a scene of a couple getting up in the morning. It could be directed that they had an argument the night before. The woman is pregnant and wants to have the baby; the man wants her to have an abortion. She asks if it is too early to call her mother, figuring that if her family is on her side she can cement the situation and avoid an abortion. What she is really asking is "Will you come around to my side or . . . ? Should I or should I not call?" When she gets on the phone, her mother reacts as her husband did. The wife is mortified and says, "Well, Grandma, act a little excited, will you?" The scene or unit is clearly not just about getting up in the morning, which is the physical action. The inner action in the unit is the event, the wife's desire to retain the baby. This scene, like most, has elements of what happened before the scene, what the characters want and what the characters' intentions are.

After the director has determined the essential task or theme of the play and has examined the author's intentions with regard to each unit, scene, character and the entire work, he next begins to determine how the scenes occur and what each character is doing in the scenes. The director should be attuned to situations as a series of events building toward a climax or resolution. He then explores the best way to visually convey the high points onstage.[7] A director creates situations as they take place in the script by taking the situations the author has sketched out and clarifying them for himself. If necessary to give the scenes urgency and definition, he may create history for the characters and the scenes to give them focus and purpose.

Even though the director investigates the spine of each character and the main objective or inner action of each character and scene, he should endeavor to retain some flexibility. A director should not be so wedded to his early ideas that he cannot change his mind when individual actors give him values he may not have perceived.

Before rehearsals begin the director should start planning what has to be created in the background for his concept of the production. He relays this concept and overall style of production to those in charge of music, costumes, props, lighting and scenery, so they too can work to evoke a consistent style. Directors can visit museums and study paintings of great painters for composition ideas. Planning sessions with heads of crews, particularly the scene designer (see glossary, "Groundplan"), help to ensure communication and common goals.

Although there have been many plays of great dramatic power performed without any scenery at all, a director should be aware that scenery or setting can have a profound effect on the audience. By creating values in the set, the director can literally change the texture of a scene. The setting of a scene may project the feeling of (or suggest a certain imagery of) a hot place, a warm nest, a cold forbidding box or another mood or atmosphere. Through such imagery the set may even introduce a character before the character appears. For example, a film scene set in an apartment or office containing much fine wood in a formal, tasteless and virtually colorless setting could reveal the occupant's bleak state of mind or drab life. The set may also project a general mood or atmosphere, such as opulence, frivolity, efficiency, decadence or decay. The mood and imagery are achieved through the use of color, geometry, furniture and objects placed in the set. Said Strasberg, "The scenery is important not as a background but as a platform literally in which the scene takes place."[8] On another occasion Strasberg elaborated, describing the set or locale as the "environment within which to play, or the world as conceived by an actor or director within which the situations will logically arise. In movies actual locations can give film directors fresh ideas, evolving behavior more real to the event."[9]

A scene in *Godfather II* between Al Pacino and his film brother was set in a park. The two had to be careful about how they spoke, for others were in the background. The effect was of a small, warm scene, two brothers talking intimately. Then in the middle of the scene the Pacino character raised the question of his brother's betrayal. "The setting in the park worked; if it had been an isolated scene, it would have been melodramatic," commented Strasberg. "Coppola has the ability to visualize not only two people talking but how they will be involved in a space."[10]

Strasberg played a part in *Godfather II*—for which he was nominated for an Academy Award—well remembered for one scene set on a veranda. A waiter asked Strasberg if he wanted some cake, and Strasberg answered, "Just a little piece," and cut the cake. "The scene worked," Strasberg noted. "Otherwise it would have been expository, but it was brought alive by placing it in that environment. People remember my

answer . . . because of the environment . . . [my] cutting the cake became symbolic of dividing properties."[11] Passing the cake around sym-
bolized an arrangement between the men, showing how they dealt with
one another to the smallest detail in their customs. Such details of Italian
life and customs were introduced throughout the film. According to then
Paramount production chief Robert Evans, Coppola was chosen to direct
The Godfather because of his Italian ancestry: "He knew the way these
men ate their food, kissed each other, talked. He knew the grit." A good
film director, through study or observation, knows how a character is
going to act in any given situation as well as what characteristic props,
costumes and makeup to use. Strasberg elaborated:

> A good director can see something in a scene that is not in the script. . . .
> That is what makes Francis a fine script writer and director—the ability to
> visualize what he's trying to get out. That's what singles one director out
> from another. For stage or screen, fine directors can take a script nobody
> else can see things in and visualize things.[12]

Then Strasberg confessed:

> Kazan brought *On the Waterfront* to me and I didn't see much that could
> be done with it, but fortunately Kazan did (e.g., when Marlon comes at the
> end like Christ being crucified). Kazan's late wife [Molly] also did not think
> it could be done, nor did studios who turned it down, but Kazan perceived
> what others could not perceive and when it was done, I had to eat whatever
> it is you eat.[13]

Scenery must be designed to permit variety of staging as well as the
development of events in a logical way. Most directors aim for a variety
of playing areas all over the stage so the audience is not bored with
groupings mainly in the same area. A good rule is to have no unused
furniture onstage. Levels and various emphases make for more interesting stage compositions. Effective compositions isolate one actor on one
area of the stage and contrast that isolation with other actors on the
other side or in another area. When a single actor is isolated from a
group, he is given emphasis while other actors appear as a mass. Composition of stage pictures can be a device for communicating to actors
perceptions about their relationships with others. It can also be a direc-
tor-actor communication to the audience.

The set, lighting and all production elements must embody the idea the director has of the play (see glossary, "Composition" and "Ground-plan") and its events. Strasberg illustrated with the following example of a play he directed:

> The set for *Night over Taos* was all wrong, as Jones's beautifully designed set had everything take place in a room. The set was a classical set with corners and a doorway. After the audience saw the marvelous set, the play died. The play was uneven too, but if I had been older . . . I would have said, "Let's get something outside too where the actors have a place to hide or to go to." The ideas I had I did in the cellar under the stage. The audience only heard sounds, since I created the actual event in the cellar, but onstage the people were only standing and talking. There was no excitement.[14]

In sum, the director subjects his play to literary, historical, artistic and theatrical analysis. Long before casting and rehearsals begin, the director researches pertinent historic and geographic factors, even visits the locale or a similar location if he thinks it useful. Plays concerned with historical events or periods require careful research. The director's goal is a creative production that accurately reflects the customs and practices of the time frame and stimulates the actors' and audience's belief.

Casting

Preliminary work completed, the director is ready to cast the play. Strasberg insisted that casting determined the fate of a production. He estimated the effort as at last half—and sometimes more—of the director's work.[15] Martin Ritt calculated casting as at least 70 percent of the director's work.[16] If a play is cast properly it "falls together," the mixture of people is just right.

The actor's talent and the pyschological dimensions he can bring to the role are sometimes difficult to judge, yet the successful director must learn to evaluate them and cast for the psychological needs of the drama.[17] When casting *The Godfather*, "Coppola saw something in Al Pacino that others in the studio could not see. Coppola's casting is not too obvious. It is just enough so the audience will accept the actor as the character."[18] Strasberg also recounted how he was cast in *Godfather II*. Pacino brought Lee the script and talked him into doing the role. Then he arranged for Lee to speak in Los Angeles (before a group including Coppola) right after coming off the plane from New York, when Lee was tired. Al wanted to see Lee like this, for Pacino knew this was one of the qualities Coppola wanted in the role.

Sometimes an actor is able to bring to a part qualities no one suspected he possessed. The director must therefore be somewhat intuitive, capable of seeing beyond type, which often depends on physical characteristics alone.

The Academy Award winning actor Dustin Hoffman was much affected by Strasberg's attitude toward "type" casting:

> I was very affected by Lee Strasberg when I studied with him; he would say over and over again, "There is no such thing as a juvenile or an ingenue or a villain or a hero or a leading man. We're all characters." I was maybe twenty-one years old, I'd just come to New York to study, and it hit me very strong, because I was a victim of casting. Even today, casting people can kill you. Because you sit down, and before you say a word they're going to look at you and without knowing anything about you tell you, "Well, you're not a leading man. You're not a juvenile. We'll cast you as a doctor, or a scientist, maybe." What's much more fun is to get to know someone, and then to see a way of casting that most people wouldn't cast them as. You start to see something coming out that is what they are underneath.[19]

Kazan's choice of Geraldine Page for *Sweet Bird of Youth* is an example Strasberg often mentioned. "He [Kazan] was able to see in her new dimensions of talent of which others were not aware. The director must perceive the essential element needed for a role."[20]

In order to plumb an actor's potential, I often use improvisation when conducting auditions (see part 2, chapter 7). Improvisation as well as repetition of a scene in a new way can demonstrate if the actor is cooperative, able to take direction and flexible.

The director's dilemma is that good "types" may not be able to do what the script calls for while actors who can develop the part may not be the type an audience will accept. In the end, the good director resolves this problem in a way that satisfies both the audience and the demands of the role.

I admire the opinion of Richard Attenborough, the director of the Academy Award winning film, *Gandhi*. A director's success, says Attenborough, depends not only on astute casting (to satisfy the demands of

The author with Kirk Douglas in New York during the filming of *The Arrangement*. Photo by Frank D. Dandridge.

the role *and* the audience) but also on the way the director handles the actor:

> You realize that casting is a massive attribute as far as a director is concerned. But if you cast right, if you balance your scenes right, really all the director has got to do, other than setting the tempo and dynamics of the scenes within their context, is to persuade the actor that he is the best . . . actor in Christendom and that he is the one actor to play that part. If you can manage to do that, you will relax the actor; if you relax the actor, the actor ventures, the actor dares, the actor gives you everything; he doesn't hold back. And he is not aware of any technical requirements, since he relies on you, and you get a performance of fire and such excitement and such daring. I think that's what happened with Ben Kingsley [in *Gandhi*].[21]

Production Scheduling

All actors (and crew members, if possible) should be present when the group first meets. By this time the director will have distributed copies of a tentative production schedule. At this first meeting rehearsal changes caused by conflicts can be made and a final schedule set. This schedule should include dates and times for scenes and acts, working props, full props, costumes, makeup, scenery and so on. An excellent general production schedule, adaptable to any play, is available from Package Publicity Service.[22] This schedule outlines suggestions for the duties and deadlines of all theatre personnel and can help the beginning director to formulate a schedule for his own production.

Basic ground rules are also laid down at the first meeting, after which the rules should be distributed and posted. Ground rules cover such matters as starting rehearsals on time, quiet in the preparation room and backstage, concentration on the role, not smoking or lounging onstage, visitors and any other guidelines the director feels necessary. I emphasize that although rehearsal schedules and rules are necessary in preparing a production, they are not intended to restrict the creative impulses of the people involved, for people are the most important element in a theatre production. The director should always keep this uppermost in his mind.

The Actor Connection

The relationship between actor and director is crucial to the success of a play or film, but the nature of this relationship is highly variable and the director must develop his own techniques of working with actors from experience.

The director's interaction with a given actor is greatly influenced by the actor's prior experience and innate talent. Beginning amateur actors will require actual teaching of basic acting craft and stage technique. Beginning as well as more experienced actors may profit from improvisation and sensory or affective memory work. Talented and skillful actors may not require sensory or affective memory guidance but may only need an atmosphere of experimentation in which the director acts as critic and advisor.

What approach should be used when directing sensitive fellow artists? Many good directors are capable of manipulating actors and on occasion will do so. Threats, wheedling and trickery have all been used to advantage, but there are obvious dangers involved. More to the point is the creation of a sound, healthy attitude, a proper emotional environment for creativity. The director should lead with an attitude of respect and compassion creating an environment that encourages everyone in the group to feel truly creative. In the ideal situation the director inspires in actors the courage to experiment, especially with unusual, creative choices. Marlon Brando is the supreme example of an actor who is innovative and unpredictable. Mark Rydell, describing Brando's acting in *A Streetcar Named Desire*, said, "Brando's intentions [or inner actions] were set. He always played the play. He never violated that, but he was unpredictable, because he was so creative."[23]

Dustin Hoffman believes in encouraging creative activity in everyone involved:

> I like collaborative filmmaking. I like to go on a set and have everyone feel that they can be a part of that film. . . . You're working with people who are really first-rate in their work and who do many more films than the directors, the producers, or the stars. The crew members go from one film to another—their credits are triple or quadruple what ours are, and they get a smell of whether the work is fraudulent or real. Some of the best ideas I've ever seen that result in the finished film have come, when allowed, from somebody on the crew. . . . I think it's a family, and I think it can be

At the Actors Studio with Mark Rydell, following a session at which he moderated. Photo © Demetrios Demetropoulos.

an emotional, spiritual experience. It still means you have a director—you have someone who has the final say—but it doesn't mean that you have an atmosphere where people are afraid to open their mouths. . . . The art director comes into it, the cinematographer comes into it, the costume-wardrobe people, the editor, etc.—those key people expand it, and all start to add input. You don't want to stifle that. I once read that Ingmar Bergman wrote a letter to his entire crew and cast before he started, saying, 'Now that we're starting production, now that we have the script, please feel that this is a family—it is our film.' . . .[24]

Hoffman also likes to be a producer of his films so that he himself can establish an atmosphere that fosters the above philosophy. Some talented directors, however, disagree with the theory of collaborative productions and make it clear from the beginning that they are in control (often by stating how things will be done). Others, equally talented, stress the collective effort where it looks like all are working together and no one is in charge. But in fact in many of these situations the director has a clear point of view and there is a sense of a director's control in that he or she guides progress and makes final decisions.

The conscientious director will feel it is part of his job to provide a sense of cohesiveness not only for work on the script but for the joint forces working on the entire project. A top-notch director takes responsibility for the ultimate product yet at the same time feels secure enough to allow a collaborative effort rather than a dictatorial one in which he imposes his will on a group of puppets.

Considering the egos, emotions and mercurial dispositions of individuals who gravitate to the theatre, an autocratic director may create an explosion rather than a production. It is clearly better for the director to be a little easy-going, to respect his colleagues as fellow human beings, theatre workers and artists. Such a director guides as a helping friend. Even when an authoritative attitude is necessary, the director's decisions can still be conveyed in a warm and friendly manner rather than in a cold, perfunctory one. The actors in this atmosphere may become hard-working, creative friends of the director who contribute much to the creative process of a production. Quite clearly, the director must ultimately make firm and definite decisions—he is in effect "the artist who paints the picture."

The director must approach criticism thoughtfully. He should know precisely what is the object of criticism, and why, and whether it should be given privately or in the presence of other cast members. The director must determine the most effective way to bring about a change in behavior. One actor may need tough criticism at a certain stage of rehearsal, or even at a certain point in his career, while another may need gentler handling. In either case some firmness is needed, whether tempered with gentleness or toughness.[25] The director's goal is to get the best work out of all involved. Each director must find the way that works best for him or her.

Frequently, the director will find himself with a cast with a wide variety of training and experience. Some will need basic advice as to the preparation of their role while others will need counsel only when they have a problem. Some need buoying up and others need only occasional reassurance. Basic advice to beginning actors and directors is available in short handouts I have prepared for the American Community Theatre Association: "Advice to Actors" (see appendix G, "Learning the Role") and "Advice to Directors."[26]

When I direct, I take some time at the first reading to comment on my concept of the theme of the play, and I tell the actors a little about what to expect from me. I tell them we will do improvisations as rehearsal procedures, and I encourage them to do homework of sensory work appropriate to the script. If there are cast members who are not familiar with sensory or affective memory techniques, I briefly explain these methods, give them applicable handouts from this book and tell them I will teach them such techniques if they are needed. At times individual sessions with actors are scheduled. I believe directors sometimes must teach, especially when directing amateur actors.

Even the experienced actor encounters problems. There are times when he cannot seem to give what the director wants—or even what he himself wants. Then I like to use a technique I learned while watching Elia Kazan direct. When Kazan perceives a problem, he enlists the actor's help. He will say, "There's a problem here," and describe the problem. Almost invariably the actor responds with "I'll think about it." Kazan then lets the actor think it over and sometimes the actor comes in with a solution. If not, the director must suggest new choices and experiment with the actor to help the actor to a solution.

A director may want to give suggestions for an actor's inner or outer justification and motivation for thinking, behavior or movement. The director may suggest imaginary circumstances or thoughts to aid an actor in justifying the script's requirements. An inner justification could simply be a reason for hurrying while in one's home or during an appointment (for instance, a friend is waiting; he must catch a bus). Simply positioning a prop in a certain place can aid an actor to motivate a particular movement the director wants (such as placing cigarettes on a table so the actor has a reason to go to the table).

Justification and motivation can be required for extras as well as main characters. When I have directed plays like *Fiddler on The Roof,* with big group scenes (over one hundred people), I have asked the extras to write biographies or I have given them individual characterizations to justify with their imaginations. I did not want the extras to be simply a mob; I wanted each actor to create a life of his own for his character.

Time is often at a premium, especially for film work, and the director cannot work with all the extras. Then a director can often get what he wants from all his actors by creating a relaxed atmosphere. John Agar, whom I directed in a Hollywood play, illustrated this theory when he told of working with his favorite director, John Ford. Ford created a relaxed atmosphere on the set and on location by leaving his actors

The author as director with the cast of *Drayman Henschel,* presented at the Marilyn Monroe Theatre.

alone. He frequently led the actors to believe they were just rehearsing when in fact the camera was rolling. Ford got a believable, relaxed quality from his actors when they thought it was just a run-through.[27]

Strasberg often counseled actors, "If you don't know what to do, do nothing. Keep it simple."[28] The rehearsal process in movies can be as creative as in the theatre. Acting in films is more demanding because of the scrutiny of the camera. It is better to do nothing than to overdo something. Many actors do nothing (and get away with it).

Regardless, trained actors should be able to achieve a spontaneous, first-time quality under any circumstances. Actors should adhere to the playwright's lines during performances, unless things go wrong and improvisation is necessary. But to achieve the spontaneous, fresh quality needed for little-rehearsed television and movies, I also recognize merit in Frank Capra's opinion:

> Seventy-five percent of the shots you see in my films are first takes, even rehearsals. I always warned my actors *not* to memorize the lines the night before, and if they came in and I thought they knew lines, we'd change 'em just enough to throw them off and keep the freshness. That was always the greatest thing about Jimmy Stewart, every time he said a line it was as if it was coming from way inside him, as if he had just thought of it at that moment.[29]

Other techniques to solve problems, particularly for the stage, include directing a variety of rehearsal procedures described earlier in chapters 8 and 9.

Shelley Winters has worked with some famous directors but claims two really helped her with her "inner life": George Cukor and George Stevens. Shelley confided: "William Wyler, an outstanding director, could tell an actor when he gave him what he wanted but could never tell him just what was wrong."[30] George Stevens, when Shelley was researching *A Place in the Sun,* had her ride on New York buses and subways to Boyle Heights so she could observe workers returning home when they were tired and let their masks down. She went to a factory to watch girls working there at mundane jobs until they became "tired and mindless." Stevens asked her to make up stories about these people and their lives.

A good director encourages his actors to research their roles: to read extensively about the play's era, visit the play's locale or a similar one, repeat the character's activities outside of rehearsals, and try to think and feel as the character at home and in rehearsals. By guiding research, aiding sensory and emotional work, exploring inner actions and suggesting imaginative choices for justification and motivation, the director fosters an actor's faith in himself.

The director should be specific. Bruce Dern was questioned, "What makes a good director?" He replied, "I like someone who is constantly suggesting ideas and making me come up with things on my own. I also like a director to embrace me, to embrace what it is that I do. By that I mean saying, 'That's it. That's it, now just try this,' and the key to it all, of course, is being verbally specific. Any director who is specific with me, I love; anyone who isn't is a struggle."[31]

Stages of Rehearsal: For the Director

The basic concepts in this section are Strasberg's, but some of the practices are ones I have learned from Kazan and from years of experience. The director, like the actor, must discover what works best for him or her. (For instance, I prefer to rehearse a play for at least two months in order to have a smooth, secure production.) Choices will vary according to what is needed for the director and actors in particular productions.

Reading Rehearsals

On the first day the director will talk about the play just a little, touching on the theme, the main intent of the playwright and the essential qualities of the play.[32] Other ideas generated in subsequent readings may reveal the inner action of each character or unit as well as basic relationships between characters. The director can also mention his concept of the play leading to the overall style of the production. Actors will be guided in their inner and outer choices by the director's concept. I advise the director not to burden the actor with a lot of talk at this time. Many ideas are better introduced gradually later when the actor is working.

Reading rehearsals should be held for three, four or five days, depending on the overall length of rehearsal time. (My suggestions here are generally for a five-week production schedule, with rehearsals five days a week during the first four weeks and daily the week before opening.) At the end of the first five days the inner line of the play is almost created as well as the individual actor's subtext. During this period, the director should be careful that the actors do not start "acting." The emphasis should be on talking easily and simply and listening to other actors. Some directors explain: "Talk to each other, find out whom you're talking to and, especially, listen to what they're saying to you."[33] The director must be alert that the actor does not get into bad attitudes or habits: mumbling, giving too much emotion, echoing another actor's tone or verbal patterns.

The director can caution the actors not to be influenced by punctuation. Tell the actors, "Do not talk in sentences. Don't worry about punctuation marks!" "Sometimes," Strasberg said, "at the Studio, we have scripts printed without punctuation marks, and the actor must fill in his own. This helps the actor get out of the sentence habit." The actor is very impressionable at the first reading rehearsal; he has not made up his mind yet and the play hits him fully. This will be the same impression he would have if he were seeing the play or film for the first time.

A director can see from the first reading some of the problems he or she will encounter and where to work with individual actors. In between the first and second day or by the third day, begin to work individually. If there's a scene in which the actor has to give emotion, the director can work separately with that individual then or later.

Reading on the second day should still emphasize a sense of talking. Keep the cast flexible, natural and relaxed. Do not give the actors drama yet or force actors to give "results." Try not to interrupt while individuals read, unless it is to stop actors from "acting" or making unsuitable choices or to correct misread characterizations and misleading stage directions.

Kazan often reads the scenes first to the actors, with pace and meaning, but always careful not to give line readings or impose his interpretation on the actors. Then, he has the actors do a read-through where he emphasizes a sense of talking. Interrupting often, Kazan points up the essential qualities of the play, sketches basic relationships between characters and corrects misread characterizations. By the second or third day the reading begins to take shape according to Kazan's suggestions. Once an actor establishes a sense of the role, Kazan leaves him alone. I too have worked Kazan's way as well as Strasberg's.

Strasberg always cautioned the director to let the actor follow his own interpretation, even if incorrect, in early rehearsals. Strasberg considered it more important that the actor work naturally at this point. He advised the director to do his talking *after* the reading if he felt the actor needed it and to schedule individual work later if necessary. Strasberg's guiding concept was: *the performance comes at the* end *of rehearsals.* The director was thus urged to let the actor initially follow his own instincts and impulses. He would grow gradually in intellectual as well as imaginative awareness of the writer's script. Working gradually aids the actor in bringing the character alive. At the same time as the actor begins to create a life for the character in accordance with the logic of the script, he begins to bring himself alive. The script's reality must be fused with the actor's reality while work progresses on a role.

This is the time to begin to block out events: What happened before? What's really happening in the scene? If the actor says, "The character comes in tired," the director tells him not to do it now but to begin sensory homework. Other sensory exercises can be suggested for homework, but if the director has worked individually on inner actions, personalization, substitution, sensory or emotional aspects with the actor, he can then let the actor try some of these techniques in reading rehearsals. Rehearsal must be the time for the actor and director to experiment.

The primary function of the director is to outline what is taking place. Gradually he verbally plans units, situations, the actors' concerns and activities, even though these may not be apparent from the dialogue. By the end of the second reading the idea of the play should be verbally blocked out. The actors should have a sense of units, events and concerns. Do not tell the actor how you anticipate doing each specific section. He or she already knows it is not going to be just talk.

Physical tasks and sense memory homework can be discussed now or later during the reading period. Some physical tasks and sensory work may be eliminated and others added as rehearsals progress. Discuss the emotional work needed so the actor has a clear idea of what will concern him. Sometimes the use of personalization or substitution in certain parts of the play is sufficient (see part 2, chapter 8, "Preparing and Learning the Role"). The director can also suggest and guide affective memory work later if the actor is not giving the director what he wants (see part 2, chapter 5, "Affective Memory").

On the third and fourth days the director works privately with individual actors. I suggest calling one actor early, then adding others as

needed. Individuals can also stay later at rehearsals. Allow thirty minutes to an hour for individual work. During the next three days the
director works individually with actors, but the group also continues to
read together. Now is the time to work on problems—*before* the actor
comes on the stage or set. I suggest individual sessions for problems and
private reading rehearsals for major scenes. Pick the tough scenes, the
big scenes, so that at the group rehearsals the actor is not just reading
anymore but has a foundation for playing a certain scene with his mind
and imagination already working.

When working individually with the actor, let him sit back in a relaxed
reading position. The lines, and what the actor is doing, will begin to
fuse. Some actors will need to improvise the event of the scene, especially if he or she is having some difficulty (see part 2, chapter 7, "Improvisation in Rehearsal"). There can be also improvisation work with
the group, so actors understand the logic of any particular scene. Improvisation can often be useful during the entire rehearsal period.

When the cast comes together as a group, actors will still be reading,
but lines and characters will continue to fuse. The actors can get up now
if they wish, sit or stand next to those with whom they must relate, and
even touch each other. But the actors still keep the script in hands while
reading. If they feel like it, the actors can simulate physical activities
and start moving in the scenes on the fourth and fifth days, permitting
their impulses to function. But they should not wander around aimlessly.

The director should see the shape of the play by the fifth day, the last
day of reading. Reading rehearsals are the last time the director gets the
overview of the whole play, until the first run-through. Even so, work
particularly on the high moments so that the actors have a sense of what
the play is about. By the end of the fifth day the actors too should have
a clear sense of the play; they should be comfortable talking to each
other, looking and listening. Some emotional moments may appear at
this time, but work on separate sections, pulling the play apart, begins
later in rehearsal.

On the sixth day the actors should have the feel of the play, so now
work can begin on the places where there are difficulties. Improvisation
helps with these problem scenes. But improvisation is of no value unless
the director has pinpointed the problem he is trying to solve. On this
basis the director sets a particular adjustment for the actors. If it does
not solve the problem, the director has chosen wrong or the actors have

picked wrong choices to play.[34] At least by the sixth day, if not before, the director should begin to move people around. Beginning directors may find these five days previous to blocking too long. If there is nothing more to do, block sooner. Do not let a stalemate set in!

Blocking

As soon as possible after reading rehearsals, the director has the stage marked with chalk or tape to indicate boundaries, doors and platforms; chairs, tables, other furniture and props should be positioned. If the real things are not available, use substitute furniture and props. Professional productions usually do not use props until technical rehearsals because union rules do not permit it unless stagehands are to be paid. It is more difficult for the actor to work with substitute objects, but much less expensive. Optimally, the final props, furniture, set and costumes or close approximations should be used for as long as possible so they become second nature for the actors.

During early rehearsals I sometimes like to be on the stage with the actors, at the front and other times moving to the side. I can watch the action closely but at the same time make notes in the script. Eventually, I move to the first row, the third and then farther back in the theatre until I am watching from all areas of the back, sides and balcony, constantly checking sight lines, energy and projection. From the earliest blocking rehearsals the director should observe the stage picture from every area of the auditorium.

The process of blocking is generally done in stages, usually one act per rehearsal. Review the last day's blocking at the beginning of each rehearsal. Never continue without walking through what you did the day before, for the actors don't always remember from one day to the next. The actors will still have scripts in their hands during the walk-throughs. Many directors change or add to blocking up to the last week. The director should always be flexible and open to new ideas from himself or the actors. Nothing should be set definitely until near the end of the rehearsal time.

Two methods of blocking will be considered here: blocking that evolves during rehearsal and blocking that is planned before the rehearsal period. Max Reinhardt, the influential Berlin director, mapped everything out in advance, writing it all in his production plan. But Strasberg confided that he preferred not to completely plan the blocking before starting rehearsals. "I have a picture in mind," he said, "and then set the people accordingly until I think they look right." In this style of blocking a picture in mind is helpful, especially when many people are in the scene. If there are high moments of confrontation, movement and blocking should be precisely in mind, for the director will want to know where various people will be in the high moments. Even then the director must trust the logic of his own thinking and that of the actors for blocking between the high moments. Sometimes an actor needs and wants to move; another may not. A director should not be constrained by pre-conceived ideas.

When a director lets blocking evolve naturally, he should not push at the first run-through. The actors usually move about unconsciously. The director can begin with an idea of where the actor starts and ends but let the actor follow his own instincts in between. Do not force an actor to do what he does not want to do. A director should use the actor's creativity when the idea is good. Some actors will do things unthought of by the director. Strasberg advised that blocking can be done through improvising. "[The actors will] stage it better than you'd think they could. Scenes the actors work on by themselves have marvelous staging. The actor goes where he has to go naturally."[35] If the actors have difficulty improvising, the director can suggest ideas and situations for them, even moods. When the actor is not improvising lines, he can hold the script while improvising blocking. The director can help him to relax and not worry about lines or emotion. "You can't have him worried about more than one thing at a time," Strasberg explained.[36]

Even when the director is allowing the blocking to develop during the rehearsal period, he should know what he wants from each scene or situation, even though only the high moments are tentatively blocked. If a director blocks loosely, it does not mean that he does not know where he is going. Blocking should be planned according to events. The director should know what the end of the play will look like, for he wants to leave a clear image with the audience.

The second method of blocking plots the actual stage movement before rehearsals begin. Some directors make miniature stages and movable models to work out the blocking. Prior blocking can also involve writing diagrams in a prompt book or writing blocking, actions, adjustments, activities and whatever else wanted in putting together a work script. The beginning director may wish to experiment with both methods. He can improvise writing blocking on paper or move his models around. I advise the director to write in a very light pencil when diagraming the blocking in the prompt book, for he is bound to erase many times.

No play should be *rigidly* blocked in advance. The director should be flexible and receptive, experimenting with creative ideas from the actors as well as exploring his own ideas. Preconceived blocking ideas do not always work and should be changed willingly by the director. Sometimes a scene will be done in ten or more different ways before the director decides which works best. Such exploration is the mark of an imaginative, creative director.

Lines

By the end of the twelfth day the play should be blocked. Up to this point the director should not worry the actor about memorizing lines. All through the early rehearsals the actor has been unconsciously memorizing, but now he can focus on the task. I suggest working on one act per day. I also recommend that the actors learn the script by alternating between the script and improvisation (see part 2, chapter 8). I find this works even for Shakespeare's plays, helping the actor to develop a depth of understanding as well as aiding him in learning lines.

The actor should not worry about "acting" or blocking during this period. His principal concern is to learn the role. Strasberg taught that the actor should concentrate on one task at a time, so at this point the director should not expect any emotional aspects of the role. I myself find that most experienced actors at this point are able to remember blocking and have some real sensations and sincerity.

The director monitors actors' stage energy and projection during the last two weeks of rehearsals (beginning approximately the sixteenth day).[37] The time to begin varies with each actor and each production. The director gives necessary directions regarding energy and projection after an actor develops an inner line and life for the character. At this point the emotional aspects of the role should be working. My experience has been that actors who become conscious of projection too soon do not always develop in the role; some have a tendency to just speak loudly with no sense of truth. There can be stop-and-go rehearsals during the sixteenth and seventeenth days.

The actors sould be ready to rehearse without scripts by the eighteenth day (approximately six days after blocking). According to Strasberg, "A stage manager or prompter then . . . is ready to jump in and help if the actor is stuck."[38] The prompter must be on the ball, to jump in quickly, but only if needed. The prompter should know the pauses so as not to jump in too quickly. He or she will need to watch the actor while following the script. It is also the prompter's or stage manager's task to write in extra or changed blocking so that the script is up to date at all times.

I prefer to rehearse with a prompter slightly differently. Once the actors are off-script, I ask them to improvise the first time they miss a line until they are back on the author's words. After the unit, scene or act is completed, it can be rehearsed again several more times. I then allow prompting or use of the script in these repetitions. Each new day of rehearsal I insist that the first time an actor gets himself into trouble he use improvisation to extract himself. Actors often tease me about one of my standard exuberant directions, "Keep going! Keep going!" Afterward, we rehearse the troublesome unit or scene more times that day, alternating between improvisation and prompting or use of the script. I have confidence that this type of rehearsing gives the actor security in performance, for the actor knows that he can respond as the character and play the event of the script no matter what goes wrong!

Run-throughs

Run-throughs of the entire play occupy days nineteen through twenty-one in a five-week rehearsal schedule. Run-throughs can take place before the fourteenth day for a professional four-week rehearsal schedule. While the actors may still be uneasy about their lines, they will already be far ahead in inner emotional work.

If original ideas have not worked out, change them. Speeches can be tried several different ways if necessary as the actors experiment with new actions or choices (including new substitutions) behind the lines. If problems persist, individual affective memory work can be guided or the director can try tapping what is really happening with the actor. Elia Kazan, for example, took advantage of Paul Newman's anxiety about playing for the first time on Broadway in *Sweet Bird of Youth*. Kazan told Newman not to be nervous so many times that the actor's worries increased and he sought more and more help from the director. Newman's nervousness, in fact, gave Kazan exactly the kind of nervous characterization he was looking for. When Kazan wanted to inspire Geraldine Page for her role as a faded movie queen, he left around old screen magazines showing Hollywood beauties in standard pin-up poses.

By the end of the fourth week (in a five-week rehearsal schedule) or the third (for professionals) the group should be playing together as an ensemble unit. Actors should be listening to, looking at and relating to one another, remaining in character at all times. Every actor must adjust to what the other actors are doing but keep his own tone and character. The director must watch to be sure that no actor is unconsciously imitating a colleague by speaking with another actor's tone or verbal pattern.

The director should now have some idea as to how the play is developing. Strasberg once said that the audience's opinion is set by the end of the second act: "The play must come alive by the end of the second act [during a three-act play] or go down the drain."[39] If rehearsals are not going well at this point, increased individual work may be necessary. The high spots and tempo of each scene should now be worked out. A director may wish to work separately with actors in key scenes or moments when precise timing and pacing are crucial.

The final week is the dress rehearsal period. One would hope by this time that the technical and production end is ready to go. By the twenty-second day the complete set should be up and painted. The director should encourage the set crew to construct the set as soon as possible. For nonprofessional groups the set crew can begin building before rehearsals start or as soon as possible after the first meetings between the director and scene designer.

At least by the twenty-third day actors should be using props on a completed set. Actors should be encouraged to familiarize themselves with the set before rehearsals, walking through doors, sitting and touching the furnishings and using the set any way they wish. Many things will feel differently and go wrong during the first day on the set. Strasberg admonished directors, "The first time the actors are on the set, be careful to close your eyes to what is happening. If you get tense then and let them know it, you could throw the actors and you'll ruin the whole performance. Take a walk, tear your hair in private, go for a cup of coffee, but don't let them know you're concerned."[40] Actors should not feel pushed or forced. Give the actor time to adjust his timing, pacing, objects of concentration and emotional work. Let the actors repeat troublesome movement, such as door openings or other physical activities. They should walk through scenes to become at ease with the set. After rehearsals actors can work with the set, and if more work is needed the actors can be called separately. Strasberg concluded one lecture, "If something goes wrong one day, don't worry—only if it happens again, worry."[41]

By the twenty-fourth day lights should be set (using stand-ins for the actors). Most professional groups will have set the lights and made changes by this time. If necessary, separate crew technical rehearsals can be scheduled to rehearse scene changes, lighting, sound and other technical cues. By the twenty-fifth day, but preferably *earlier,* casts should have a complete dress rehearsal with lights and all technical aspects functioning. Some light changes may need to be made at this time, and occasional stop-and-go rehearsing may be necessary until crews operate on cue and all goes smoothly technically.

If possible, the director should try not to interrupt the actors or crews during final run-throughs, particularly on the twenty-sixth and twenty-seventh days (for example, if an actor forgets to sit on a chair at a certain time). The director can take notes and give the actors and crews the notes later. An uninterrupted run-through lets the actors feel the continuity and flow of the play.

I believe that a director can reach his or her people best if he or she gives notes and suggestions privately to each individual actor and crew member. As the director talks softly to the individual, there is a special attention and intimacy involved so that the person listens better and is more receptive. An astute director can also respond to the actor's needs, which are often quite private.

Strasberg concluded a directing lecture as follows:

> Don't worry now about being a director! . . . at the end, tell them the things you want, from notes you took. Don't stop during the run-through. Keep reminding them, emphasizing the important things. If there's still work to be done, do it separately, after the run-through is over. Don't do it so the other actors have to sit around while you work on a scene with the more important individuals.[42]

Complete run-through dress rehearsals with final costumes take place on the twenty-sixth and twenty-seventh days. Makeup changes can be made on or before the twenty-seventh day. These final dress rehearsals pose a serious problem if the actors, crew members and friends present engage in criticism. The director should caution the actors that people will attempt to advise them in various ways but that anything bothering the actor should come to the director. The actors should *never* listen to anyone but the director; friends' comments can ruin a performance. The actor could exaggerate onstage or be conscious only of what the friend says to the detriment of other elements. Outsiders do not know the director's intentions and do not have a perspective on the play as a whole.

The actors and the crew should not criticize one another. All suggestions or complaints should go directly to the director, who can evaluate their validity. The director can then decide whether to take any action.

Some actors solve problems with coworkers ingeniously. A case in point is Susan Strasberg's experience when she appeared on Broadway with Joseph Schildkraut in *The Diary of Anne Frank*. She found that Schildkraut would hold her head against his shoulder and keep it there even when she had a line to say. She did not want to complain to Schildkraut about it, fearing he might think, "Who the hell does this kid think she is, telling me what to do?" Finally in desperation, she appealed to her father for help. Lee advised her not to worry but to take his hand away from her head when she had a line and then put his hand back after she had spoken. Susan did this once and Joseph Schildkraut never buried her head again. The lesson is that it is always better to talk to the director about problems and let him handle them—rather than bruise an actor's ego.[43]

I advise amateur groups to rehearse five days per week for the first four or more weeks.* Rehearsals in the last or fifth week (up to the twenty-seventh day) should be fairly steady, although the actors may have a day off while lights are being set. A simple and easy line rehearsal can be scheduled that day if needed. Professional groups can adopt this rehearsal schedule for a four-week rehearsal period or for shorter or the preferred longer periods.

Near the end of rehearsals, or once a play is in performance and pick-up rehearsals are called, the director may want to prescribe new choices,

---

*I actually prefer to rehearse for at least eight weeks if possible. I then adjust the above schedule with more time allowed for the actors to learn lines and more stop-and-go rehearsals.

strengthening of previous choices, exercises, improvisations, gibberish or speaking out in order to keep the performance fresh and spontaneous. All actors are subject to anticipation, so the director needs to watch for this problem during all rehearsals as well as after the production is running.

During a play's run the audience or other actors may affect an actor's playing of a scene, sometimes to the detriment of the play. Constantly striving for top-quality work, a diligent director will take notes during each performance and discuss them with the actors afterward. The director may notice that an actor's original inner action has weakened or changed altogether because of repetition, his partner's playing or audience response. The director may need to review the actor's original objectives or even work with the actors on scenes that have altered. Individual notes can be given after the show or early enough before the next performance so as not to interfere with preparation work. If time is at a premium, the telephone may be used, but face-to-face communication is preferable.

Martin Landau tells how important notes are to Elia Kazan.[44] Kazan directed the original production of *J. B.* Landau sat with him one night after the play had been running about two months and Kazan took reams of notes. He confided that an actor can go off by just a little bit (illustrated by a half inch between fingers)—a mistake as simple as moving two steps too much or not being in the right light. And sometimes little embellishments added by actors are not right for the play, explained Kazan.

After the play Pat Hingle, who was appearing in the title role, told Landau: "I just have to listen to a few notes from Kazan. Then we can go out to eat." The "few notes" were finished an hour and a half later!

Conclusion

The Method developed by Strasberg, his peers and his disciples provides a foundation for training in all phases of acting and directing. Many are critical of the Method because some actors trained in it become self-indulgent in their release of emotions or inject sensory and affective memory work not appropriate to the role. I do not advocate this, as such excessive "Methodism" may prevent the actor's responsiveness to fellow actors in the scene or may preclude his playing the scene's intention. Another criticism of Method actors is that they tend to carry improvisation into performance. While improvisation for a specific reason during rehearsal is a good practice, it has no place in performance of a play unless something has gone wrong. At some point the director must demand adherence to the playwright's words. "The play's the thing."

Much has been written about Strasberg's teaching, but no detailed study has described his latest techniques in a precise and understandable way. This is what I have attempted here. I wish to clarify that I do not present Strasberg's ideas and thoughts literally but as my memory and notes have retained them. Others who trained and worked with Strasberg may perhaps disagree with some of the ideas put forth in this book. But it is not the aim of this book to be argumentative. Rather, as the former senior faculty member at the Los Angeles Lee Strasberg Theatre Institute, I have tried to describe the Strasberg teaching techniques as I observed, remembered and used them. From Strasberg's teachings I have evolved my own techniques, as every teacher must do.

Stanislavski and Strasberg have both been extensively memorialized—and deservedly so. We must always remember them. But we must also remember that both these great teachers repeatedly reminded us that the Method is a living, changing process that demands never-ending experimentation.

At the Actors Studio West with Martin Landau. Photo © Demetrios Demetropoulos.

Finally, in memory of Lee Strasberg and his contribution to American theatre, I would like to remember my own favorite quotation from the master:

"An actor's tribute to me is in his work."[1]

Appendix A
Strasberg's Relationship to Stanislavski and Vakhtangov

Stanislavski's influence on Strasberg was considerable. Lee Strasberg and Arthur Miller were the only two Americans officially attending the Stanislavski Centennial in the Soviet Union in 1963, and in 1973 Lee Strasberg and Tennessee Williams were two Americans invited to the International Film Festival there. Following the second of these trips, in a talk at the Strasberg Theatre Institute, Strasberg told of his interest in Soviet theatre events stemming from "the influence and importance of Stanislavski and Russian theatre in my own life."

Constantin Sergeyevich Alexeiev was born January 18, 1863. His father was a wealthy Moscow businessman who owned a factory that made gold and silver thread. From an early age Constantin and his brothers and sisters were often taken to the theatre, sometimes with the servants and their children. Starting at the age of seven, Constantin performed in various types of family theatricals, at first organized by his parents but later carried on more by the children themselves.

When Constantin was 14, his father built a little theatre as a wing of their country house and six years later provided a small family theatre in their Moscow home. After Constantin finished school he worked diligently in his father's business but gave almost all his spare time to his theatrical efforts, for by now he wished to make acting his profession. He began to act with some groups outside his family circle and then started to appear anywhere he had the chance. Some of these performances were with dramatic groups of questionable reputation with whom he did not want to appear under his real name, so he assumed the stage name Stanislavski.

Encouraged by his father and armed with a substantial bonus from the family business, Stanislavski helped found the "Society of Arts and Literature" in 1888. This was originally an amateur group with a professional director, but soon Stanislavski became its principal director and producer as well as actor. Later, professional actors performed with this group, and many of its amateur members approached professional caliber themselves. One of these was Marie Perevoschikova, who had assumed the stage name of Lilina and whom Stanislavski married in 1889. With touring companies in the provinces Stanislavski finally had an opportunity to work with some talented professional actors, and the experience stimulated what was to be a lifelong study of the methods these actors used to achieve their goals.

The productions of Stanislavski attracted the attention of Vladimir Nemirovich-Danchenko, an accomplished playwright and teacher at the Philharmonic School of drama in Moscow. In 1897 these two joined forces to form the Moscow Art Theatre, destined to become world famous. As the artistic director of this organization, Stanislavski continued to challenge almost every old convention of the theatre, including overacting, bad scenery, false pathos, declamation, and all "theatricality" in general. He focused more and more on the actor as the key to a successful production, and he carefully observed those actors with natural talent, seeking to discover what it was that made them great. Gradually over the years he formed these observations into a system he thought could be used in teaching the art of acting to young people. He began to test this idea in 1909 with the aid of Leopold Sulerzhitsky, an associate, and his efforts were so successful that in 1912 the First Studio of the Moscow Art Theatre was formed with Sulerzhitsky as director. At the suggestion of the famous playwright Maxim Gorky, the studio adopted the technique of improvisation, which was used with much success. Many outstanding young actors emerged from the studio, including Richard Boleslavsky, Maria Ouspenskaya, and Eugene Vakhtangov, the last becoming in 1920 the head of the Third Studio of the Moscow Art Theatre.

This Third Studio was Vakhtangov's own school of acting and directing. After Vakhtangov's death in 1922, the Third Studio became the Vakhtangov Theatre. Vakhtangov was probably the most outstanding director and teacher of the whole group, and certainly the most articulate. His descriptions and explanations of the Stanislavski system were clear and effective, and doubtless had much influence on Strasberg. Some of Vakhtangov's lectures to students were preserved and translated and came to Strasberg's attention through the Group Theatre.[1]

In 1922 Stanislavski decided to take the Moscow Art Theatre on a two-year tour of Europe and America. Their performance in New York inspired Lee Strasberg to become a professional actor, and he joined the American Laboratory Theatre, founded by Boleslavsky and Ouspenskaya. From them Strasberg learned the rudiments of the Stanislavski system; he learned of discoveries about the psychological nature of the actor and ways of training based on those discoveries which Stanislavski had tested for many years. As an actor, director and teacher, Strasberg would subsequently modify Stanislavski's approach, developing and adapting his method to the modern American theatre. This modification was not irreverent, for Stanislavski himself continually changed and adapted his system, and urged others to do so. Joshua Logan reported that when asked about his method, Stanislavski replied, "Create your own method. Don't depend slavishly on mine. Make up something that will work for you. But keep breaking traditions, I beg you."

Strasberg clarified Stanislavski's system. "The important thing in the Stanislavski method is that it is the opposite of a system. A system implies a theory with precise rules of what to do exactly at each moment. The Stanislavski method is no system. It does not deal with the results to be obtained and therefore sets no rules for what should be done. It only tries to show the actor the path to be followed . . ."[2]

In the late 1920s Stanislavski wrote an article on his acting theory.[3] He concluded that an actor must discover the fundamental motive of the play, believed to be the force that moved all characters toward the final goal of the playwright. After discovering the "through line of action" for the play, each actor had the task of finding his own "through line of action," relating that discovery to the total play and then internally re-creating appropriate emotion (see part 3). This discovery process was one of gradual evolution for the actor.

To Stanislavski muscular tension and rigidity were a barrier to believable acting. He interpreted such static form as a contradiction to an essential dynamism. He insisted that his actors develop the ability to free their bodies of such tensions, usually through physical exercises. Actors were encouraged to develop control of each muscle separately. He linked outer dynamism to inner fluidity of energy. Stanislavski defined the problem but let each actor find his own method of solving it. In *An Actor Prepares*[4] Stanislavski described what did not work for muscle relaxation and stated that inner justification for an action on stage was the path of relaxation. In addition, Stanislavski insisted that his actors be able to control their voices. He felt that each actor should be the complete master of his own body and voice, using both in a manner consistent with the playwright's intentions for the character.

Stanislavski insisted that his actors create "the circle of attention" to develop concentration. The actor's maximum energy must be directed toward the action of the play. As the actor enters into a mutual communion with the action of the play, he excludes all but the most peripheral awareness of the audience. Stanislavski also emphasized the "sense of truth." He cautioned actors to continually search for the inner truth in what they were doing in order to justify behavior.

One of the most important discoveries made by Stanislavski was that an actor could re-create on stage an emotion he had previously experienced in his own life. Stanislavski observed that recollections of particular sensations associated with an emotional experience were especially potent in aiding such recall. He called this whole process "affective memory." Strasberg extensively studied and experimented with this technique and emphasized the use of the senses of touch, taste, sight, smell and hearing in emotional recollection. This explains what Strasberg means when he says affective memory means "memory of sensation, memory of emotion."[5] In this book, I have referred to memory of sensation as "sense memory" and memory of emotion as "affective memory." Affective memory and emotional memory are considered synonymous terms.

Stanislavski developed the theory of affective memory as a method for creating and stimulating the emotions. This method used an actor's feelings about an actual event in his past in which the feelings were similar to those occurring in the play. Having recalled this similar feeling, the actor applied the memory of his emotions to the event in the play. Stanislavski believed the proper use of affective memory gave the actor a credibility that no other method could produce. The basis of Lee Strasberg's modification of Stanislavski's theory is his adaptation of affective memory. Both Stanislavski and Strasberg encouraged actors to take an active part in the creation of the truth of the performance. Additionally, Strasberg sought to develop techniques of discovery related to the American experience. Truth in performance can be generated through an actor's homework as he re-creates reality through exercises and inner techniques developed by the Method. The work is based on what the actor knows—his own reality.

Strasberg and his trained teachers discussed the "through line of ac-

tion" with students, probing to find the intent of the playwright. Strasberg was adamant that the actor and the director understand the intent
of the playwright and agree on this understanding. Strasberg's guidance,
comments and discussions led students to develop objects of concentration and a through line of action for a script and for an entire role, plus
specific thoughts for particular scenes. He developed concentration and
a sense memory repertoire for students through exercise classes; the
techniques learned were then applied in scene study classes. This process
promotes consistency in the actor's work.

Three areas important to the training of the actor (as recognized by
Stanislavski and Strasberg) should be compared: body language, affective memory, and concept of reality.

Stanislavski defined the problem of muscular tension as a barrier to
creative activity. He insisted that his actors free their bodies of superflu-
ous muscular tension through physical exercise or through other means
that worked best for each actor. Each actor tried to develop his own
relaxation technique. Strasberg developed exercises for relaxation, and
these were taught first in the classes conducted by him and his trained
instructors. Relaxation exercises are guided individually, with tension
spots identified, as the first step in the teaching of acting.

It appears that Stanislavski relied chiefly on direct emotional recall
when an actor remembered an event in his past, not caring too much if
the senses were activated or not. Having recalled a similar event, the
actor applied the memory of his emotions or his imagination to the event
in the play. Strasberg, however, after years of experimentation, concluded that emotional recall is easier and more consistent if the actor
does not work directly for the emotion but rather attempts to recall all
the sensations and circumstances associated with the event that produced
the emotion originally. He guided actors to reproduce the emotion by
concentrated efforts of sense memory until the sequence became logical
and orderly through practice so that one word, sensation, image or
"knowing what the experience is" produced the desired emotional response. Thus, Strasberg's training stimulated the sense memory of the
actor so that the experience the actor is trying to create can be recaptured not only mentally, not only externally, but by the actual sensory
and emotional reliving of that experience. This developed the actor's
sense of truth.

Stanislavski, Vakhtangov and Strasberg all searched for the sense of truth, reality and conviction for the actor. Each believed that actors should justify their actions by continually seeking an inner truth, which would lend credibility and a sense of reality to their roles. And although each may have used slightly different techniques and devices, they conceded that ultimately an actor must find his own truth in the work he does.

Appendix B
Vakhtangov as a Director

Perhaps the most important difference between the teachings of Stanislavski and Vakhtangov was pointed out by Strasberg at the Actors
Studio:

> Very often I see you people following the Stanislavski formulation, as op-
> posed to the Vakhtangov formulation, which I happen to favor. The Stan-
> islavski formulation states: "Here is a girl who falls in love. I have been in
> love. When I am in love, what do I do?" That is the way Stanislavski
> formulated the acting problem; therefore, he never solved any of the basic
> problems in any of the classic plays that he did outside of the Russian
> repertoire. Vakhtangov rephrased the approach . . . He said, "If I am play-
> ing Juliet and I have to fall in love overnight, what would I, the actress,
> have to do to create for myself belief in this kind of event?" . . . We have
> tried both approaches, and in certain circumstances the Stanislavski ap-
> proach does not work. The Stanislavski formulation often leaves you high
> and dry in something that is natural and easy and simple but is just not
> what is needed by the play. The Stanislavski formulation often does not lead
> the actor to seek the kind of reality which the author conceived and which
> underlies the lines he wrote. It becomes almost a way of bringing every
> dramatic thing down to a naturalistic level, which cannot support the drama.
> Stanislavski's formulation will then only help the actor by accident. . . .[1]

> Stanislavski in approaching Shakespeare through his peculiar formulation
> was a little too deliberately realistic in the use of time and consequently
> broke the fabric of the wonderful constructions that Shakespeare
> created. . . .

> Stanislavski's productions of Shakespeare were not successful. People
> blamed the Method but to me they were not successful only because Stan-
> islavski had this strange tendency to stress such superficial and naturalistic
> details.[2]

We see here that Stanislavski asked the actor how *he* would feel and
behave in a certain circumstance facing a character in a given scene.
Stanislavski asked, "What would I (the actor) do in this situation?"

Vakhtangov asked the actor to motivate himself to feel and behave as the *character* would.

Strasberg referred to the first and second Vakhtangov formulations.[3] In the first formulation Vakhtangov responded to the question: What is the event? By asking "What is the significance behind the event?" The second formulation involved how to motivate the actor to accomplish the aims of the director and author.

I have been impressed with reports of Vakhtangov's imagination and creativity as a director. He was one of the greatest theatrical innovators of the twentieth century. Vakhtangov was noted for his creation of boldly exciting theatrical forms in which the acting, though not naturalistic, was always truthfully based. Vakhtangov insisted that his actors portray their roles with an inner truthfulness based on the teachings of Stanislavski. For those who wish to study Vakhtangov's directorial methods further, the following books describe accounts of his techniques:

The Vakhtangov School of Stage Art by Nikolai M. Gorchakov
Habima by Raikin Ben-Ari
Stanislavski's Protégé: Eugene Vakhtangov by Ruben Simonov
Vakhtangov's Legacy by William Kuhlke

Although these books are out of print, they may be found in certain large libraries. Gorchakov's work was considered, "the best book on directing" by both Strasberg and Kazan. I found it truly inspiring to read of Vakhtangov's months of rehearsals through improvisational and other techniques.[4]

Gorchakov relates excerpts from what Vakhtangov said to his directing students:

> Before a director can start rehearsing, he has to live (that is to play) all the roles in his mind. And how can he do it if he has never been an actor himself? . . . Most directors hide the fact that they've been actors in their youth, amateurs, perhaps, but still actors. . . . But there are exceptions to every rule. . . . Put everything you have into studying acting [he taught Stanislavski's system at his school] and always bear in mind that in the future you have to play any role: comedy, tragedy, man, woman or even child. Such are the diverse demands made on a real director. . . .
>
> A director is first and foremost an organizer—an organizer of his own thoughts and dreams, an organizer of his colleagues. He should be modest to the utmost. But he is at the same time one of the most important men

in the theatre, a sort of "goblin" who pokes his nose into everything. He is the best friend of the actor and the spectator. . . . The director is the stimulating element of a theatrical company. . . .[5]

Improvisation was Vakhtangov's basic experimental technique. Vakhtangov allowed the form of his plays to develop through a series of improvisations by his actors from which he would select the interpretation he considered most appropriate. Then with a more dictatorial attitude, he carried out the final honing. But the discovery through improvisation was a collaborative endeavor.

Vakhtangov elicited cooperation in fulfilling as much as possible, under his guidance, a vision shared by an entire production group to which each member had contributed. Of course, as the director, it was Vakhtangov who rejected some ideas and accepted others, but his choice was recognized by the group as not dictated by the will of a director/dictator but by the demands of a vision shared by the entire unit. This kind of directing is no longer unique, but Vakhtangov was a master at it with extraordinary documented success.

How interesting to note that Carroll Baker in 1983 made a similar statement about Elia Kazan. Baker wrote:

He [Elia Kazan] made everyone involved in the project [the filming of the movie *Baby Doll*] feel like a full participant. His crew would have walked through fire for him, because no other director had ever made them sense that enormous satisfaction of being an equal contributor to the whole. On his sets, everyone was encouraged to come forward with an idea. When Gadge Kazan had a problem he discussed it openly. For example, the opening shot of the film was of the old southern mansion. Gadge was concerned that the audience might get the impression of a period piece. It was a gaffer who stepped forward and said, 'Hey Gadge, why not wait until a jet flies overhead?' It was a brilliant idea which Gadge jumped at, one by the way which has been imitated many times since. Imagine the feeling of pride that will forever be with that gaffer![6]

Vakhtangov advised his directors, "The actor's task is to represent life and give a vivid portrayal of human character, a task, which is full of joy and satisfaction though sometimes full of torture."[7] Gorchakov illustrated this by writing how Vakhtangov directed actors in *Turandot*:

But the important thing was not to carry out Vakhtangov's [the director's] instructions mechanically [by the *Turandot* company].

To make the production a success it was necessary to harmonize extremely sincere performances of the actors (who did their best to convey the idea underlying the play and acted boldly in the circumstances that were offered) with original, seriously executed (without departing from the character, so to speak) tricks—such as wiping one's face with a towel thrown from the wings, helping Tartaglia to "collect tears" and showing them to the audience, and so on and so forth. It was necessary, in other words to harmonize a childish naiveté with a truly realistic performance, bold eccentricity with tempestuous, dramatic emotion. . . . "Never be afraid of an unknown genre," he would say. "But never ignore the peculiarities inherent in it. . . . Respect the author, but don't kowtow to him. Remember that it is the duty of the theatre to use the talents of the actor, director, set designer and composer to enrich the playwright's drama, to make it tangible and exciting."[8]

Ruben Simonov, Vakhtangov's favorite student and subsequent head of the Vakhtangov Theatre (in 1969), speaks of Vakhtangov's relationship to Stanislavski in *Stanislavski's Protégé*:

He [Vakhtangov] fought the old theatre, destroying its out-of-date forms and replacing them with new forms which were both brilliant and honest. [Vakhtangov never allowed the form to overpower the production as a whole. He always strived for an ensemble production which would convey the basic idea of the play.] Vakhtangov never betrayed the eternal realistic basis of the teachings of Stanislavski; he never doubted the validity of Stanislavski's system. But he criticized it, pointing out some of its weaknesses, and he expressed new thoughts which Stanislavski often accepted. . . . Here is how Vakhtangov put it: 'The correct theatrical means, when discovered, gives to the author's work a true reality on the stage. One can study those means, but the form must be created, must be the product of the artist's great imagination—fantasy. This is why I call it fantastic realism. It exists in every art'. . . . His rehearsals were a thrilling example of it [inspiration]. Here he revealed an extraordinary enthusiasm in his work; a sparkling fantasy which would picture suddenly the enormous possibilities of his work and would inspire all those participating; inventive, daring, brilliant ideas for portraying the meaning of the play, which sprang suddenly to his mind; and the courage to discard bravely what he had painstakingly discovered earlier and start again to search for the means whereby he might express the essence of the play more pointedly, more vividly. As a natural consequence of all this, Vakhtangov had an extraordinary ability to arouse in his actors the same creative mood he himself had. . . .[9]

In *Vakhtangov's Legacy* William Kuhlke claims:

> This method of discovering organic form, form which grows spontaneously out of situation and emotions, was surely one of the sources of Vakhtangov's great success with young actors. Reuben Simonov asserts that the one indispensable facet of any director of talent is not his ability to assimilate research nor his active and detailed imagination, but his ability to communicate successfully his vision of the play to actors, designers, costumers, and musicians in concrete terms capable of realization, and then to lead them step by simple, concrete step to that realization. This process, of course, is not just a matter of transmitting information, but also of engendering in the actor or designer that spark of inspiration which sets his own creative forces in motion along the indicated path.[10]

Gorchakov concluded, "The teacher lives on in his pupils!"[11]

Gorchakov's and Simonov's attitudes and feelings about Vakhtangov exemplify mine about Strasberg. Lee Strasberg's daughter, Susan, beautifully expressed such thoughts in a note to me shortly after her father's death, "It's all a challenge and the dream goes on."

Appendix C
Behavioral Psychology as a Basis for the Method

According to Michael Schulman, a practicing psychologist, members of his profession recognize the scientific facts prevalent in the Method. Schulman wrote of Stanislavski's and Strasberg's principles and procedures of responsive acting. He claimed that while Stanislavski was rejecting two traditional ideas—that acting was imitation and that inspiration could not be controlled—Ivan Pavlov was first demonstrating the conditioning of reflexive and emotional behavior in animals. The two Russians knew each other, and while Stanislavski drew his discoveries primarily from the laboratory of the theatre, there is evidence that his contact with Pavlov helped root his method firmly in the principles of modern psychology. Stanislavski was also aware of Freud's theories, including the psychologist's conclusion that the ultimate forces at work in a personality were instinctual. Schulman explained:

> Method actors and behavioral psychologists have a common intention: they are both in the business of controlling behavior of others, but where the psychologist observes the behavior of others, the actor's only subject is himself. He must learn which stimuli to apply to himself so that, on cue, he will experience the proper feeling and give the proper response.[1]

Schulman identified three critical phases of the Method actor's training: the internal work, the external work and the creative work, each of which can be analyzed in behavioral terms. The intent of the actor's internal work is to provide for himself stimuli that evoke actual feelings and responses while he is acting. Schulman elaborated:

> Contemporary behaviorism distinguishes three main classes of stimuli: unconditioned, conditioned, and discriminative. Unconditioned (or unlearned) stimuli are effective without learning because of the biological arrangement of the body; they evoke what Pavlov called reflexive behavior and what B. F. Skinner calls respondent behavior. An animal salivates when one places food in its mouth; one's eye waters if a particle is trapped under the lid. Emotions also are respondent behaviors; except that the stimuli that evoke them usually are more complex than food or a speck of dust. For

example, failure that occurs in the face of high expectancy (or reliable indicants) of success is very likely to provoke anger.

Pavlov discovered another set of stimuli—conditioned stimuli—that could produce physiological and emotional responses. In his classical experiment, Pavlov sounded a bell just before he gave food to a dog. At first the dog salivated only when it received the food, but eventually it began to salivate whenever it heard the bell. The sound of the bell became a conditioned stimulus. Through the same process, the sight of food can become a conditioned stimulus and can cause one to salivate.

Many persons will salivate upon merely thinking about food. In fact, imaginary stimuli (visual, auditory, olfactory, etc.) can evoke responses that closely correspond to those that real stimuli evoke. This is the basis of the internal work of the Method actor. He learns how to create and use imaginary stimuli when he is playing a role. Ultimately, he develops a repertoire of images that he can rely upon to evoke in him a broad range of emotional responses. . . .

There is evidence that the internal work produces corresponding physiological changes in addition to affecting the actor's subjective experience. Robert Stern and Nancy Lewis measured the galvanic skin responses (GSRs) of Method and non-Method actors. The GSR usually is a reliable indicator of changes in a person's emotional state. Stern and Lewis asked their actor subjects to make as many GSRs as possible during a 10-minute period, then asked them to reverse the direction of the galvanometer by relaxing 10 minutes. (As part of their training in emotional and bodily control, Method actors learn procedures for concentrated relaxation.) The researchers found large differences between the two groups—Method actors had significantly better voluntary control over GSRs than other actors had.

The Method actor in contrast to the traditional one, is more concerned with selecting the proper evocative stimuli than with predetermining the precise movements of his body or the tone of his voice. However, the external work phase of his training does concentrate on his physical and vocal behavior on the stage.[2]

B. F. Skinner has called operant conditioning and operant behavior that behavior affected or conditioned by its consequence. Schulman claimed the manner of physical and vocal expression in the Method is operant conditioning, and he called the stimuli that signal particular operant behaviors and their consequences discriminative stimuli. The actor's external work helps him respond realistically or naturally on stage because Method acting teaches the student to bring real-life behavior to the stage. An example is the actor listening and reacting to the words of his acting partners as if he were hearing them for the first time instead of simply responding to anticipated cues with lines with preplanned vocal and postural pattern. Realizing the importance of training in improvisation, Schulman reinforced that an actor must rely only on the external realities of the moment when improvising—on what he sees, hears, smells, touches and tastes, and on the private, internal realities of what he thinks and feels.

From a psychologist's viewpoint Schulman also related how the Method actor deals with stage fears: "The Method actor learns to produce responses that are incompatible with fear. To do this, he may concentrate on muscle relaxation or on either of two forms of stimuli: 1) the real objects and persons on the stage, or 2) the imaginary stimuli he has created by his internal work.[3]

Method acting can increase and improve an individual's problem-solving behavior. In Strasberg's classes actors answered the question "What did you work for?" in a discussion after scene work. When the actor's goal is to fulfill the requirements of the character and the play, he must formulate the problems that he tried to solve and the solutions that he used. Strasberg often taught students to rely on the given circumstances of the play by asking: What was the character doing just prior to this moment? What did he come here to do? Where is the event taking place? What are the stimuli affecting him—the objects, the odors, the time of day, the temperature? What are his relationships to and what does he want from the other people in the situation? The answers to these and similar questions should influence an actor's choice of action. An actor finally should select a stimulus that would evoke the proper response.

Consequently, when we judge an artist's creativity, we are often responding to the choices he makes in his work. As Stanislavski emphasized, it is largely the choices of physical actions that distinguish the creative actor from the conventional one.

Method-trained teachers praise students according to the uniqueness of their choices and the degree to which their acting fulfills their stated intentions. Schulman concludes his article with the conviction that "Method acting and behavioral psychology find common interests in the control of behavior, and they also share an enthusiasm for an empirical path to discovery."

Appendix D
Professional Acting Training as Summarized by Lee Strasberg

The highest skill and responsiveness is demanded of the actor. The actor deals not with the word but with the act, the deed. He performs an action. The word is not an isolated element, of tonal value, but it is always part of a character, of a situation, of a relationship between characters. The training of purely verbal dexterity is valuable as a part of the actor's mechanical skill. But the same words placed in different circumstances assume totally different meanings. The actor does not read or recite; he speaks lines as a character in an event. He always acts. Any training that stresses the verbal is a return to the old-fashioned form of declamation. Instead, the poem, or soliloquy, or song is placed in different situations and spoken by different characters (Whitman's poem, "I Sing the Body Electric," spoken by a meek little clerk as he steps into his morning cold shower; the gravedigger's scene done by a flirtatious flapper asking answers of a shy teacher; etc.). Words are acted out to find the imaginative possibilities (the word "America"—the actor is asleep, the alarm rings, the actor awakes, he is late, dresses frantically, rushes into the subway, arrives at the office, settles himself quickly, and then leans back, puts his feet on the desk and lights a cigar; or the actress starts as the Statue of Liberty, torch uplifted high, slowly the torch descends, turns into a cocktail glass, and the actress becomes slightly tipsy). The actor is given a series of simple lines:

"Hello, how are you?"
"Fine."
"What happened today?"

This abridgment of an article on actor training in the United States by Lee Strasberg explains some of the fundamentals of Mr. Strasberg's work "Professional Acting Training as Summarized by Lee Strasberg," *Educational Theatre Journal* (Washington, D.C.: American Educational Theatre Association, November 1966), pp. 333–335. The "Use of Memory" quotation is from an interview of Lee Strasberg by Edwin Newman for NET television, November 1969.—*L. Hull*

"Nothing much."

He learns to place these in different situations—husband who has just found out his wife is unfaithful; a man who has lost his job; etc. All of these and many more exercises of this kind develop the actor's awareness of the possibilities inherent in the word, and also heighten the actor's imagination. The words are always acted never just spoken.

The training of the actor deals primarily with helping him to experience, to live and think on the stage. This is achieved through the training of will, intelligence (thought), emotion, imagination, and the stirring of the unconscious. To achieve this, the actor must be able to relax and to concentrate. Many problems in acting disappear when the actor learns to relax, and many difficulties are overcome when the actor learns to concentrate. These are elements basic to all acting in any period and in any kind of play. The ability to experience is a necessary foundation for the actor to find the most expressive form for that experience.

The actor's means of expression (voice, speech, movement, rhythm, etc.) must be especially trained to permit the greatest and most vivid expressiveness, precisely because the creative approach to acting does not permit mechanical or conventional results. Exercises in acrobatics, gymnastics, rather than ballet, some elements of Meyerhold's biomechanics that stress relation to the partner, Chinese training that develops relaxation and flexibility at the same time that it strengthens are especially valuable.

Essential to this approach is the element of improvisation. This helps the actor to think, to follow logical rather than preconceived conventional solutions, expands the actor's imagination, helps him to explore the nature of a situation, and leads to true feeling on the stage. Exercises with masks are useful but not to be confused with this more fundamental function of improvisation. Improvisation is the only means that helps the actor to break the grip of the cliché, the conventional and mechanical form of expression which still rules the stage today as in the past and must always be fought.

Exercises can start with tasks that use "imaginary objects" and with simple unmotivated acts—to sit, to open a door, to shine shoes—and then go on to purposeful or motivated [acts]—to sit in order to rest, or to hide oneself, etc. The entire life of a man is re-created by means of imaginary objects (sense memory) and of simple purposeful controlled behavior that develops the sense of truth and logic in the actor. This work is then carried on in the approach to the inner and outer problems of a role and finally of a play.

Use of memory is essential to understanding the entire process that goes into acting. In acting every thing is done unconsciously as a process of memory. The important thing in Stanislavski and our approach is that we point to the fact that there is a third kind of memory which we all are aware of and yet which we have not recognized. That may be called affective memory, which means memory of sensation, memory of emotion.

When we come to an experience on the stage, the good actor, rather than externally imitating, has unconscious sensation and emotion functioning; by means of an association, which is set off by a word or by the fact that the actor knows what the experience is, the actor incites the reliving of the experience itself, not just the mental idea of the experience. This is, by the way, what is new . . . because otherwise, experiencing on the stage cannot be done night after night . . . without an inner technique, which previously was left up in the air when an actor did not stimulate the emotions.

Strasberg thus indicates that his approach and Stanislavski's approach are similar in the use of affective memory. But Strasberg believes his training stimulates the sense memory of the actor, so the experience that he is trying to create can then actually be recaptured not only mentally, not only externally but by the actual sensory and emotional reliving of the experience. It does not matter what an actor remembers, so long as the remembering stirs the proper degree of belief and the proper stimulus to make the actor behave as he would under those conditions in the play. What will stimulate one person may not another. In Strasberg's opinion the entire problem of acting deals with the actor's approach to the play. A director must aid the actor to use all the tools of his craft.

Appendix E
Strasberg as a Director

**Notes on Directing from Lee Strasberg's
June 1967, Racine, Wisconsin, Directors' Seminar and
Faculty Meeting, Friday, January 9, 1981,
The Lee Strasberg Theatre Institute, Los Angeles**

A director needs technical knowledge, and most good directors were previously actors or playwrights, the best training ground.

A director can do a brilliant job in one play and fall apart in the next if he's not clear on what a director does.

You can learn more from your failures than your successes. Why a play fails gives you more insight, than why it succeeds.

The way in which you cast decides the fate of the production. (At another time Lee stated that casting can be 70 percent of a good production.)

A director who is not a good director casts well, then lets the actors alone.

Any individual properly directed can be as believable as a professional actor.

A director conceives the situation, [he] must visualize the scene. He cannot simply permit people to just act. Don't try to make pictures, but work on scenes. Play the event.

In blocking, work out the high points of a scene, where you will want the people to be, and this determines the best way of placing the people.

The director must tell the actor anything that will support him. However, it takes an actor at least two weeks before the actor is prepared to give.

A director of any kind never caters to the weakness of the actor but builds on the actor's strength.

The play must come alive at the end of the second act or go down the drain. Audience opinions are set by then.

[In response to a comment about Method actors being criticized for mumbling, Strasberg quipped,] They wouldn't get the jobs if they couldn't be understood. None of the reviews of plays directed by me had that criticism.

From Strasberg's Directing Classes, The Lee Strasberg Theatre Institute, Summer 1980

I agree with Kazan that one of the best books for directors is *The Vakhtangov School of Stage Art* by Nikolai Gorchakov. [At this time the book was out of print, so I xeroxed Strasberg's copy for my personal library.] "I [learn] from two basic sources: life and art," said Strasberg. "Directors should learn lighting and composition." Strasberg advised directors to read the following books:

> *From Stage to Screen* by Vardac. This book has an interesting description of the way the stage influenced the way movies were made.
>
> Adolphe Appia books on lighting are excellent: *Music and Stage Setting, The Work of Living Art,* and *Man Is the Measure of All Things.*
>
> Gordon Craig's books: *The Art of the Theatre, On the Art of the Theatre, Towards a New Theatre* and *The Theatre Advancing.*
>
> Prompt books of Stanislavski, Vakhtangov and Meyerhold.
>
> The most useful books on scenery are Kenneth Macgowan's *Theatre of Tomorrow,* which has extraordinary sketches of scene design; books by Robert Edmund Jones (*Drawings for the Theatre* and *The Dramatic Imagination*); Macgowan and Jones, *Continental Stagecraft*—the two went to Europe and Jones has brilliant illustrations; and books by other scene designers, such as Denis Bablet and Mordecai Gorelik, *New Theatres for Old.*
>
> *Outline for Directing for Cinematography* by Sergei Eisenstein is the most conclusive ever done. It outlines the entire area of directing.

Excerpts from "The Bottomless Cup,
an Interview with Geraldine Page," *Tulane Drama Review,*
with Particular Emphasis on Strasberg's Practices
as a Play Director and Teacher

Miss Page: Lee left us alone when we didn't expect it and he told us to do things when we didn't expect him to. . . . He visualized certain moments very strongly. Masha [Kim Stanley] kept wanting to get up off the couch in the beginning of the fire scene. Lee wouldn't let her . . . he brought out a Japanese print and said, "This is how I see the fire scene . . ." This visualization struck like a nail in his head . . .

When asked if she thought Strasberg was a good director, Geraldine Page answered:

Yes, I do. . . . His was a good way. For example, I kept saying: "I'm so busy over here." And he explained to us that as long as we all kept busy, it wouldn't be distracting. But if we stood stock-still during somebody's speech, and then one of us made a gesture, the whole thing would fall apart. As long as life kept moving the focus naturally came out where it was supposed to be . . . only in certain spots [he blocked carefully], like the first picture. From then on we would go according to where our characters went. And we gradually evolved a pattern. But it was completely free.

The interviewer, Richard Schechner, asked if the production was "unusual and good" because of what Strasberg did? Miss Page replied:

Because of what he made us do. You see, it would have been a marvelous production with other people—but not as good [the actors were Actors Studio people] because others couldn't do what we can do with what Lee tells us.

Schechner continued the interview as follows:

Question: Then his creative contribution to you as an actress was to leave you alone?
Page: And to insist on certain things. I have to sit at the beginning. I have to stand still at certain points. I have to look up at the balcony at the end, and I have a tendency in moments like that to blur, to make them naturalistic so nobody can catch me being hammy. . . .

Question: Did he give any talks to the whole cast at once?

Page: Oh, yes, he talked all the time. . . . Lee says "You gotta chop them in otherwise they sound like speeches. I want to hear talk. If you listen and think and talk it becomes acting. Cut into it. . . ." He felt there was no point in doing exercises [at rehearsals]. He kept saying, "Why aren't you people doing your homework? . . . all the ad-libbing is improvised."

Question: What's the value of improvisation?

Page: Oh, I think it's marvelous! I love it. As a matter of fact, I adore it in performance. The candle fell over the other day, so I had to reblock Olga. . . . It helps me relate to the play, it weaves a logic. If you just say the lines as written, you often have to leap from mountain crag to mountain crag in your own thinking. But if you can improvise and stretch the fabric and poke around in it for a while, then you find the links that aren't immediately observable. . . .

Question: How did you react when Masha tells you of her infidelity?

Page: Lee was in there right away—because of his Japanese print— saying that it should be like Olga's caught in great horror. And he said, "What you must do, after Natasha leaves, is stand completely still, since you're always doing some little naturalistic thing."

SOURCE: Richard Schechner, "The Bottomless Cup, an Interview with Geraldine Page," *Tulane Drama Review* 9: 2 (T26, Winter 1964), pp. 115–124.

Appendix F
Strasberg's Influence on American Theatre through the Group Theatre, the Method, the Actors Studio, and the Lee Strasberg Theatre Institute

Strasberg's influence on the American Theatre began when he became a founder and head of actor training for the Group Theatre in 1931. Realizing the importance of Lee Strasberg and the group on the American Theatre scene, Paul Gray of the *Tulane Drama Review* concluded:

> . . . it was obvious that the Group Theatre had found its voice and range—and that a company carefully trained by Strasberg in his version of the system after four bitter years was about to become the core of the American Theatre. . . . Strasberg's interpretation of Stanislavski—now called the Method—prevailed. More or less behind the scenes in the forties, Strasberg became very much the man of the hour.[1]

In one of his textbooks for colleges and universities, O. G. Brockett, the theatre historian, lists important actors and directors fostered by the Group Theatre and analyzes the group's significance:

> Probably one of the most significant American organizations of the 1930s was the Group Theatre . . . During the 1930s it produced some of the finest plays seen in New York. . . . The Group Theatre also fostered talents of a number of important directors (among them Harold Clurman and Elia Kazan) and actors (such as Lee J. Cobb, John Garfield, and Morris Carnovsky). Some former members of this troupe were to be the principal popularizers of the Stanislavski system of acting in America. Some former members such as Lee Strasberg . . . have continued to teach this method.[2]

Robert Herridge, a teacher, director and author, also stressed the importance of the Group Theatre, naming Lee Strasberg in particular as altering the course of the American Theatre through the Method:

> . . . its experiment and its achievement remains a dominant one in the American Theatre. . . .

For out of the experience of the Group emerged one of the theatre's finest artists, undoubtedly the greatest American teacher of acting in our time, Mr. Lee Strasberg. His work and influence in the modification, development, and practical application of Stanislavski's System of training actors to use themselves consciously as instruments to attain truth and reality onstage is now general and decisive. In fact, it might be hard to find an American actor of stature who has not been influenced directly or indirectly by Mr. Strasberg's years in the theatre.[3]

Examples of this extraordinary influence are many:

When I was a professor at Ripon College, I asked Roddy McDowall to critique my students' acting and directing scenes. Believing him to be English-trained, I assured him, "Your approach will be good exposure for the students, as I assume it is different from mine." He in turn confided, "I work as a Method-trained actor because I studied with a woman in New York who is an offshoot of Lee, having studied with him." Indeed, McDowall's terms and approach were similar to what I had been teaching, and his astute critiques were understood by all students.

I met Warren Beatty at the 1976 Democratic national convention in New York and he promised to talk to my classes in Los Angeles, explaining, "I've always admired Lee's teachings. Of course, I acted for 'Gadge' Kazan, who was in Lee's actor training program of the Group Theatre."

Before Robert De Niro became a studio observer in 1967 and subsequently studied with Lee, he studied with people of the "so-called Method, Actors Studio people, who had studied with Strasberg,"[4] emphasizing the through-line of Strasberg's teaching.

Even actors who have not taken classes with Method teachers try to practice Strasberg's concepts. An illustration is Peter O'Toole, who one time while in London ran down the street after Strasberg to introduce himself and tell Strasberg he tries to work in Strasberg's way and has read everything he can on Strasberg's Method. Indeed, I too was told this by people from all over the world when I was conducting acting and directing workshops at international theatre conferences in Sweden and Monaco. Time after time participants told me that they tried to work according to "Strasberg's Method" in their native countries.

Elia Kazan, the Pulitzer Prize and Academy Award winning director who trained with Strasberg in the Group Theatre, later asked Strasberg

Lorrie Hull with Roddy McDowell following a seminar at Ripon College.

to teach at the Actors Studio. In personal conversations Kazan told me, "Lee is one of the greatest teachers of acting in the world."[5] In the book *Kazan on Kazan,* Kazan expresses his opinion regarding Strasberg's influence:

> Strasberg . . . [is] a superb teacher. The Actors Studio and he became synonymous, which is the way I wanted it. The Actors Studio and this kind of acting have become the central tradition of American acting. Now, not only all these actors have become famous, but they have followers.[6]

At another time Kazan noted: "Lee is one of those few people who by their very nature are teachers . . . Cliché criticism that Actors Studio actors scratch and mumble is all so much garbage from the gossip writers and the night club comics."[7]

Elia Kazan made the keynote remarks on the occasion of the Actors Studio eightieth birthday party for Lee Strasberg:

> Bobby Lewis and I, with Cheryl Crawford, started the Actors Studio, but Lee made it. . . . Lee did the work here, until this place became a shrine in the world. His work with actors is unique and it seeps down. . . . Lee has given meaning to thousands of actors' lives—actors we don't see and don't know. . . . All of us tonight, Lee, give you our thanks.[8]

Rod Steiger, the Academy Award-winning actor, has been eloquent on the subject of the Actors Studio as offering the finest dramatic training in the world. He believes in actor training, and in an interview with the *Los Angeles Herald-Examiner,* Steiger told syndicated columnist Harold Heffernan:

> It [the Actors Studio] is the only place in America an actor can practice for free . . . And don't let anybody get you off on the wrong track about that "method" stuff. The term "method" was invented by the press and ever since they've made a ridiculous three ring circus about those who attend acting schools.[9]

William Glover, the AP drama critic and correspondent, endorsed Strasberg in 1965 as a worldwide theatrical leader. He wrote:

> Strasberg . . . is the organization's [Actors Studio] paradoxical inspiration and undisputed leader—teacher. Equally undisputed is the interest which the Studio has generated in international theatrical circles. This spring the Actors Studio Theatre . . . participates in London's World Theatre Festival.

"We consider ourselves to be the outstanding educational unit in theatre throughout the world—one of the greatest idealistic achievements in America," says Strasberg.[10]

Theodore Hoffman, former associate editor of the *Tulane Drama Review,* described Strasberg's significant contribution to the American Theatre:

> The Actors Studio is the only major coalition of talent, ambition and experiment we can point to. . . . The Group and Studio experience . . . generated most of the worthwhile theatre we possess. It can weather the withering tongue of controversy, fulsome tribute and the malpractice of *faux devots* and imitators. The artists and teachers of the American Stanislavski tradition have been active for forty years. It is time their work received full and honest scrutiny. They cannot be measured against any exposition of the System because they have produced their own practice and methodology, both substantial and admirable. They have created our American theatre, which is to them as they are to Stanislavski. Its resentment and resistance only prove a point. Elia Kazan is already a major figure in American theatre, whether Lincoln Center proves a phase or apotheosis in his career. Lee Strasberg is the touchstone of our mid-century theatre, possibly its most significant thinker.[11]

The many testimonials by other successful theatre people reaffirm Lee Strasberg's widely spread influence and abilities:

> *Kim Stanley*: Strasberg was the man who made it possible for the whole world to open up for me. . . . I mistook showing off for acting. He taught me the difference. He is interested not in exploiting talent but in nurturing it and making it grow.[12]

> *Eli Wallach*: The Studio is an antidote to cliché acting. . . . I believe in the Method. As long as it's part of what I can use, I'm for it.[13]

> *Anne Jackson*: In your worst work Lee will always find something good, even while he is exposing the trickery and fears that lead an actor to resort to trickery. He always leaves the actor his self-respect.[14]

> *Jane Fonda*: [At their first meeting Strasberg told Fonda that she had too much of a phony facade, and that it would limit her acting if she held onto it. She didn't.] Strasberg gave me a technique that gave me confidence. I was learning a craft—drawing on my own experience. He shows you how to use yourself, and not something borrowed from someone else. If I have

problems, I use private moments, sense memory and relaxation. I talked to
Lee about how to work on *Julia*.[15]

Shelley Winters: Lee's the best teacher in the world. He's a genius.[16]

Paul Newman and Rod Steiger: We both decided after seventeen beers, Lee,
that you can take either the credit or the blame for what we have become.[17]

Martin Balsam: I have to come back to the studio every so often to refurbish
my artistic soul and hear it again from the master's lips.[18]

Tony Richardson: It has been claimed, and on the record not unjustly, that
he [Strasberg] has done more for the American Theatre than any other man
in history.[19]

Eva Marie Saint: He makes you think you can do anything.[20]

To evaluate actors' opinions means to recognize that Strasberg was an
expert teacher of actors because of the confidence he inspired in them
and because of the techniques he taught to enable them to use their
instrument. William Glover supports the belief that Strasberg's major
contribution is the training of actors and directors, labeling him "the
world's greatest drama teacher."[21]

C. Robert Jennings, a newspaper man with the *Los Angeles Times*,
describes Strasberg's molding of theatre artists thus:

> Since Strasberg seems so magically able to mine sapphires out of common
> ore and put mermaids on mountaintops, he has been regarded by his dis-
> ciples almost as Christ was regarded by the monks of the Middle Ages.
> Cleveland Amory dubbed him 'God of the Methodists.'[22]

Mr. Jennings also describes Strasberg's Paris Seminar in 1967, attended by many of the top directors and actors in Europe including
Jeanne Moreau, Alan Resnais, Delphine Seyring, Louis Malle, Jean-
Louis Barrault, and over 440 other foreign professionals from twenty-
six countries. They found him "a great teacher, the kind who doesn't
mold an actor but makes him discover simple things he has never really
considered, or important things he has forgotten."[23] The seminars were
regarded as "the event of the theatrical season" by *Le Monde* (*Time*,
October 1967). In 1978 Strasberg taught a foreign seminar in Germany.
Many foreign professionals subsequently followed Strasberg to the
United States to study at the Lee Strasberg Theatre Institute in New
York and Los Angeles.

Alan Schneider, director of *Tiny Alice, Who's Afraid of Virginia Woolf?, The Ballad of the Sad Cafe, The American Dream,* and many other award-winning plays, studied with Strasberg when he first came to New York. In the following quotation Schneider verifies the value of training with Lee Strasberg:

> . . . it was very valuable in the sense that Lee gave me my first concrete training or discipline in the Stanislavski Method in a directing class. . . . Lee was very valuable to me in opening up the whole area—of exploring the subtext, of the off-stage life, the life in the other rooms of the house— and the whole idea of working with actors creatively.[24]

In their *Actors on Acting,* Toby Cole and Helen Krich Chinoy label Strasberg the best known acting teacher in America who has turned Stanislavski's Russian system into an "American Method":

> The best-known acting teacher in America, Lee Strasberg, is credited with turning Stanislavski's Russian system of acting into an "American Method." Although his contributions to acting and to theatre in America are the subject of acrimonious debates between disciples and critics, there is little doubt that his early work in the Group Theatre was one of the major avenues through which a new approach to acting reached the American theatre, and he has been one of the most influential figures in acting for almost forty years.[25]

Not only do some believe that Strasberg has been one of the most "influential figures in acting" but they describe him as "the most widely known and respected acting teacher in America."[26] The well-known writer and historian John Gassner labeled Lee Strasberg the "greatest American teacher of acting in our time."[27] The *New York Times* called Strasberg, "Sage and guru, legend and symbol."[28] *TV Guide* asserted about the Actors Studio, "For 26 years has been the single most profound and pervasive influence upon American acting styles."[29]

Dramatics magazine gave Strasberg more space than has ever been accorded an interview subject in its forty-eight years of existence. The editor stated that Strasberg's "opinion carries much weight. Few professionals have as deep an intellectual understanding of the theatre as does Strasberg."[30] The editor added: "[Strasberg] seems more like a scholar who should be debating the relative merits of teaching methods than a person who has left the imprint of his method—if only by reaction in some cases—on virtually every stage in America."[31]

Lee Strasberg is the first American ever asked by the *Encyclopaedia Britannica* to write its article on "Acting." Strasberg's article, appearing in the current as well as past editions of the encyclopaedia, replaces earlier articles by Constantin Stanislavski and Max Reinhardt among others.

The entertainment magazine *Footlights,* printed Strasberg's "The Definition of Acting" from the fifteenth edition of the *Encyclopaedia Britannica* (1974). The article was preceded by the following introduction:

> Lee Strasberg is back in Hollywood. And we welcome him. Los Angeles and, in fact, the United States and the world are the richer for Mr. Strasberg's long and diligent efforts to awaken in some and create in others the ancient but ever modern Art and Skill of Acting.[32]

The Christian Science Monitor interviewed Strasberg and printed his defense of the Method, pointing out "that audiences—not theorists or partisans—have made the success of Actors Studio veterans from Karl Malden and Robert De Niro to Rod Steiger and Geraldine Page and so many others." Strasberg summed it up this way:

> They have a distinctive quality that makes them stand out. Their work seems spontaneous, not as if they were reciting or "speaking well." They seem to be speaking like you and me. They don't seem to be acting. That's the strange thing. Sometimes it seems so natural they don't get enough credit! Often our actors are confused with their parts. . . .[33]

The approximately 557 members of the Actors Studio represent a significant percentage of the most respected actors in the United States. Between 1947 and 1976, 112 Actors Studio members received Academy Award nominations, of which 30 won the award.[34] Over 28 members won Emmys and 26 won Tonys. Today the number of Actors Studio Academy Award, Emmy, Tony and Obie winners has increased considerably.

Strasberg realized the importance of carefully chronicling the Method when he was in Moscow in 1963 for the Stanislavski Centennial. He was the only American invited to speak from the stage of the Moscow Art Theatre for the centenary. Returning to Moscow in 1973, he found that some of Stanislavski's most profound precepts were not only misunderstood but also had been disregarded by those who carry on the Stanislavski tradition in Stanislavski's own country. In 1973 it appeared to Lee that the Russian theatre did not reflect the quality and standards set by Stanislavski before his death only thirty-five years before.[35]

In 1976 members of the Moscow Art Theatre were in Los Angeles and sought to speak with Strasberg. One of the MAT members visited my classes at the Lee Strasberg Theatre Institute and told me that Strasberg had been right about what Stanislavski had intended, about the MAT's growing away from Stanislavski's teachings and not following the teaching correctly. The visitor explained that after Strasberg had left the Soviet Union, the director of MAT had been fired. The Russian visitor wanted to tell Lee that Strasberg had been right about their productions and work at the MAT!

At the time of Lee Strasberg's death news media coverage was extensive. Stories lauded Strasberg as "the man whose development of 'method acting' had a profound influence on the American Theatre"[36] and as "the foremost teacher and implementor of the Stanislavski 'Method' in the United States."[37]

Appendix G
Sample Handouts from Dr. Hull's Classes and Private Coaching*

1
What Is a "Simple" Scene?

1. Has a clear physical line of behavior.

    (e.g. getting up in the morning: washing, showering, shaving or putting on makeup, making breakfast, getting dressed, going to work—or getting ready for bed at night: drinking a glass of hot milk, bathing, getting undressed, reading, turning off the lights, going to sleep.)

2. Does not call for intensity of reaction or have a high emotional content.

    (e.g. someone just dies or you're contemplating suicide or having a mental breakdown, etc.)

3. Does not call for heavy characterization.

    (e.g. an old person, an accent or a peculiar type—for instance, Charlie in *Charlie*.)

4. Answer the following questions:

    A. Is the character close to your own nature?

    B. What would you be doing if this scene never took place?

    C. What physical activities can be explored for your objects of concentration?

    D. What sensory object (or objects) must be created?

    E. What do you want in this scene? What is your need?

    F. What makes this time different from any other time when you would be doing the same tasks?

    G. Who . . . are you and what is your relationship to others in the scene?

    What . . . are you doing in this place? What do you want?

    Where . . . is this happening?

    When . . . is this happening?

---

*Appendixes A, B, C, D and E, and part 3, "Directing," are also handouts.

Why . . . is this happening? *Why* are you doing what you are
doing?
What are the given circumstances? What preceded the scene?
What adjustments, if any, must you make in order to do what the
character does?

2A
Scene Suggestions for Men and Women
Key: SS (Short Story)
P (Play)
N (Novel)
by Lorrie Hull

Scenes for One Man and One Woman

Simple

P	*All Summer Long*	Robert Anderson
P	*All the Girls Came Out to Play*	Richard Johnson and Daniel Hollywood
SS	*And You Want a Mountain*	John O'Hara (Great Short Stories of and other O'Hara Stories)
N	*The Arrangement*	Elia Kazan
P	*At Home* (published with *Actors*)	Conrad Bromberg
P	*The Bachelor Party*	Paddy Chayefsky
P	*Barefoot in the Park* (older man/girl, older woman/boy, boy/girl)	Neil Simon
P	*The Beautiful People*	William Saroyan
P	*Birdbath*	Leonard Melfi
P	*Blithe Spirit*	Noel Coward
P	*Born Yesterday*	Garson Kanin
P	*Bus Stop*	William Inge
P	*Butley*	Simon Gray
P	*Butterflies Are Free*	Leonard Gershe
SS	*By Way of Yonkers*	O'Hara (Great Short Stories of)
P	*Cactus Flower*	Abe Burrows
P	*Career*	James Lee

SS	*Cat in the Rain*	Ernest Hemingway (and other Hemingway Stories)
N	*Catcher in the Rye*	J. D. Salinger
P	*Champagne Complex*	Leslie Stevens
P	*Come Blow Your Horn*	Simon (and other Simon Plays)
SS	*A Day Like Today*	O'Hara (Great Short Stories of)
P	*Dark at the Top of the Stairs*	Inge
P	*Death of Bessie Smith*	Edward Albee
P	*Double Solitaire*	Robert Anderson
P	*Echoes*	N. Richard Nash
P	*Encounters* (6 one acts)	Melfi
SS	*The Engineer*	O'Hara (The Cape Cod Lighter)
P	*Enter Laughing*	Joseph Stein (adapted from Carl Reiner's novel)
P	*Entertaining Mr. Sloan*	Joe Orton
P	*Forty Carats*	Jay Allen (adapted from Barillet and Gredy)
P	*The Four Poster*	Jan de Hartog
P	*The Gentle People*	Irwin Shaw
SS	*The Gentleman in the Tan Suit*	O'Hara (Great Short Stories of)
P	*The Gingerbread Lady*	Simon
SS	*Girls in Their Summer Dresses*	Irwin Shaw (Short Stories of)
P	*Girls of Summer*	Nash
SS	*Give and Take* (mother/son)	O'Hara (Great Short Stories of)
P	*The Glass Menagerie*	Tennessee Williams
P	*Golden Boy*	Clifford Odets
P	*Gloria and Esperanza*	Julie Bovasso
SS	*Goodbye Columbus*	Philip Roth (and other Roth stories)
SS	*Goodbye Herman*	O'Hara (Great Short Stories of)
P	*A Hatful of Rain*	Michael Gazzo
P	*Hole in the Head*	Arnold Schulman
SS	*Homage to Switzerland*	Hemingway
P	*House of Blue Leaves* (first act)	John Guare

SS	*How Can I Tell You*	O'Hara (The Hat on the Bed)
P	*Huui-Huui*	Anne Burr
P	*I Am a Camera*	John van Druten (adapted from Christopher Isherwood)
P	*I Love My TV*	Lance Lane
P	*I Never Sang for My Father*	Robert Anderson
P	*Joe Egg*	Joe Nichols
P	*La Ronde*	Arthur Schnitzler
P	*Last of the Red Hot Lovers*	Simon
SS	*The Last Tea*	Dorothy Parker (Short Stories of)
P	*Later Encounters* (7 one acts)	Melfi
P	*Liliom*	Ferenc Molnar
P	*Little Black Book*	Jean-Claude Carriere (trans. by Jerome Kilty)
P	*Look Homeward Angel*	Ketti Frings (from the novel by Thomas Wolfe)
P	*A Loss of Roses*	Inge
P	*Lou Gehrig Did Not Die of Cancer*	Jason Miller
SS	*Lovely Leave*	Parker
P	*Lovers and Other Strangers*	Joseph Bologna and Renee Taylor
P	*Lunch Hour*	Jean Kerr
P	*Lunchtime*	Melfi
P	*Marty*	Chayefsky
P	*Mary, Mary*	Kerr
P	*Middle of the Night*	Chayefsky
P	*Mixed Doubles*	Fred Carmichael
P	*Miss Julie*	August Strindberg
P	*The Moon Is Blue*	F. Hugh Herbert
P	*No Place to Be Somebody*	Charles Gordone
P	*Not Enough Rope*	Elaine May
SS	*Nothing Machine*	O'Hara (The Cape Cod Lighter)
P	*Oh Men, Oh Women*	Edward Chodorov
P	*One Flew Over the Cuckoo's Nest*	Dale Wasserman
P	*Only Game in Town*	Frank Gilroy
SS	*Our Friend the Sea*	O'Hara (The Hat on the Bed)

P	*Owl and the Pussycat*	Bill Manholt
P	*Pastels*	Lane
P	*The Perfect Setup*	Jack Sher
P	*Peterpart (Marriage Gambol)*	Enid Rudd
P	*Picnic*	Inge
P	*Plaza Suite*	Simon
P	*Prisoner of Second Avenue*	Simon
SS	*Public Dorothy*	O'Hara (The Hat on the Bed)
P	*The Rainmaker*	Nash
SS	*Screen Test*	O'Hara (Great Short Stories of)
SS	*The Sexes*	Parker (Short Stories of)
SS	*Short Walk from the Station*	O'Hara (The Cape Cod Lighter)
P	*The Shy and the Lonely*	Irwin Shaw
SS	*Sidesaddle*	O'Hara (Great Short Stories of)
P	*The Sign in Sydney Brustein's Window*	Lorraine Hansberry
P	*6 Rms Riv Vu*	Bob Randall
P	*Star Spangled Girl*	Simon
P	*Subject Was Roses* (older woman/young man)	Gilroy
P	*Suggs*	David Wiltse
SS	*Things You Really Want*	O'Hara (The Cape Cod Lighter)
P	*A Thousand Clowns*	Herb Gardner
P	*Time of Your Life*	Saroyan
P	*Two for the Seesaw*	Gibson
P	*What Time Does It Get Dark?*	Travilla Deming
P	*Will Success Spoil Rock Hunter*	George Axelrod
P	*You Know I Can't Hear You When the Water's Running*	Robert Anderson
SS	*You Were Perfectly Fine*	Parker
SS	*Here We Are*	Parker (Short Stories of and other Parker Stories)

Advanced

P	*After the Fall*	Arthur Miller

P	*Antigone (and other plays by Sophocles)*	Sophocles and Jean Anouilh
P	*Antony and Cleopatra (and other plays by Shakespeare)*	William Shakespeare
SS	*Appearances*	John O'Hara (The Cape Cod Lighter)
P	*Arms and the Man*	George Bernard Shaw
N	*The Arrangement*	Elia Kazan
P	*At Home*	Conrad Bromberg
P	*The Balcony*	Jean Genet
P	*The Big Knife*	Clifford Odets
P	*Birdbath*	Leonard Melfi
P	*Blithe Spirit*	Noel Coward
SS	*Bucket of Blood*	O'Hara (The Cape Cod Lighter)
P	*Bus Stop*	William Inge
SS	*The Butterfly*	O'Hara (The Cape Cod Lighter)
P	*Caesar and Cleopatra*	George Bernard Shaw
P	*Cat on a Hot Tin Roof*	Tennessee Williams (and other Williams plays)
P	*Come Back, Little Sheba*	Inge
P	*The Country Girl*	Odets
SS	*The Crisis*	DeMaupassant
P	*The Crucible*	Arthur Miller (and other Miller plays)
P	*The Dark at the Top of the Stairs*	Inge (and other Inge plays)
P	*The Death of Besse Smith*	Edward Albee
P	*Deep Purple Dream*	Sage Allen
P	*Desire under the Elms*	Eugene O'Neill
P	*Detective Story*	Sidney Kingsley
P	*The Dirty Old Man* (girl and older man or girl and boy)	Lewis John Carlino
P	*A Doll's House*	Henrik Ibsen
P	*Dutchman*	LeRoi Jones
P	*Dylan*	Sidney Michaels
P	*Electra (and other plays by Euripides)*	Euripides
SS	*The Father*	O'Hara (The Cape Cod Lighter)
P	*The Ferryboat*	Melfi

P	*5th of July*	Lanford Wilson
N	*Focus*	Arthur Miller
P	*Fool for Love*	Sam Shepard
P	*The Fox*	Alan Miller (adapted from D. H. Lawrence)
P	*The Gin Game*	D. L. Coburn
P	*Gingerbread Lady*	Neil Simon
P	*The Girl on the Via Flaminia*	Alfred Hayes
P	*Hamlet*	Shakespeare
	He Done Her Wrong: The Saga of Frankie and Johnny	Tara Untiedt
P	*Hay Fever*	Coward
SS	*Hills Like White Elephants*	Ernest Hemingway
N	*The Hustler*	Walter Tevis
P	*Idiot's Delight*	Robert Sherwood
P	*I Love My TV*	Lance Lane
P	*I'm Herbert* (older woman and older man)	Robert Anderson
P	*Importance of Being Earnest*	Oscar Wilde
P	*Incident at Vichy*	Arthur Miller
P	*I Never Sang for My Father*	Robert Anderson
SS	*In the French Style*	Irwin Shaw
SS	*Intimacy*	Jean-Paul Sartre
P	*The Lark*	Anouilh (adapted by Lillian Hellman)
P	*JB*	Archibald MacLeish
P	*Lady Windemere's Fan*	Wilde
SS	*The Lesson*	O'Hara (The Cape Cod Lighter)
P	*The Lion in Winter*	James Goldman
P	*The Little Foxes*	Hellman
P	*Look Back in Anger*	John Osborne
P	*The Loveliest Afternoon of the Year*	John Guare
P	*Lovers and Other Strangers*	Renee Taylor and Joseph Bologna
P	*Lysistrata*	Aristophanes (trans. by Douglass Parker)
P	*Macbeth*	Shakespeare
P	*The Master Builder*	Ibsen
P	*Medea*	Euripides

P	*Merchant of Venice*	Shakespeare
P	*Middle of the Night*	Chayefsky
P	*A Midsummer Night's Dream*	Shakespeare
P	*Miss Julie*	August Strindberg
P	*Mobile Home*	Sage Allen
P	*A Month in the Country*	Ivan Turgenev (trans. by Ariadne Nicolaeff)
P	*Moon for the Misbegotten*	O'Neill
P	*Next*	Terrence McNally
N & P	*Of Mice and Men*	John Steinbeck
P	*On Golden Pond*	Ernest Thompson
P	*Orpheus Descending*	Williams
P	*Othello*	Shakespeare
P	*Period of Adjustment*	Williams
P	*Petrified Forest*	Sherwood
P	*Picnic*	Inge
P	*Plaza Suite*	Simon
P	*The Price*	Arthur Miller
P	*Prisoner of Second Avenue*	Simon
P	*The Rainmaker*	N. Richard Nash
P	*Red Peppers*	Coward
P	*The Rehearsal*	Anouilh (trans. by Pamela H. Johnson)
P	*Requiem for a Heavyweight*	Rod Serling
P	*Reunion*	David Mamet
P	*Richard III*	Shakespeare
P	*Rocket to the Moon*	Odets
P	*The Rose Tatoo*	Williams
SS	*Sailor off the Bremen*	Irwin Shaw
P	*Same Time, Next Year*	Bernard Slade
P	*Sarah and the Sax*	Carlino
SS	*Sea Change*	Hemingway
P	*The Seagull*	Anton Chekhov
P	*School for Scandal*	R. B. Sheridan
P	*Seduced*	Sam Shephard
P	*Separate Tables*	Terence Rattigan
P	*She Stoops to Conquer*	Oliver Goldsmith
P	*6 Rms Riv Vu*	Bob Randall
P	*Snowangel*	Carlino

P	*A Streetcar Named Desire*	Williams
P	*The Subject Was Roses*	Frank Gilroy
P	*Taffy's Taxi*	Melfi
P	*Talk to Me Like the Rain*	Williams
P	*Tally's Folly*	Wilson
P	*Taming of the Shrew*	Shakespeare
P	*A Taste of Honey*	Shelagh Delaney
P	*A Thousand Clowns*	Herb Gardner
P	*The Tiger*	Murray Schisgal
P	*Three Sisters*	Chekhov
P	*27 Wagons Full of Cotton* (one act plays)	Williams
P	*Two for the Seesaw*	William Gibson
P	*Uncle Vanya*	Anton Chekhov
P	*Venus Observed*	Christopher Fry
P	*A View from the Bridge*	Arthur Miller
P	*Watch on the Rhine*	Hellman
P	*Waiting for Lefty*	Odets
P	*The Way of the World*	William Congreve
SS	*Welcome to the City*	Irwin Shaw
P	*Winners*	Brian Friel
P	*Winterset*	Maxwell Anderson
P	*Who'll Save the Plowboy?*	Gilroy
P	*Who's Afraid of Virginia Woolf?*	Albee

2B
Scene Suggestions for Two Women
Key: SS (Short Story)
      P (Play)
      N (Novel)

by Lorrie Hull

Simple

P	*And Miss Rearden Drinks a Little*	Paul Zindel
P	*Bell, Book and Candle*	John van Druten
SS	*Between Two Men*	Doris Lessing
P	*Blithe Spirit*	Noel Coward
SS	*Burlesque*	Howard Mandel

P	*Butterflies Are Free*	Leonard Gershe
P	*Cactus Flower*	Abe Burrows
P	*Calm Down Mother*	Megan Terry
P	*Captains Paradise*	Alec Coppel
P	*The Chalk Garden*	Enid Bagnold
SS	*The Chorus Girl*	Anton Chekhov
P	*Cry Havoc*	Allan R. Kenward
P	*The Dark at the Top of the Stairs*	William Inge (and Other Inge Plays)
P	*The Days and Nights of Beebee Fenstermaker*	William Snyder
P	*Dream Girl*	Elmer Rice
P	*The Effect of Gamma Rays on Man-in-the-Moon Marigolds* (2 girls or 1 girl and 1 woman)	Paul Zindel
SS	*Friends of Miss Julia's*	John O'Hara (The Hat on the Bed)
P	*Gigi*	Anita Loos (adapted from Colette)
P	*Gingerbread Lady*	Neil Simon
P	*The Glass Menagerie*	Tennessee Williams
P	*The Holly and the Ivy*	Wynyard Browne
P	*In the Boom Boom Room*	David Rabe
P	*Ladies Alone* (3 women or girls)	Florence Ryerson and Colin Clements
P	*Ladies of the Alamo*	Zindel
SS	*Letting Go*	Phillip Roth
P	*Liliom*	Ferenc Molnar
P	*Lovers and Other Strangers*	Joseph Bologna and Renee Taylor
P	*Ludlow Fair*	Lanford Wilson
P	*Marty* (2 old women)	Paddy Chayefsky
P	*Member of the Wedding*	Carson McCullers
P	*Middle of the Night*	Chayefsky
P	*Moonchildren*	Michael Weller
N	*Mosquitoes*	William Faulkner
P	*No Time for Comedy*	S. N. Behrman
P	*Picnic*	Inge
P	*The Recluse*	Paul Foster
P	*Saturday Night*	Jerome Kass

P	*Scenes from American Life*	A. R. Gurney, Jr.
P	*The Serving Girl and the Lady*	Myrna Lamb
P	*The Shy and the Lonely*	Irwin Shaw
P	*Stage Door*	Edna Ferber and George S. Kaufman
N	*Such Good Friends*	Heywood Gould
P	*A Taste of Honey*	Shelagh Delaney
P	*Tea and Sympathy*	Robert Anderson
SS	*Uncle Wiggly in Connecticut*	J. D. Salinger
P	*Veronica's Room*	Ira Levin
P	*The Warm Peninsula*	Joe Masteroff
P	*What Time Does It Get Dark?*	Travilla Deming
P	*The Women*	Clare Boothe Luce
N	*Women in Love*	D. H. Lawrence

Advanced

P	*Agnes of God*	John Pielmeier
P	*Ah Wilderness*	Eugene O'Neill
P	*All My Sons*	Arthur Miller
P	*Anastasia*	Guy Bolton
P	*Antigone (and other Greek and Roman plays)*	Sophocles
SS	*Appearances*	O'Hara (The Cape Cod Lighter)
P	*Autumn Crocus*	Anthony
P	*Autumn Garden*	Lillian Hellman
P	*The Balcony*	Jean Genet
P	*Blithe Spirit*	Coward
SS	*The Broken Giraffe (other O'Hara stories)*	O'Hara
SS	*The Butterfly*	O'Hara (The Cape Cod Lighter)
P	*Camino Real* (1 young girl and 1 older woman)	Williams
P	*Children's Hour*	Hellman
P	*A Couple of White Chicks*	John Noonan
P	*Crimes of the Heart*	Beth Henley
P	*The Dark at the Top of the Stairs*	Inge (and Other Inge Plays)
P	*A Doll's House*	Henrik Ibsen
P	*Extremities*	William Mastrosimone

P	*Fallen Angels*	Coward
P	*Father's Day*	Oliver Hailey
SS	*The Fox*	Lawrence
P	*The Fox*	Alan Miller (adapted from D. H. Lawrence)
P	*Getting Out*	Marsha Norman
P	*The Girl on the Via Flaminia*	Alfred Hayes
P	*The Glass Menagerie* (1 young girl and 1 older woman)	Williams
P	*Hedda Gabler*	Chekhov (and Other Chekhov Plays)
P	*Hello from Bertha (in 27 Wagons Full of Cotton)*	Williams
P	*The House of Bernarda Alba*	Federico Garcia Lorca
P	*The Killing of Sister George*	Frank Marcus
P	*Ladies of the Corridor*	Parker and d'Usseau
P	*Lady of the Larkspur Lotion*	Williams (and Other Williams Plays)
P	*Lady Windemere's Fan*	Oscar Wilde
P	*Lemonade* (2 older women)	James Prideaux
P	*Letters Home*	Rose Goldemberg (based on Sylvia Plath's letters to her mother)
P	*Look Back in Anger*	John Osborne
P	*The Maids*	Genet
P	*Mary of Scotland*	Maxwell Anderson
P	*Mary Stuart*	von Schiller (translated by Mellish and Eric Bentley)
P	*Monday after the Miracle*	William Gibson
P	*Night Mother*	Marsha Norman
P	*No Exit*	Jean-Paul Sartre (adapted by Paul Bowles)
P	*Othello*	William Shakespeare
P	*Perfect Analysis by a Parrot*	Williams
P	*Pride and Prejudice*	Helen Jerome (adapted from Jane Austen)
P	*Romeo and Juliet* (1 young girl and 1 older woman)	Shakespeare
P	*The Rose Tattoo* (1 young girl and 1 older woman)	Williams

P	*Separate Tables*	Terence Rattigan
P	*Stevie*	Hugh Whitemore
P	*A Streetcar Named Desire*	Williams
P	*The Stronger*	August Strindberg
P	*Trifles*	Susan Gaspel
P	*Twelfth Night*	Shakespeare (Viola and Olivia and other Shakespeare plays)
P	*Uncle Vanya*	Chekhov
P	*A View from the Bridge* (1 girl and 1 woman)	Arthur Miller (and other Miller plays)
P	*Vivat, Vivat Regina*	Robert Bolt
P	*Mrs. Warren's Profession* (1 young girl and 1 older woman)	George Bernard Shaw
P	*Watch on the Rhine*	Hellman

2C
Scene Suggestions for Two Men
by Lorrie Hull

Simple

P	*Actors*	Conrad Bromberg
P	*All American Boy*	Barkley Jones
P	*American Buffalo*	David Mamet
P	*The Andersonville Trial*	Saul Levitt
P	*Bachelor Party*	Paddy Chayefsky
P	*Back to Back*	Al Brown
P	*The Basic Training of Pavlo Hummel*	David Rabe
P	*Born Yesterday*	Garson Kanin
P	*Botticelli* (2 young men)	Terrence McNally
P	*Boys in the Band*	Mart Crowley
P	*Butley*	Simon Gray
P	*Caine Mutiny*	Herman Wouk
P	*Career*	James Lee
P	*Changing Room*	David Storey
SS	*A Clean, Well-lighted Place*	Hemingway
SS	*Coffeepot*	John O'Hara (The Short Stories of)

P	*Come Blow Your Horn*	Neil Simon
SS	*Defender of the Faith*	Phillip Roth
N	*The Disenchanted*	Budd Schulberg
P	*Does a Tiger Wear a Necktie?*	Rabe
P	*The Dumbwaiter*	Harold Pinter
P	*End as a Man*	Calder Willingham
SS	*Fifty Grand* (1 young man and 1 older man)	Ernest Hemingway
P	*Fortune and Men's Eyes*	John Herbert
SS	*Goodbye Herman*	O'Hara (The Short Stories of)
P	*A Hatful of Rain*	Michael Gazzo
SS	*The Hat on the Bed* (John Barton Rosedale)	O'Hara
N	*The Hustler*	Tevis
P	*La Ronde*	Arthur Schnitzler
P	*Luv*	Murray Schisgal
SS	*The Man Who Had to Talk to Somebody*	O'Hara (The Short Stories of)
P	*Marty*	Chayefsky
P	*Odd Couple*	Simon
P	*Oh Men, Oh Women!*	Edward Chodorov
SS	*On His Hands*	O'Hara (The Short Stories of)
P	*Ross*	Terence Rattigan
SS	*Shave*	O'Hara (The Short Stories of)
P	*Short Eyes*	Miguel Pinero
P	*Tea and Sympathy* (2 young men)	Robert Anderson
SS	*Three Day Blow* (2 young men)	Hemingway
SS	*To Esme with Love and Squalor*	J. D. Salinger
SS	*Two Turtle Doves* (1 young man and 1 older man)	O'Hara (The Cape Cod Lighter)
P	*The Zoo Story*	Edward Albee

Advanced

P	*Actors* (1 young man and 1 older man)	Conrad Bromberg
P	*All My Sons* (1 young man and 1 older man)	Arthur Miller
P	*American Buffalo*	David Mamet

P	*The Andersonville Trial*	Saul Levitt
P	*Becket*	Jean Anouilh
SS	*The Battler* (1 young man and 1 older man)	Ernest Hemingway
P	*Blood Knot*	Athol Fugard
P	*Butley*	Simon Gray
P	*Candida*	George Bernard Shaw
P	*The Cage*	Rick Cluchey
P	*The Championship Season*	Jason Miller
N	*Darkness at Noon*	Arthur Koestler
P	*Death of a Salesman*	Arthur Miller
P	*Deathwatch*	Jean Genet
P	*Detective Story*	Sidney Kingsley
P	*The Dresser* (2 older men)	Ronald Harwood
P	*Emperor Jones*	Eugene O'Neill
P	*End as a Man*	Calder Willingham
P	*Equus* (1 young man and 1 older man)	Peter Shaffer
N	*Focus*	Arthur Miller
P	*The Iceman Cometh*	O'Neill
P	*The Importance of Being Earnest*	Oscar Wilde
P	*The Indian Wants the Bronx* (2 young men)	Israel Horovitz
P	*JB*	Archibald MacLeish
P	*Julius Caesar*	William Shakespeare
P	*Long Day's Journey into Night* (2 young men or 1 young man and 1 older man)	O'Neill
P	*Macbeth*	Shakespeare
P & N	*Of Mice and Men*	John Steinbeck
SS	*Pursuit Race*	Hemingway
P	*Quare Fellow*	Brendan Behan
P	*Seduced*	Sam Shepard
SS	*A Simple Inquiry* (1 young man and 1 older man)	Hemingway
P	*She Stoops to Conquer*	Oliver Goldsmith
P	*Sleuth*	Anthony Shaffer
P	*Staircase*	Charles Dyer
P	*Streamers*	David Rabe
P	*Tiny Alice*	Edward Albee

P	*True West*	Shepard
P	*A View from the Bridge*	Arthur Miller
P	*Waiting for Godot*	Samuel Beckett
P	*Who'll Save the Plowboy?*	Frank Gilroy
P	*Who's Afraid of Virginia Woolf?*	Albee
P	*The Zoo Story*	Albee

FOR ALL SCENES

In addition to Shaw, Hemingway, Salinger, O'Hara and Parker, Strasberg suggested scenes to acting students from short stories of Colette, De Maupaussant, Sartre and Chekhov (Los Angeles, May 6, 1981). Beginning *directors* are advised to direct simple scenes from plays rather than from short stories or novels.

3
Suggested Scenes and Monologues for Teenagers
(Some simple scenes listed for adult
actors are also appropriate)

Guides to Scenes

Play	Author	Act	Scene
Male-male			
All American Boy	Barkley Jones		
Bernadine	Mary Chase		
Billy Liar	K. Waterhouse & W. Hall	I	
Blue Denim	J. L. Herlihy & W. Noble	I & II	1
Botticelli	Terrence McNally		
Cheaper by the Dozen	Frank Gilbreth, Jr. and Ernestine Gilbreth Carey. Dramatized by Christopher Sergel		
Chicken Every Sunday	Julius J. and Philip G. Epstein. Based on book by Rosemary Taylor		

The Dumb Waiter	Harold Pinter		
Enter Laughing	Joseph Stein. Based on book by Carl Reiner	I	1
Equus	Peter Shaffer		
The Family Nobody Wanted	Helen Doss		
Look: We've Come Through	Hugh Wheeler	III	1
Of Mice and Men	John Steinbeck		
Take Her She's Mine	Phoebe and Henry Ephron		
Tea and Sympathy	Robert Anderson	II	1
A Thousand Clowns	Herb Gardner		
Tom Sawyer	Paul Kester		
Tom Sawyer's Morning	Regina Brown		

Female-female

The Advertisement	Natalia Ginzburg	III	
Antigone	Jean Anouilh and Sophocles		
The Chalk Garden	Enid Bagnold		
Cheaper by the Dozen	Frank Gilbreth, Jr. and Ernestine Gilbreth Carey. Dramatized by Christopher Sergel		
Chicken Every Sunday	Julius J. and Philip J. Epstein. Based on book by Rosemary Taylor		
Children in Uniform	Christa Winsloe	II	1
The Children's Hour	Lillian Hellman		
Dark at the Top of the Stairs	William Inge		
Dream Girl	Elmer Rice		
The Effect of Gamma Rays on Man-in-the-Moon Marigolds	Paul Zindel	II	1
The Girl on the Via Flaminia	Alfred Hayes	I	
The Haunting of Hill House	F. Andrew Leslie	I	2
Junior Miss	J. Chodorov and J. Fields		
Jupiter Laughs	A. J. Cronin		
Lace on Her Petticoat (15 yrs.)	Anne Stuart	I	1
Liliom	F. Molnar		
Look: We've Come Through	Hugh Wheeler	I	1
Ludlow Fair	L. Wilson		
Middle of the Night	Paddy Chayefsky	II	1
A Month in the Country	Ivan Turgenev		

Moonchildren	Michael Weller		3
Mosquitoes (a novel)	William Faulkner		
My Sister Eileen	J. Fields & J. Chodrov		
One Sunday Afternoon	James Hagan	I	2
Our Hearts Were Young and Gay	Jean Kerr (Based on book by Cornelia Otis Skinner and Emily Kimbrough)	II	1
Page Miss Glory	J. Schrank & P. Dunning		
Picnic	William Inge		
The Recruiting Officer	George Farquhar	I	2
The Relapse	Sir John Vanbrugh	II	
The Shy and Lonely	Irwin Shaw		
Stage Door	E. Ferber & G. Kaufman	I	2
Thieves Carnival	Jean Anouilh		
Wait until Dark	Frederick Knott		
Wedding Breakfast	Theodore Reeves		
The Young and Beautiful	Sally Benson		
A Young Lady of Property (15 yrs.)	Horton Foote	I	

Female-Male

The Advertisement	Natalia Ginzburg		
Ah, Wilderness! (15 yrs.)	Eugene O'Neill	III	2
Alice in Wonderland	V. Italie & E. LaGalliene		
American Plays (vol. 4)			
Billy Liar	K. Waterhouse & W. Hall	III	
Blue Denim (15 yrs.)	J. L. Herlihy & W. Noble	I	
Bringing It All Back Home (15 yrs.)	Terrence McNally		
But for the Grace of God (young)	Leopold Atlas		
Butterflies Are Free	Leonard Gershe	II	2
The Catcher in the Rye (novel)	J. D. Salinger		
Cheaper by the Dozen	Frank Gilbreth, Jr. and Ernestine Gilbreth Carey. Dramatized by Christopher Sergel		
Chinaman	Michael Frayn in *The Two of Us*		
Come Back Little Sheba	William Inge	I	2

Comings and Goings	Megan Terry		
Cop Out	John Guare		
Dark at the Top of the Stairs	William Inge		
David and Lisa	James Rench		
A Day for Surprises	John Guare		
The Diary of Anne Frank	Goodrich & Hackett	II	2
Enter Laughing	Joseph Stein	I	
The Family Nobody Wanted	Helen Doss		
Ferryboat (15 yrs.)	Anna Marie Barlow		
The Girl on the Via Flaminia	Alfred Hayes		
The Glass Menagerie	Tennessee Williams		7
The Lark	Jean Anouilh		
Liliom	F. Molnar		1
Look Homeward Angel (based on Thomas Wolfe's book)	Ketti Frings		
Look: We've Come Through	Hugh Wheeler	I	
		II	
Lovers	Brian Friel		'Winners'
The Male Animal	James Thurber		
A Month in the Country	Ivan Turgenev		
Moonchildren	Michael Weller		7
One Sunday Afternoon	J. Hagen		
Our Hearts Were Young and Gay	Cornelia Otis Skinner and Emily Kimbrough (Dramatized by Jean Kerr)		
Pastels	Lance Lane		
Peter Pan	J. M. Barrie		
The Philadelphia Story	Philip Barry		
A Raisin in the Sun	Loraine Hansberry	III	
Romanoff and Juliet	Peter Ustinov	I	
The Rose Tattoo (15 yrs.)	Tennessee Williams	III	2
The Sound of Music	Rodgers & Hammerstein		
The Star Spangled Girl	Neil Simon	II	1 and 2
Suddenly Last Friday	Clay Frankon in *Two for a Happening*		
Take a Giant Step	Louis Peterson	I	3
A Taste of Honey	Shelagh Delaney	I	2
There's a Girl in My Soup	Terence Frisby	II	
They Knew What They Wanted	Sidney Howard	I	
This Property Is Condemned (13 yrs.)	Tennessee Williams		

The Time of Your Life	William Saroyan	II	
Tom Sawyer's Morning	Regina Brown		
The Ugly Duckling	A. A. Milne	I	
Up the Down Staircase	Bel Kaufman		
A View from the Bridge	Arthur Miller	II	
Where Has Tommy Flowers Gone	Terrence McNally	I	6
Where Have All the Lightning Bugs Gone?	Louis E. Catron		
You're a Good Man Charlie Brown (Available in paperback in most book stores) (Based on Charles Schulz' comic strip)			

Monologues

Play	Author

Male

Alice in Wonderland	Van Italie and Eva LaGalliene
The Andersonville Trial	Saul Levitt
Belles on Their Toes	Frank Gilbreth, Jr. and Ernestine Gilbreth Carey (Dramatized by William Roos)
Bernadine	Mary Chase
Cheaper by the Dozen	Frank Gilbreth, Jr. and Ernestine Gilbreth Carey (Dramatized by Christopher Sergel)
Dark at the Top of the Stairs	William Inge
Dear Ruth (Albert)	Norman Krasna
Equus	Peter Shaffer
The Flea Gang's First Cigars	Wetmore Declamation Bureau Catalog
George Washington Slept Here (Newton)	Moss Hart and George S. Kaufman
Joan of Lorraine (Dauphin)	Maxwell Anderson
Laura (Mark)	Vera Caspary and George Sklar
My Sister Eileen (Frank)	Joseph Fields and Jerome Chodorov
Of Mice and Men	John Steinbeck
Once Upon a Playground	Jack Frakes
Pastels	Lance Lane

Pick-up Girl (Larry)	Elsa Shelley
Pick-up Girl (Peter)	Elsa Shelley
Saint Joan	George B. Shaw
Snafu (Ronald)	Louis Solomon & Harold Buchman
The Wizard of Oz	E. Goodspeed
The Youngest	Philip Barry
You're a Good Man Charlie Brown	Charles Schulz

Female

The Belle of Amherst	William Luce
The Beautiful People	William Saroyan
A Bell for Adano (Tina)	Paul Osborn
Bernadine	Mary Chase
Butterflies Are Free	Leonard Gershe
A Church Mouse	Lasislaus Fodor
The Days and Nights of Beebee Fenstermaker (1st scene)	William Snyder
Dear Ruth (Miriam)	Norman Krasna
Deep Are the Roots (Genevra)	Arnaud d'Usseau and James Gow
The Diary of Anne Frank	Goodrich & Hackett
The Doughgirls (Vivian)	Joseph Fields
Dream Girl	Elmer Rice
The Effect of Gamma Rays on Man-in-the-Moon Marigolds (Tillie)	Paul Zindel
The Fifth Season	Sylvia Regan
Flight to the West (Hope)	Elmer Rice
The Flying Gerardos	Kenyon Nicholson
For Keeps (Nancy)	F. Hugh Herbert
Heart of a City (Judy)	Lesley Storm
Heart of a City (Toni)	Lesley Storm
I Remember Mama	John Van Druten
Joan of Lorraine	Maxwell Anderson
Kiss and Tell (Corliss)	F. Hugh Herbert
Kiss and Tell (Mildred)	F. Hugh Herbert
The Lark	Jean Anouilh (Adapted by Lillian Hellman)
Liliom	F. Molnar
The Little Foxes (Alexandra)	Lillian Hellman
Loss of Roses (Lila)	William Inge
Ludlow Fair (older teen)	L. Wilson

Member of the Wedding	Carson McCullers
Night Must Fall	Emlyn Williams
Once upon a Playground (13 yrs.)	Jack Frakes
Ondine	Jean Giraudoux
Only the Heart (Julia)	Horton Foote
Our Town	Thornton Wilder
Pastels	Lance Lane
Pick-up Girl (Elizabeth)	Elsa Shelley
The Rainmaker	N. Richard Nash
Rebecca	D. Du Maurier
Saint Joan	George B. Shaw
Stage Door	Edna Ferber
State of the Union (Mary)	Howard Lindsay & Russel Crouse
Sweet Aloes	Jay Mallory
And Things That Go Bump in the Night (seriocomic, 13 yrs.)	Terrence McNally
Time and the Conways	J. B. Priestley
Up the Down Staircase	Bel Kaufman
The White Carnation	P. C. Sheriff
The White Cliffs	Alice D. Miller
The Wizard of Oz	E. Goodspeed
Years Ago	Ruth Gordon
You're a Good Man Charlie Brown (Lucy)	Charles Schulz

Play scripts plus "More Actors Guide to Monologues" may be purchased at the following places, among others:

> Larry Edmunds Cinema Bookshop Inc.
> 6658 Hollywood Blvd.
> Hollywood, CA 90028
> Tel.: (213) 463-3273
> Hours: 11:00 A.M. to 6:00 P.M.

> or

> Samuel French, Inc.
> 7623 Sunset Blvd. (near Preview House)
> Hollywood, CA 90046
> Tel.: (213) 876-0570

Hours: 9:30 A.M. to 5:00 P.M.

or

Dramatists Play Service, Inc.
440 Park Ave. South
New York, NY 10016
Tel.: (212) 683-8960

or

Drama Bookshop
723 Seventh Avenue (48 St.)
New York, NY 10011
Tel.: (212) 944-0595

or

Samuel French, Inc.
45 West 25th Street
New York, NY 10010
Tel.: (212) 206-8990

4
ADVICE TO ACTORS
Learning the Role
by
Lorrie (Loraine) Hull, Ph.D.

When learning a role, **do not ever memorize lines by rote**. Study lines by reading them aloud over and over until they begin to come naturally and spontaneously. When reading aloud, strive for a sense of talking. It is helpful to have someone read the other parts as you do this. If necessary, you may silently read the lines of the other characters in the scene yourself, but preferably read your own lines aloud by reading them simply at first and then in character.

In the beginning do not worry about projection or emotion.* Stay

---

*A director is advised to check projection and stage energy approximately two weeks before a performance—after an inner line is developed for the character. Only then are directions given for more energy or projection.

relaxed and emphasize naturalness and a sense of talking. You should be asking yourself: What is the present situation? Where is it taking place and what has happened just before? What did the character you are portraying do just prior to this scene? What is your condition at the beginning of the scene? What did you come here to do? What is your relationship to the other people in the scene? What are the stimuli affecting you in the scene—physical (sight, touch, odors, sounds, tastes) and emotional stimuli? What is the character's action? What do I want? Why am I here? Also, how far will I go to get what I want? What are the obstacles? Is the scene logical? Are the responses logical? What would I do if I were the character? The above questions can aid an actor to choose sensory and emotional homework on which to work.

In rehearsal it is desirable to alternate between using the script and improvising the scene. Improvisation leads actors to think—to discover the behavior of the scene. Improvisation forces the actor to think as the character, to feel and behave as the character. It helps the actor to create the role, and gives him the assurance to remain in character even when things go wrong in performance. If necessary, the actor can improvise in performance and go with whatever happens.

In directed work, blocking is guided by the director, often with actors contributing through improvisation. The actor now continues to discover and experiment with the director's advice, continuing to develop and add depth to the character he is creating. Once the script is put aside and the scene is "off book," it is helpful for actors to stay in character even when lines may be forgotten. When lines are "dropped," actors can remain in character and improvise until they are back "on track" with the script. Only then should they stop and go back and correct whatever was forgotten by running the scene more times using the script or with prompting. Adherence to this practice gives the actor a confidence in performance which cannot be achieved in any other way.

As soon as possible in the course of rehearsals the actor should experiment with preparation techniques to be used prior to the beginning of the scene. Preparation can involve relaxation, overall sensations and other sense memories, affective memories (emotional recall) when needed, creating the place and developing specific thoughts and a train of thought as the character. The instructor or director may guide the actor in the use of these and other techniques. For example, the actor may be asked to speak out the character's thoughts and feelings before beginning the scene and also during rehearsal of the scene while other actors are speaking.

An actor should write or know the complete biography of the character up to the time of the scene. Many directors require written biographies from their actors where imaginations are utilized to fill in what the playwright has not provided. Never ask only "What would I do in this situation?" Also ask "What would I do if I were the character in this situation?" Teachers and directors should guide actors to come up to the level of the character rather than allow the character to come down to the level of the actor. All of the above methods help the actor discover what works for him and what he must do as the actor to create a specific character with a life of its own.

5
Audition Tips*

1. Know two short monologues that show your ability and range. One serious and one comic are preferable, but if you are auditioning for regional theatre, a classical choice would be appropriate. Audition with characters you would be cast to play. If you are twenty, do not audition with an old character.
2. Practice cold reading at home and in class, so you feel secure and readings can flow smoothly.
3. Try to see the script several days ahead of the audition. Keep or photo a copy, if possible. Read the entire script. As you work, really think of the character for which you are reading and explore choices for the character.
4. If number 3 is impossible, go to the audition early and ask to see the script.
5. If all else fails, ask to read the audition scene silently before reading it for the casting person. If you can't read the entire script, make up a story for yourself or your acting will be too general.
6. Try to find out who will be auditioning you and what they are looking for. Ask your agent, other actors who have auditioned and the stage manager.

*See also part 2, chapter 7, "Improvisation in Casting."

7. Never be late.
8. Dress to give an impression of the character. If you go in with an overdone production of a costume, it can affect you psychologically and make you feel foolish. An example would be if auditioning for a bum, it would be better to take off your jacket, loosen your tie, and roll up your sleeves rather than to come in looking like a real bum from skid row.
9. Ask questions if there is something important you must know.
10. Relax and concentrate (as in all acting).
11. Be aware of the other actor or actors. Talk and listen.
12. Have as much eye contact as possible with the person with whom you are reading, whether it's another actor, the casting person, or someone in the room you choose as a partner. Try to connect with someone. If the person reading with you stays uninvolved, personalize—use your imagination.
13. Be aware of the relationships involved. Listen to the other person. Be fully involved in the role, follow choices. Some of your choices may be decided after you ask the casting persons questions about the character.
14. Recognize the lights and space. Use them.
15. Follow your instincts. Move around with physical actions as the character.
16. If the audition is for the theatre, have more energy. When in a small room, ask the casting person, "Do you want me to audition for a large theatre or this room?" Be sure you are heard.
17. Cooperate with any requests, such as improvising or doing the scene over differently.

6
One-page List of Basic Sensory Exercises
(Handout for all Hull classes)

1. *Coffee Cup* (or Breakfast Drink) Actor's sense of truth
   a. Real thing
   b. Imaginary thing
2. *Mirror* Awareness of themselves

     a. Man shaving

     b. Woman putting on makeup

3. *Sunshine* Sensation; inhibitions—embarrassments

     a. Putting on shoes

     b. Getting undressed

4. *Three Pieces of Material*

5. *Sharp Pain* Test the intensity of the reaction

6. *Sharp Taste and Smell* Lemon, vinegar

7. *Sight and Sound*

8. *Overall Sensations* Inhibiting and confining factors; muscle and nerve system of the actor

     a. Shower

     b. Bathing

     c. Wind

     d. Rain

     e. Elements of nakedness

9. *Personal Objects* (sometimes together with overall sensations)

10. *Private Moments*

    Daily activity and sound; different adjustments

11. *Song and Dance*

12. *Affective Memory*

13. *Improvisations*

14. *Scenes*   performed by all acting class members

7

Additional Sensory Exercises
(not necessarily in this order)

Inner senses: taste, smell

Outer senses: sight, sound

Overall sensation: touch

---

1. Go from hot to cold liquid

2. Go from cold to hot liquid

3. Two personal objects

4. One sense and one or two personal objects

5. One sense and overall
6. Two senses (inner and outer)
7. Inner and outer senses and place
8. Overall and personal object
9. Two senses and overall
10. One sense, overall, and place
11. Inner objects
12. Textures
13. Daily activity
14. Two senses and personal object
15. One sense, overall and personal object
16. Two senses, overall and personal object
17. Three senses and overall
18. Two senses and two personal objects
19. Shaving or makeup with extreme heat the first half of exercise and extreme cold the second half
20. Several traits from animal with sensory choices
21. Animal exercise, one sense and overall
22. Affective memory or private moment and two senses
23. Affective memory or private moment and overall
24. Affective memory or private moment and place or re-create a place alone
25. Affective memory or private moment and personal object
26. Inner monologue and one task
27. Inner monologue and two tasks
28. A private moment combining one or two more of the above (private and personal)
29. Animal exercise evolving as described in chapter 4, and combining one or more of the above
30. Narrative monologue exercise

Place exercise:	All sensory aspects of the place are created. The environment influences how the actor as the character reacts and behaves. Actors sometimes forget the environment in their concern with the dramatic continuity of the play.

Combination exercises:

When the actor is able to concentrate and accomplish one object at a time, he is then guided to carry more than one object (e.g., the overall sensation and the personal object exercise stimulates two strong reactions; personal object, overall sensation, daily activity and other tasks and exercises in combination allow the actor to carry on more than one task while maintaining sensory and emotional aspects).

Combination exercises with private moment:

Combination exercises are done with the private moment, then words are added and physical and rhythmic adjustments are made that prepare the actor for the numerous tasks he will have to perform onstage.

Inner monologue:

Often things are going on in the actor which interfere and inhibit what he is trying to achieve. By making contact with these disturbances and speaking them out in a procedure called the inner monologue, the actor frees his expression and at the same time achieves a greater degree of vividness and color.

Animal exercise into character:

After the animal is stood up, the next step is to stand up as the human character with animal characteristics. Then the animal/character can be put into a private moment, into some other exercise or into a scene so that he is able to do anything he wishes to do. The animal exercise is a good introduction to character work.

Narrative monologue exercise:

An actor can be acting quite well, and yet may be missing what is happening in a scene. The narrative monologue is an exercise in which the actor, speaking as the character, describes what the character is clearly doing and thinking. The actor is

consequently led to discover the behavior,
logic and reality of a particular scene.

8
Capsule Advice to Directors

Reading rehearsals should be held for at least five days. At the end of five days the inner line of the play should have been created. During this period be careful that the actors do not start acting. The main emphasis should be on talking easily and naturally. The first day talk about the play just a little, then add other ideas in subsequent readings or rehearsals.

Continue to emphasize a sense of talking on the second day of reading. Guide your actors to stay relaxed. Begin to outline for actors situations that are taking place. Plan units, situations, and actors' concern with objects. When the play is finally planned, the actors should have a sense of units and what they have to be concerned with at each moment. Sometimes sensory memory is created later for a particular sensation or a certain emotion. The director discusses the emotion or feeling to give the actor a clear idea of what will concern him.

On the third day work privately with individual actors. For the next three days work individually, then come together as a group. The cast will still be reading, so lines and characters should begin to fuse. Improvisation can begin, so the actors understand the logic of the scene.

The director should see the shape of the play by the fifth day, which would be the last reading. By the end of the fifth day the actors should be able to talk and listen to each other with awareness and some emotional moments. The actors can be moving in the scenes at the end of the fifth day.

By the sixth day the actors should have the feel of the play; now it can be pulled apart and work can focus on the places where there is difficulty. There can be improvisation work with these difficult scenes. At least by the sixth day, if not before, the director should begin to move people around. For beginning directors these five days previous to blocking may be too long. If there is nothing more to do, block sooner. Do not let a stalemate set in! The process of staging can be done with two people at a time or in mixed stages.

Block the play for the next six days—up to the twelfth day. Stage one act each day followed by a review of the blocking on the next day. In blocking a scene the director can let the actors stage the scene through improvisation. Often the actors will do good things not thought of by the director. If actors have difficulty in improvising, block moods. Let the actor hold the script, aid him to relax and don't worry him about lines or emotion.

Do not block the play rigidly in advance. The director can nevertheless have a picture in mind when many people are in the scene; if there are high moments of confrontation, blocking ideas should be precisely in mind. These ideas can be written for a beginning director with the understanding that the director will be willing to change his preconceived ideas because of contributions from the actors. Blocking should be planned according to events. A director should ask himself, "What is taking place onstage at the moment?" Sometimes a scene can be done ten or more different ways before the director decides what works best. If the high moments of the play are tentatively blocked, try to trust the logic of your own thinking and that of the actors for blocking in between the high moments. Sometimes an actor needs and wants to move while another does not, so do not stick too much to preconceived ideas. Motivate movement. You can create objects (like placing cigarettes on a mantel) to get the actor to the place where you want him to be and give him a reason for going there.

Do not say anything about memorizing dialogue yet. By the end of the twelfth day, the play should be blocked. By the end of the next six days, the eighteenth day, actors should be ready to rehearse without scripts. Have actors improvise the first time lines are missed until they are back on the author's words or until you wish to stop the improvisation. Rerun units; actors can then alternate between using the script, improvising when things go wrong or being prompted. For the next three days, until the twenty-first day, the prompter, when used, must be on the ball and jump in quickly with the line. Yet he must also know the pauses so he does not jump in too soon. He will need to watch the actor but also follow the script.

By the twenty-second day, the complete set should be up. If it is possible to have the set earlier, encourage the set crew to construct it as soon as possible. They should begin after meetings between the director and scenery designer. These meetings would be held before rehearsals begin.

At least by the twenty-third day the actors should be able to work on a complete set with complete props. Many things will go wrong during the first day on the completed set. A director should close his eyes and not get tense! Relax—do not show the actors your nerves or you can throw them! Let the actors walk through the scenes to become at ease with the set. Let them practice movements first, such as door openings and whatever might bother them. If more work needs to be done, actors can be called separately.

On the twenty-fourth day set the lights without the actors present.

On the twenty-fifth day a complete dress rehearsal with lights takes place. Some light changes may need to be made at this time.

On the twenty-sixth and twenty-seventh days have complete run-through dress rehearsals. Poor makeup can be changed on the twenty-seventh day.

It is advisable to rehearse five days per week for the first four weeks. The last seven days of rehearsals should be fairly steady, with the possible exception of a day off for actors while lights are being set. The actors can have a line rehearsal that day if it is needed.

Caution actors to be careful about comments from friends, as actors are vulnerable. Actors should never listen to friends but should come to the director with what bothers them. The actors should not criticize the crew and the crew should not criticize the actors. All suggestions or gripes should come to the director, who can evaluate their validity. The director decides what to do—if anything—about gripes and suggestions.

Some of the preceding suggestions are original, but most were learned from Lee Strasberg and Elia Kazan. (See Section 3 of Lorrie Hull's book for more detailed suggestions for directors.)

9
Recommended Reading List
for Directors and Actors
(see also Strasberg's list for directors in appendix E)

Acting: The First Six Lessons (Richard Boleslavsky)
Actors on Acting (Toby Cole and Helen Krich Chinoy)

Advice to the Players (Robert Lewis)
Directors in Action (ed. Bob Thomas)
Directors on Directing (Toby Cole and Helen Krich Chinoy)
The Empty Space (Peter Brook)
Habima (Raikin Ben-Ari)
Improvisation for the Theater (Viola Spolin)
Kazan on Kazan (Michel Ciment)
Method or Madness (Robert Lewis)
On Directing (Harold Clurman)
The Open Stage (Richard Southern)
Play Directing (Francis Hodge)
Respect for Acting (Uta Hagen)
Stage Management (Lawrence Stern)
Stanislavski Directs (Nikolai M. Gorchakov)
Stanislavski Directs Othello (Nikolai M. Gorchakov)
Stanislavski's Protege—Eugene Vakhtangov (Siminov-Goldina)
Stanislavski (any books by him; see bibliography)
Strasberg at the Actors Studio (ed. Robert H. Hethmon)
To the Actor (Michael Chekhov)
The Vakhtangov School of Stage Art (Nikolai Gorchakov)

10
Suggested Projects for Directors in
Hull's Teachers/Directors/Writers/Actors Class

I recommend that beginning directors work on two-character scenes
from plays. Sample scenes were listed earlier for actors (see also "Notes
and Comment," part 2, chapter 9, "Class Scene Studies," note 23).

Play	Author	Cast	Where to Get
The American Dream (and other one-acts by Albee)	Albee	3 women, 2 men	Dramatists Play Service, Inc.
The Sandbox	Albee	2 women, 2 men	*2 by Albee* Signet book
Blues for Mister Charlie (one act or scenes)	Baldwin	large cast	Samuel French
The Elephant Calf	Brecht	4 men	*3 by Brecht* Evergreen

Actors	Bromberg	1 woman, 2 men	Dramatists Play Service, Inc.
At Home (and other one-acts by Bromberg)	Bromberg	1 woman, 1 man	Dramatists Play Service, Inc.
The Dirty Old Man	Carlino	1 girl, 2 men	Dramatists Play Service, Inc.
Junk Yard	Carlino	1 woman, 4 men	Dramatists Play Service, Inc.
Used Car for Sale (and other one-acts by Carlino)	Carlino	1 woman, 3 men	Dramatists Play Service, Inc.
The Bear	Chekhov	1 woman, 2 men	*American Blues* (other suitable plays in this book)
The Boor	Chekhov	1 woman, 2 men	*Thirty Famous Plays*
Swan Song	Chekhov	2 men	*Short Plays by Chekhov,* Bantam Books
Fumed Oak (and other one-acts by Coward)	Noel Coward	3 women, 1 man	*Thirty Famous One-act Plays,* ed. Cerf and Cartmell
Escurial	de Ghelderode	4 men	*Modern Theatre,* ed. E. Bentley, vol. 5
Waiting for the Bus	Delgado	2 women, 2 men	*10 Great One-Acts* Bantam Books
White Whore and the Bit Player	Eyen	2 women	*New American Plays,* Mermaid, vol. 2
Unexpurgated Memoirs	Feiffer	1 woman, 1 man	*Collision Course,* Vintage drama
Who'll Save the Plow-boy (one-act or scenes)	Gilroy	2 women, 4 men	Samuel French
No Place to Be Somebody (one-act or scenes)	Gordone	5 women, 11 men	Samuel French
Rising of the Moon	Lady Gregory	4 men	*The Mentor Book of Short Plays*

Bosoms and Neglect (one-act or scene)	Guare	2 women, 1 man	Dramatists Play Service, Inc.
House of Blue Leaves (act one only)	Guare	2 women, 1 man	Dramatists Play Service, Inc.
The Loveliest Afternoon of the Year	Guare	1 woman, 1 man	Dramatists Play Service, Inc.
Something I'll Tell You Tuesday	Guare	3 women, 2 men	Dramatists Play Service, Inc.
Vanities (one-act)	Heifner	3 girls or women	Samuel French
Crimes of the Heart (one-act or scenes)	Henley	4 women, 2 men	Dramatists Play Service, Inc.
The Indian Wants the Bronx	Horovitz	2 boys, 1 man	Dramatists Play Service, Inc.
Rats	Horovitz	2 men	*Collision Course,* Vintage drama
The Quannapowitt Quartet (and other one-acts by Horovitz)	Horovitz		Dramatists Play Service, Inc.
"Spared"		1 man, taped voices	
"Stage Directions"		2 women, 1 man	
"Hopscotch"		1 man, 1 woman	
"75th"		1 woman, 1 man	
Soul Come Home	Hughes	1 woman, 3 men	*5 Plays by Hughes,* Midland
People in the Wind	Inge	5 women, 3 men	*Eleven Short Plays*
To Bobolink, for Her Spirit (and other one-act plays by Inge)	Inge	4 women, 3 men	*The Mentor Book of Short Plays*
The New Tenant (and other one-acts by Ionesco)	Ionesco	4 men	*3 Plays Ionesco* Evergreen
The Dutchman	Jones	1 woman, 1 man	Samuel French
If Men Played Cards as Women Do	Kaufman	4 men	*Thirty Famous Plays*
American Buffalo (one act or scenes) (and other scenes or plays by Mamet)	Mamet	3 men	Samuel French
Botticelli	McNally	2 men	*Collision Course*
Next	McNally	1 woman, 1 man	Samuel French

Tour (and other one-acts by McNally)	McNally	1 woman, 4 men (3 are extras)	*Collision Course*
Sand	Mednick	1 woman, 4 men	*New Underground,* Bantam World Drama
Ferry Boat (and other one-acts by Melfi) (and other plays in *Encounters* and *Later Encounters*)	Melfi	1 woman, 1 man	Samuel French
Lou Gehrig Did Not Die of Cancer	Jason Miller	2 women, 1 man	Dramatists Play Service, Inc.
Camera Obscura	Patrick	1 woman, 1 man	*Collision Course,* Vintage drama
Upstairs Sleeping	Perr	2 women, 2 men	*New Theatre in America,* Delta
The Dwarfs	Pinter	2 women, 2 men	*8 Review Sketches,* Dramatists Play Service, Inc.
Man with a Flower in His Mouth (Pirandello's one-act plays)	Pirandello	2 men	*Pirandello One-acts* (Anchor paperback; Samuel French)
The Autograph Hound	Prideaux	2 women, 1 man	Dramatists Play Service, Inc.
Lemonade	Prideaux	2 women	Dramatists Play Service, Inc.
Hello Out There	Saroyan	1 woman, 1 man, extras	*Eleven Short Plays,* Grove Press
For Colored Girls Who Have Considered Suicide When the Rainbow Is Enuf (one-act or scenes)	Shange	7 women	Samuel French
How He Lied to Her Husband	Shaw	1 woman, 2 men	*10 Great One-Acts,* Bantam Books
Chicago and Other Plays	Shephard		Samuel French
Four Two-act Plays (one-act)	Shephard		Samuel French

Red Cross	Shephard	2 women, 1 man	*New Underground,* Bantam World Drama
True West (and other scenes or plays by Shephard)	Shephard	1 woman, 3 men	Samuel French
The Unseen Hand and Other Plays	Shephard		Samuel French
Barefoot in the Park (one-act or scenes)	Simon	2 women, 4 men	Samuel French
The Gingerbread Lady (one-act or scenes)	Simon	3 women, 3 men	Samuel French
Last of the Red Hot Lovers (one-act or scenes)	Simon	3 women, 1 man	Samuel French
Plaza Suite (one-act) (any other act or scenes from Simon plays)	Simon	Small cast for each act	Samuel French
The Stronger	Strindberg	2 women	*Plays of Strindberg,* Vintage paperbacks, vol. 1
Riders to the Sea	Synge	3 women, 1 man	*The Mentor Book of Short Plays*
Three One-act Plays (and other one-acts by Terry)	Terry		Samuel French
The Carpenters (other Tesich plays)	Tesich	2 women, 3 men	Dramatists Play Service, Inc.; Samuel French
Powder-puff Squad No. 219	Untiedt		
The Tenor	Wedekind	2 women, 2 men	*15 International One-acts,* Pocket books
Happy Journey (and other one-acts by Wilder)	Wilder	2 women, 3 men	*The Mentor Book of Short Plays*
The Case of the Crushed Petunias	Williams	2 women, 2 men	*American Blues* (other suitable plays in this book)

Hello from Bertha	Williams	4 women	*27 Wagons Full of Cotton and Other Plays* (other suitable plays in this book)
Portrait of a Madonna	Williams	2 women, 4 men	*27 Wagons Full of Cotton and Other Plays* (other suitable plays in this book)
Something Unspoken (and other one-acts by Williams)	Williams	2 women	*10 Great One-Acts,* Bantam Books
Ludlow Fair (and other Wilson plays)	Wilson	2 women	Hill & Wang
Purgatory	Yeats	2 men	*Eleven Short Plays* Grove Press
The Effect of Gamma Rays on Man-in-the Moon Marigolds (one-act or scene)	Zindel	4 women	Dramatists Play Service, Inc.

All of the above are in paperback and at public libraries or available from Samuel French, Dramatists Play Service, Inc., and other play publishing companies. These short plays have been selected because they all have merit—plus mostly small casts. Scenes from longer works are also appropriate. Regardless all projects must be approved by the instructor.

If a director has access to an unpublished scene or play that fits into the above category it would be acceptable. Works of class members who are writers are especially encouraged as projects to be performed for an audience.

11
Information Sources for the Writer

American Theatre Association, 1010 Wisconsin Avenue, NW, Suite 630,

Washington, D.C. 20007

The Playwrights Program of the ATA is looking for new, living theatres and theatres looking for new, original, unpublished plays; it is therefore preparing two catalogs: (1) new, original, and unpublished plays that will be available without charge to all theatres in North America or abroad to those who request them; and (2) names of theatres interested in producing such plays.

Copyrights, U.S. Copyright Office, Library of Congress, Washington, D.C. 20540

Write for Form D, Class D Copyright Form. Send application, plus copy of script and $6. Plays may be copyrighted before publication.

Information about copyrighting can be obtained from *The Copyright Book* by William Sitron, $12.50, published by MIT Press, Cambridge, Ma. The book answers writers' questions.

Dramatists Guild, 234 West 44th Street, New York, NY 10036

Professional organization for produced playwrights. Associate membership available for continuing playwrights ($20.00 per year by application and approval). The *Dramatist Guild Quarterly* (subscription $6 per year) is an excellent source for current playwriting trends and statistics; it also features in-depth articles by popular playwrights.

The Hollywood Scriptletter, 1626 North Wilcox Avenue, Suite 385, Hollywood, CA 90028

Publishes specific, practical information on how to write and sell TV and film scripts.

Drama-Logue presents *The Playwright's and Scriptwriter's Market* by Larry Ketchum, $3.50. $3.71 in California.

This book offers complete information about theatres across the country looking for new plays to produce, as well as playwriting and scriptwriting contests, TV and motion picture production, companies, agents and the guilds. Order from Drama-Logue, Department PG, P.O. Box 38773, Los Angeles, California 90038, or buy at bookstores and newsstands.

Prolog, Michael R. Firth, editor; 4712 Northway Drive, Dallas, TX 75206 (50¢ per copy)

One of the best newsletters for exchange of information among playwrights. News of theatres seeking new plays, contests, meetings, and anything else this ambitious editor can find out. News not found anywhere else.

Show Business, Leo Shull, editor; 136 West 44th Street, New York, NY 10036
Weekly trade paper on what's going on in show business and TV. Also publishes *Who's Where*, 10,000 names and addresses of people and places connected with show business.
Simon's Directory of Theatrical Materials, 1564 Broadway, New York, NY 10036
(Package Publicity) A where-to-find-it guide comprising all fields of theatre arts in the U.S. and Canada.
The Writer, 8 Arlington Street, Boston, MA 02116
Writers Digest, 9933 Alliance Road, Cincinnati, Ohio 45242
These two magazines offer occasional articles about playwriting. Both list current playwriting contests as well as play producers and publishers.
Writers Guild of America West Inc., 8955 Beverly Blvd., Los Angeles, CA 90048
Treatments of scripts as well as scripts may be registered here for protection.
Good Basic Playwriting Books
William Archer, Playmaking. Old but good.
Jackson G. Barry, *Dramatic Structure*.
Charlotte Chorpenning, *Twenty-one Years with Children's Theatre*. Excellent for writing children's plays.
Toby Cole, ed., *Playwrights on Playwriting*.
Foster-Harris, *The Basic Patterns of Plot*.
Bernard Grebanier, *Playwriting*. Available in paperback.
Bernard Grebanier, *How to Write for the Theatre*. Exercises for a writers class.
Walter Kerr, *How Not to Write a Play*.
Lajos Egri, *The Art of Creative Writing*.
Lajos Egri, *The Art of Dramatic Writing*.
John Howard Lawson, *Theory and Technique of Playwriting*.
Lehman Engel, *Words with Music: The Broadway Musical Libretto*. A manual for the musical theatre playwright.
Kenneth MacGown, *A Primer of Playwriting*.
Josefina Niggle, *New Pointers on Playwriting*.
Georges Polti, *The Thirty-six Dramatic Situations*.

Sam Smiley, *Playwriting: The Structure of Action.*
Walter Wager, *The Playwrights' Speak.*
The O'Neill Theatre Center Inc., 305 Great Neck Road, Waterford, CT
06385
National Playwright Directory 400 living playwrights with short biographies, plays in synopsis form. Publication updated periodically.
Yearly playwrights' conference.
Theatre Communication Group (TCG)
Dramatists Source Book Lists college developmental programs,
awards, managers of theatres involved with TCG and other items of
interest to writers.

American Theatre a monthly forum for news, features and opinions.
The magazine includes features stories and opinions from influential
critics and artists; it covers the realms of acting, directing, design,
playwriting, media government, trustees and volunteerism, management and developments in related art forms.

New Plays USA 2 the second volume of its anthology series of contemporary writing from this country's permanent professional
theatres. Contains plays by four American writers and a new translation of Franz Xaver Kroetz' *Mensch Meier* by Roger Downey.

Theatre Facts 3 a statistical guide to the finances and productivity of
the nonprofit professional theatre in America.

Other Publications:
  Monthly Newsletter: Informing theatre writers of new funding and
    production opportunities.
  New Plays: Brochure distributed twice a year with newsletter. New
    plays may be nominated for listing and then made available to
    theatres with interest in producing.
  Theatre Profiles: Information for playwrights; lists organizations
    geared to aiding playwrights, publications of interest and a directory of theatres expressly interested in reading new and unsolicited scripts.
  Theatre Directory: Contact information for the 181 constituent and
    56 associate theatres who are members of TCG. Describes programs and services of arts organizations for theatres and individual artists. Address: TCG, 335 Lexington Avenue, New York,
    NY 10017 (212/677–2530).

Midwest Television Workshop, Play Selection Committee, 702 West 35th Street, Chicago, IL 60616

Here's a chance to get your play produced on television.

Open to anyone; preference given to midwestern playwrights. Entry requirements: the play must be full length (two acts or 90 minutes), it must be suitable for television, and it must be capable of being produced in a studio. Only writers having no prior professional television or film experience are eligible.

All plays received will be read by a committee which will pick four for production. Deadline is February 28.

Recommended Reading List for the Screenwriter

James Agee, *Agee on Film, Five Film Scripts,* and *Agee on Film: Reviews and Comments.*

A. S. Barnes (publisher), *Screenwriting.* A thorough how-to guide for the screenwriter.

Bjkorman, Mannis and Sima, *Bergman on Bergman.*

Richard Corliss, ed., *The Hollywood Screenwriters.*

Syd Field, *Screenplay.* Excellent.

Lewis Herman, *Screen Playwriting.*

Robert Lee and Robert Misiorowski, *Script Models.* Contains glossary of terms and model script pages of correct form.

Joseph McBride, ed., *Filmmakers on Filmmaking.*

Constance Nash and Virginia Oakey, *Screenwriters Handbook.*

Pudovkin, *Film Technique and Film Acting.*

F. A. Rockwell, *How to Write Plots That Sell.*

J. Michael Straczynski, *The Complete Book of Scriptwriting.* Scriptwriting for all media, plus information on marketing script.

Coles Trapnell, *Teleplay: An Introduction to Television Writing.* Course format for a workshop.

Wells Root, *Writing the Script.* Excellent.

12
Terms and Phrases for a Writing Class *

1. Lead character: protagonist

---

* Written by Paul Zindel, Pulitzer Prize-winning playwright and moderator of the Los Angeles Actor Studio writers' unit.

2. Villain: 2nd character
3. Third character (used to pinpoint climactic action)
4. What's the *root* of the problem of your play?
5. What *raises the question* in your play?
6. What is your play *about*?
7. Theme?
8. What plot point occurs about 25 minutes into a two-hour play to turn the action around?
9. What plot point occurs around 85 minutes to turn that action around again?
10. What do you know about the ending of your play?
11. What do you know about the *dark moment,* the *climax,* the *epiphany,* the *insight*?
12. Is your language interesting, stage size?
13. There are sometimes *conflicts to a happy ending.* (A happy ending is really a solution to a personal problem, and hopefully something the world could use.)
14. *But all the rules in the world cannot write a play. Its life lies deeply, uniquely inside you.*

13
Suggestions for Reviews for
"Drama Appreciation" Classes

This supplement sheet is for you to read carefully in order to guide you in the writing of your review. You should probably ask these questions:
1. Did you like the play as a play or the script as a film?
   Support your opinion by stating *why* you did or did not like the production. Remember: there are good productions of bad scripts and bad productions of good scripts. These must be separated in your mind.
2. Did you like the acting?
   You might ask yourself a few questions about the acting. Did you believe the actor? Did you find the whole cast working together in convincing ensemble playing? Was the acting truthful or exciting? Did it accomplish what you felt it should? Whether your answer is

yes or no to these questions, be sure to say *why* it was successful or unsuccessful in your opinion.

3. Did you like the production?
   Consider the lights, sets, costumes—the technical aspects of the production.
4. Did you like the direction?
   Was the movement of the actors good and motivated in the general blocking? Was the overall idea of the script communicated to you? Did you understand what the script was about? The director's point of view? Do you think that the director interpreted the script correctly? If the script was interpreted differently, did you like the interpretation? Note: This part of your review will necessarily be tied up with your answers about the production as a whole, for the director fuses *all* elements together to create a good production.
5. If there is music, singing or dancing in the production, did it add or detract from the production?

All of these suggestions are guides. They should be dealt with, although more emphasis should be placed on the acting, the direction and the script than on the details of lighting, sets, costumes, etc.

State your honest opinion, be it positive or negative, but support your opinion with reasons and examples. Use your intelligence in answering these questions. The evaluation of your work does not depend on whether you liked the production but on how well you support what you say.

14
Listing of Other Handouts for Teachers

The following handouts were originally printed in my Master of Arts thesis, *A Theatre Specialist for School and Community Drama* (University of Wisconsin, Madison). This thesis may be published into a book entitled *Inspiring Creativity through the Method and Creative Dramatics*. The handouts are available for members of my teachers class and those coached privately:

1. Exploring Creativity and Its Relationship to Creative Dramatics
2. Why Creative Dramatics
3. Background, Description and Philosophy of a Representative Creative Dramatics Lesson

4. Creative Dramatics, Drama, and Speech Activities for Grades K-12.
5. Format of Creative Dramatics Using "The Sleeping Beauty" as a Sample Story
6. Format of Types of Questions Suggested to Stimulate Creative Dramatics Activities in Elementary Grades
7. A Creative Dramatics Reading List. Includes *Creative Dramatics for the Classroom* by Nellie McCaslin, D. McKay, New York; *Development Through Drama* by Brian Way, Humanities Press; *Course Guide,* Secondary School Theatre Conference of the American Theatre Ass., 1010 Wisconsin Ave., N.W., Suite 630, Washington, D.C. 20007.
8. The Theatre Specialist: A Definition
9. Beginning the School–Community Program
10. Implementation and Maintenance of Elementary Drama Program
11. Implementation and Maintenance of Secondary Drama Program
12. Proposed Class Schedule for a School System's Dramatics Instructors
13. Continuing an Adult Drama Program
14. Community Theatre, U.S.A.
15. Definitions and Terms for the Stage
16. Theatre Conventions
17. Pantomime Ideas to Develop Sensory Aptitudes

Notes and Comment

Introduction

1. *The Actors Studio at Pickfair,* benefit program, "The Actors Studio Speaks," October 28, 1979.
2. *The Actors Studio at Pickfair.*
3. From notes taken during an interview with Delia Salvi, actress and UCLA theatre and film professor, September 30, 1977. Ms. Salvi has studied with numerous well-known professional acting instructors in New York and Los Angeles, besides studying with Lee Strasberg at the Lee Strasberg Theatre Institute and the Actors Studio.

Part 1, chapter 1: The Rewards of Studying Method

1. Lainie Kazan concurred, writing, "Thank you, thank you Actors Studio. Now at last there is 'Method' to my madness." *The Actors Studio at Pickfair* benefit program. Vic Damone told Mary Martin on "Over Easy" television, "I use emotional memory when I sing my songs" (December 16, 1981).

Part 1, chapter 2: The Evolution of Strasberg's Method

1. Currently, members of his family are all very much involved in theatre: wife Anna, daughter Susan and son John. His young sons Adam and David were appearing in a play at the New York Actors Studio at the time of their father's death.
2. Strasberg admired Eagels for a "strange vibrancy" in *Rain*; Eva Le Galliene for her "fragility and beauty"; Joseph Schildkraut for a "somewhat exaggerated forerunner of what would today be labeled the Actors Studio style"; Pauline Lord for "the driving quality" she possessed in *Anna Christie* and *They Knew What They Wanted*; Jacob Ben-Ami for his "flair and emotional depth" in *Samson and Delilah*; Alfred Lunt for his "creation of levels of perception and characterization"; and the Barrymores for their "glamour and excitement." Lee Strasberg, "Renaissance?" *The New York Times,* July 20, 1958, section 2, p. 1.
Strasberg spoke of many others whom he had admired through the years, Charles Chaplin and his use of the whole body and his ingenious physical expressivity. Chaplin was important to Strasberg because "he could not do anything that was purely verbal or mental." Strasberg enjoyed meeting Chaplin through their mutual friend Clifford Odets and recalled, "I remember Charles Chaplin coming to our house in Hollywood. He sat at the piano, and was so good with the children. He played hide-and-seek with them and had a child's sense of playfulness and imagination."
3. Richard Boleslavsky, *Acting: The First Six Lessons* (New York: Theatre Arts, 1933).
4. Lee Strasberg faculty meeting, Los Angeles, September 12, 1977.
5. Richard Findlater, "Acting. Direction and Production," *Encyclopaedia Britannica,*

14th edition (1967), Vol. I, p. 109. From the "Direction" section by Findlater. Lee Strasberg wrote the "Acting" section of the article, "Acting, Directing and Production," for
the 1959 printing of the 14th edition of *Britannica*. It was included in the article through
the final printing of the 14th edition (1973).

6. Robert H. Hethmon and Lee Strasberg, *Strasberg at the Actors Studio* (New York:
Viking Press, 1965), p. 15.

7. Findlater, *Encyclopaedia Britannica*, Vol. I, p. 109.

8. Other Group productions directed by Strasberg included *Night Over Taos, Success
Story, Men in White* between 1932 and 1934) and *Johnny Johnson* in 1936. Various other
New York productions directed by Strasberg through the years include *Hilda Cassidy*
(1933); *Gentlewoman* (1934); Gold Eagle Guy (1934); *The Case of Clyde Griffiths* (1936);
Many Mansions (1937); *Roosty* (1938); *All the Living* (1938); *Dance Night* (1938); *Summer
Night* (1939); Hemingway's *The Fifth Column* (1940), starring Franchot Tone and Lee J.
Cobb; *Clash by Night* (1941); *The Big Knife* (1949) and *The Country Girl* (1966) by Clifford
Odets; *R.U.R.* (1942); *Apology* (1943); the drama *South Pacific* (1943); *Skipper Next to
God*, starring John Garfield (1948); *The Closing Door* (1949); *Peer Gynt* for ANTA (1951);
and *The Three Sisters* (1964), with Geraldine Page, Kim Stanley and Shirley Knight.

9. Paul Gray, "Stanislavski and America: A Critical Chronology," *Tulane Drama Review* 9 (2) (T26, Winter 1964): 32–33.

10. Strasberg also was a producer of Odets's *The Country Girl* in 1950. Information
about how he and Odets worked together on the script was printed in a *Theatre Arts* article
(Armand Aulicino, "How the Country Girl Came About," *Theatre Arts Magazine* (May
1952):54–57 and again with revisions by Lee Strasberg in Stanley A. Clayes and David G.
Spencer, eds., *Contemporary Drama* (New York: Charles Scribner's Sons), pp. 332–39.

11. Paul Gray, "Stanislavski and America," pp. 32–33, 35.

12. Lee Strasberg, "Acting," *Encyclopaedia Britannica*, vol.1, 15th edition (1974),
p. 61. At another time Strasberg answered the question, "Do Studio actors act alike?"
"In that they all have aliveness and ability to be real, yes, those characteristics they share
in common. But there is a wide difference between them. There is no typical Method
actor. Marlon Brando and James Dean were the first two to become stars on the screen,
so those two set the criteria. Both played parts of characters who had difficulty in expressing themselves, so it became common to assume all Method actors are the same way. But
Marlon was completely different in *Viva Zapata* and Irwin Shaw's movie (*The Young
Lions*). Many actors could be mentioned. Kim Stanley to me is the epitome of the thing
we are working toward. Marlon's work recently has been on a very high level; *The Godfather* and *Last Tango in Paris* were extraordinary. His ability to create the character in
The Godfather was startling to me. Everyone agrees Marlon is the outstanding actor in
today's movies, but we do feel an actor like Marlon should have played great parts in the
theatre and in movies. He has been limited, so there is a degree of dissatisfaction" (Lee
Strasberg, September 19, 1977).

13. Sylvie Drake, "Confronting Theatre at the Frontier," *Los Angeles Times,* March 23,
1977, part 4, pp. 1, 15.

14. John Gassner, *Directions in Modern Theatre and Drama* (New York: Holt, Rinehart
and Winston, 1966), pp. 129, 130, 132.

15. Bobby Lewis told me that everything he knew about acting training he learned from
Lee. (Personal conversation, Minneapolis, Minnesota, August 12, 1974).

16. The studio is one organization but has an East Coast branch in New York City and
a West Coast branch in Los Angeles. In fall 1982 Al Pacino and Ellen Burstyn became
co-artistic directors of the Actors Studio for three-year terms, and Paul Newman was

selected president of the studio's board of directors. In Los Angeles Mark Rydell, Martin Landau and Sydney Pollack were the executive directors. Elia Kazan, Joseph Mankiewicz and Arthur Penn were appointed leaders of the playwrights/directors unit, New York and Martin Ritt led the directors' unit, Los Angeles. Paul Zindel headed the writers' unit, Los Angeles.

17. I am also a member of the Actors Studio Directors and Writers units, Los Angeles.

18. The Actors Studio in New York received a Ford Foundation Grant of $250,000 in 1962 and produced on Broadway O'Neill's *Strange Interlude* for its opening production. The studio produced several plays in professional theatres, including James Baldwin's *Blues for Mr. Charlie, Marathon 33, Baby Want a Kiss* and *The Three Sisters* directed by Strasberg.

19. My daughter played one of the leads in *The Secret Thighs of New England Women* when it opened at the New York Studio November 11, 1980. The play was one of several produced by Carl Schaeffer as an outgrowth of the Playwrights Lab directed by Israel Horovitz. Until his death Harold Clurman led a similar director's unit at the New York Actors Studio. As of this writing, fall 1982, Kazan is writing and directing *The Chain,* based on *Agamemnon,* at the Actors Studio, New York. My daughter is portraying Iphegenia.

20. Written by Michael Gazzo and directed by Frank Corsaro.

21. Lee Strasberg, ed., *Famous American Plays of the 1950's* (New York: Dell Publishing Co., 1962), p. 20.

22. *The Actors Studio at Pickfair,* benefit program, "The Actors Studio Speaks," October 28, 1979.

23. S. Loraine Hull, private interview with Lee Strasberg, Los Angeles, California, July, 1971.

24. Writers were encouraged to experiment with their new material in my Teachers/ Directors/Writers/Actors Workshop. As the workshop leader I found it exciting when a play evolved to a professional premiere. I instigated, organized, developed and taught the teachers workshops. At first all participants audited Strasberg's classes, and they additionally took my "Understanding of the Method" course, which was originally entitled "Introduction to the Method." Eventually, the workshops evolved to a continuous teachers/ directors/writers/actors class, which I taught for twelve years.

25. Information compiled from lecture notes by Lorrie Hull, Monday, July 26, 1971, Los Angeles.

26. Edwin Newman interview, NET telecast, November 1969.

27. Ibid.

28. Ibid.

29. Ibid. He maintained that the Method is not new insofar as it draws attention to procedures and processes that have been unconsciously used by every actor who was ever good in his life, even by actors who argue against the Method. Supporting both sides of the question "Is the Method new or not?" Strasberg concluded the interview as follows: "That is the peculiar thing about the Method—that on the one hand there is nothing new in it, and if anybody thinks it is new, he misunderstands completely what the Method is about. On the other hand, the fact that we have drawn attention to facts which hitherto were not known, were not understood, and therefore, tried to suggest for the future what could help solve these kind of problems, that in a way, is new!"

30. Ibid. Strasberg emphatically disclaimed any set of rules. He compared great actors' finding their way to great results to John Harvey's discovery that the blood circulates: the blood did not wait for Harvey's discovery.

Part 2, chapter 1: Relaxation

1. "Working With Live Material: An Interview with Lee Strasberg," *Tulane Drama Review* 9 (1) (T25, Fall 1964):119–20.

2. "To make the sound without movement is meaningless. It means you are closed inside. This has to do with Pavlovian psychology or Skinner, which insists on a relationship between physical and mental" (Lee Strasberg, May 11, 1981). To make the actor aware of why it may be difficult to make a sound, the instructor can ask if there is any reason why he does not want to do so (e.g., "In your house did you have to be quiet?").

3. Technically, the sounds come from the larynx, which is in the throat, but Strasberg always taught, "Let the sound vibrate from the lungs." Possibly, the key here is supporting the sound with a deep breath, so the throat does not become tense.

4. At times, the student is asked to make the sound, to put the tension in the sound, connect with the sound and get rid of the tension through the sound. During a demonstration of relaxation work Strasberg said: "Make an even and easy sound to get rid of repression inside, or emotion wells up. If emotion appears, we want good relaxed breathing, then make sound even and easy. Breathe out and breathe in when you make the sound. Once you command your breath, already your body is beginning to respond to your will. Control the muscles. The actor should have control over the sound, so the impulses come through."

Another relaxation technique, which a radiologist friend uses with patients and which I have shared with actors, is to tell the actor to inhale very slowly while counting backward slowly from five, then to exhale very slowly counting backward from five. Repeat approximately five times.

5. "The actor has to go through the process of relaxation, or he will never solve problems in performance. He will learn what to do, so he can go on with the performance" (Lee Strasberg, July 27, 1981).

6. The student's body should not be completely straight. One side may need more relaxation than the other because of uneven tenseness. "When a student wiggles around, he may find that the body is unequal, or the body is 'aligned' differently on each side" (Lee Strasberg, May 13, 1981).

7. A further illustration: During the sensory exercise the student can think of the head as growing out of the spine and hold the head upright by balancing it (e.g., like a person balancing a pole on his finger with an object on the top of it. The pole has flexibility like the spine).

8. Strasberg made the student aware that his back can be the seat of traumatic tension. Back muscles should be moved to relax them.

9. I learned this from several phsyical therapists.

10. When the sensory exercise has started, the student moves to check for tension, locates it and then moves to relax the tension. Thus, he moves to make contact with the area that may be tense and continues moving and working on relaxation as he does the sensory exercise.

11. Before going onstage in *The Effect of Gamma Rays on Man-in-the-Moon Marigolds* in Milwaukee, I saw Shelley enter the theatre, talk to us in the audience and then, since she is a highly trained and talented actress, spend only a few minutes relaxing and preparing before the play began.

12. Lee Strasberg, faculty meeting, August 18, 1979.

13. Lee Strasberg, The Lee Strasberg Theatre Institute class, May 6, 1981. At another time Strasberg told a class, "Relaxation for the actor is nothing more than the equivalent

of tuning the violin. If some of the strings on a violin don't respond, you are in trouble. Relaxation is a test of the extent to which you can use your own talent. After learning the skill to relax at will, actors ultimately get freedom and the ability to relax and concentrate under the pressures of production" (Lee Strasberg, May 11, 1981).

14. Robert H. Hethmon and Lee Strasberg, *Strasberg at the Actors Studio* (New York: Viking Press, 1965), pp. 92–93.

15. Personal conversation with Lee Strasberg, May 11, 1981.

Part 2, chapter 2: Concentration

1. According to Strasberg, one may also use as objects emotions, characters, specific thoughts, situations or events, either as experienced by the actor or as imagined by him.

2. A similar exercise is to ask two actors to go onstage or in front of the room, telling them to "act." The teacher lets them go for five minutes, during which they usually pretend to know each other or make up a situation. Then they are encouraged to ask real questions about people, why they are in the class, why acting, etc. This exercise, too, demonstrates that when one really thinks and listens one becomes more believable.

3. Robert H. Hethmon and Lee Strasberg, *Strasberg at the Actors Studio* (New York: Viking Press, 1965), p. 98.

Part 2, chapter 3: Sense Memory

1. Lee Strasberg lecture, notes by Lorrie Hull, Actors Studio, August 8, 1977.

2. Lee Strasberg, "Acting," *Encyclopaedia Britannica,* 15th edition (1974), vol. 1, p. 63. Strasberg told a class, "Only in constant repetition and in exercise work lies the security an actor needs. Take fifteen to twenty minutes at home for exercise work every day. Continuity of practice makes for the perfection we all seek—not three hours at once, then not do it again for awhile. Continuity is important just as a musician practices" (May 11, 1981). This class was comprised mainly of actors who had studied with Lee for several years.

Another suggestion to the same class: "Remembering in bed at night becomes an exercise test" (Lee Strasberg, May 6, 1981).

And at another time: "When in bed try to remember an occurrence during the day to recreate sensorily: sight, sound, touch, taste, smell, someone or something you saw, etc., so reexperiencing what happens to you becomes an automatic process. You can develop high intense experiences to become Golden Keys" (Strasberg, October 25, 1979).

3. Lee Strasberg class, May 13, 1981.

4. Lee Strasberg faculty meeting, September 18, 1977. The sequence of exercises is important, as Strasberg pointed out when he carefully described their sequence, logic and value.

5. Robert H. Hethmon and Lee Strasberg, *Strasberg at the Actors Studio* (New York: Viking Press, 1965), p. 100. At another time Strasberg declared, "Senses of all individuals are unevenly developed. One [person] sees more and hears less, and another vice versa" (August 18, 1979).

6. John Gassner, *Producing the Play* (New York: Holt, Rinehart and Winston, 1953), pp. 143–44.

7. Ibid., p. 143.

8. Ibid., p. 144.

9. Notes on Strasberg lecture by Lorrie Hull, September 12, 1977.

10. Lee Strasberg, July 18, 1981.

11. Ibid.

Part 2, chapter 4: Sequence and Description of Sensory Exercises

1. "We evolved the exercises, so now an actor can do six to eight exercises at one time" (Lee Strasberg, June 18, 1981).

2. Lee Strasberg faculty meeting, August 18, 1979.

3. Lee Strasberg faculty meeting, January 9, 1981.

4. Strasberg told a class of mostly longtime students, "No exercise is of value that you have not practiced. Only something you have worked on shows you have trained yourself to do it. Work a few minutes every day, so you develop skill to do it. [The time should be much longer for beginners.] It is the ability to hit it every time you want it that makes the craft (e.g., You can hit a high note once and it does not mean a thing. The ability to train yourself to hit it time after time is what counts). The same holds true for our sensory work" (Lee Strasberg, Los Angeles, May 11, 1981).

At another time Strasberg suggested, "Tell your students to practice the exercises at home four hours a day, five days a week" (Lee Strasberg faculty meeting, The Lee Strasberg Theatre Institute, Los Angeles, January 9, 1981). This would be the ideal way to progress in the sensory work by practicing twenty hours per week while doing the work daily.

5. Lee Strasberg faculty meeting, August 18, 1979.

6. Ibid.

7. Ibid.

8. Ibid. In a Lee Strasberg class, July 27, 1981 Strasberg further explained kinetic senses operating all through the body, using heat as an example: "Define [and experience] heat in every place [in the body] so it begins to work." He encouraged the student to move his body in specific places as the student sensorily tried to recreate heat.

9. "An actor does not need to work with the real personal object at home; sometimes he won't have it anymore. Some can get it better with the real object, while others clam up and don't get it so well" (Lee Strasberg, August 18, 1979).

10. Strasberg, August 18, 1979.

11. Strasberg faculty meeting, September 18, 1977.

12. Lee Strasberg class, September 21, 1980. He added, "You can also add other things to the private moment. Keep working on it and don't go to something else. You can add whatever you have to work on, so [the aloneness] becomes full."

13. Strasberg class, July 8, 1981.

14. Robert H. Hethmon and Lee Strasberg, *Strasberg at the Actors Studio* (New York: Viking Press, 1965), pp. 118–19.

15. Ibid., p. 118.

16. Richard Schechner, "Working with Live Material: An Interview with Lee Strasberg," *Tulane Drama Review* 9 (1) (T25, Fall 1964): 126.

17. Students have informed me that their psychiatrists have told them to do certain private moments or affective memories in my classes. After doing so, they reported back that the work had been a great catharsis and their psychiatrists were pleased. My policy is to check directly with the doctor before taking responsibility for such exercises.

18. Hethmon and Strasberg, p. 119.

19. September 18, 1977.

20. Ibid. See beginning of the chapter regarding awareness and control, the exercise's purpose.

21. "Choose an animal like a gorilla if you're supposed to be paralyzed or if you have to dance badly onstage or on screen" (Strasberg in class, May 4, 1981).

22. Michael Ciment, *Kazan on Kazan* (New York: Viking Press, 1974), p. 18.

Part 2, chapter 5: Affective Memory

1. Richard Schechner, "Working with Live Material: An Interview with Lee Strasberg," *Tulane Drama Review* 9 (1) (T25, Fall 1964): 133.

Strasberg further explained, "Great actors are great onstage as somehow they are able to achieve an intense living through, an emotional living through, but before modern psychological discoveries no one knew how it was achieved or if inspiration struck again or why" (July 13, 1981).

2. John Gassner, *Producing the Play* (New York: Holt, Rinehart and Winston, 1953), p. 144. Strasberg also told his faculty, "Stanislavski separated sense and emotional memory, even though he started with emotional memory" (January 9, 1981).

3. Lee Strasberg class, September 24, 1980. "Sense and emotional memory give wonderful, powerful human results rather than just a naturalness" (Lee Strasberg, July 13, 1981).

4. Learning how to effectively use sensory and affective memory can involve specialized guidance. I suspect that is why actors like Sally Fields, Barbra Streisand, Marilyn Monroe, Edward Albert, Jr., Shelly Duvall, Tanya Tucker and many others came to Strasberg for training after they had become well known. Freddie Prinze wanted Shelley Winters to teach him privately because he was afraid if he tried to work correctly at the Actor's Studio, he could not do it. Jon Voight's wife, who was in my class, asked me if I would teach them privately, because she claimed Jon did not want to work in a class even though he wanted more training.

5. Marcel Proust, *Remembrance Of Things Past: Volume I*, "Swann's Way," trans. C. K. Moncrieff and Terence Kilmartin (New York: Random House, 1981), pp. 48–51. The narrator in the novel remembers how his mother served him tea with "those squat, plump cakes called *petites madeleines*." He soaks a piece of madeleine in the tea, takes a spoonful of tea and crumbs and immediately experiences a powerful feeling of joy. He drinks another mouthful of tea and cake and then another, but the sensation of joy appears to lessen. After contemplating briefly, he concentrates on recalling the sense of taste finally recognizing "the taste of the piece of madeleine soaked in . . . decoction of lime blossom" and suddenly a flood of recollection from his childhood is released. He recalls Sunday mornings at Combray where his aunt dipped madeleine into her cup of lime-flower tea prior to giving a piece to the boy. He reexperiences this situation, letting it develop into the detailed recollection that becomes *Remembrance Of Things Past*. Proust's Volume I and Volume II of *Remembrance Of Things Past* contain other examples of affective memory.

6. Michael Schulman, "Back Stage Behaviorism," *Psychology Today,* June 1973, pp. 51–54, 88.

7. Ibid., p. 52.

8. Edwin Newman interview, NET telecast, November 1969.

9. Ibid.

10. Martine Bartlett and Dianne Hull.

11. Strasberg class, July 13, 1981.

12. Ibid.

13. Robert H. Hethmon and Lee Strasberg, *Strasberg at the Actors Studio* (New York: Viking Press, 1965), p. 110.

14. Helen Krich Chinoy, "Reunion: A Self-Portrait," *Educational Theatre Journal* (December 1976): 546.

15. Ibid., p. 549.

16. The relived emotion is always different, sometimes only slightly, but emotion relived is never exactly the same as the original, just as in life emotion is never the same again.

17. Lee Strasberg, October 18, 1979.

18. Even though verbalization is preferred most times so the actor can be checked to determine if the exercise is being properly done, there are times when speaking out can take away from the exercise and its fullness. In an affective memory exercise if the experience is extremely personal, it can be better just thought rather than spoken. In either case the actor does not need to tell what the situation is. An astute instructor or director may at times tell an actor to remember silently and relive the answers to the questions or may ask the actor if he or she prefers to do this.

19. Western Springs, Ill., ACTA National Play Contest, August 1971.

20. The idea is to perform the task, such as combing the hair, applying makeup, cleaning the room, getting dressed, mowing the lawn or anything familiar needing minimum concentration.

21. Strasberg class at the Los Angeles Lee Strasberg Theatre Institute, July 23, 1980. Lee also told how he worked on his sensory and affective memory exercises while riding on the subway.

22. At times the emotion not only lingers but even becomes fuller after the exercise or scene is completed. One time at a party the Actors Studio gave some fun awards. Al Pacino was named the best after-the-scene-was-over actor.

23. Examples are "She never put her arms around me before, and I wondered why," "I think it was wrong to do this," "He is such a jerk," "It is an ugly coat." When the latter was related to Strasberg during an affective memory exercise, he retorted, "You are giving me emotional reaction. I want sensory objects. *Ugly* describes. [It is subjective.] Don't give me that."

24. The Actors Studio, May 8, 1982. On November 12, 1982, Shelley referred to affective memories as "the most powerful tool Lee ever taught me."

25. Chinoy, "Reunion: A Self-Portrait," pp. 485–86.

26. The trained professional actress Jody Carter, portraying the first Frau Henschel in Hauptmann's play *Drayman Henschel,* worked several times individually with me, her director, at my home. She explored an affective memory for the opening scene as well as one for later in the act. Finally, she was secure that she could create real emotion that was right for the character. Every night of performance she was able to silently prepare by doing an affective memory that propelled her into the opening scene. She fully concentrated on the affective memory as she lay on a bed in full view of the audience entering the Marilyn Monroe Theatre, Los Angeles. The exercise took less and less preparation time each night, but the actress just lay there in her spot for the opening scene, as if in her own home, creating specific thoughts and feelings as Frau Henschel. She also did her homework for the latter part of the act where another affective memory came in on cue, giving her a reality and truthfulness in the role. The first act with Ms. Carter was performed

several times at the Actors Studio, Los Angeles, with Sydney Pollack or Lee Strasberg as moderators. This was prior to the professional run.

27. Lee Strasberg class, July 13, 1981.

28. Schechner, "Working with Live Material," p. 134.

29. That night we did the play for Strasberg and the public as an example of a play directed by a Strasberg student. Strasberg asked me later, in our dialogue for the audience, if I was satisfied with the actor's performance; I had to say no and tell him why. Lee knew what my answer would be when he asked me how I should have worked with the actor. I answered that we should have explored affective memory exercises to find one to fuse with the scene in case there should be a problem. Since the actor, George Caldwell, had only taken one acting class from me—a Univesity of Wisconsin extension adult class—he was not at that time well trained in sensory work. I should have trained him, as I directed him, by working individually with him.

30. I assume that through Strasberg's acting training sessions they experimented, found what worked and practiced with repeated homework until the sequence of sensory steps was logical and orderly so one word, image, sensation or remembering of the experience would set off the proper result. I advise students to strive for this goal during their home-work practice as well as during affective memory work prior to an improvisation, scene and rehearsal. If the homework is well done, an actor trained in affective memory pro-cedures can recall the desired emotion in the middle of a scene by the trigger, which could be a word, image or sensation.

31. Chinoy, "Reunion: A Self-Portrait," p. 547.

32. Strasberg class, July 23, 1980.

33. Ibid.

34. Chinoy, "Reunion: A Self-Portrait," pp. 546–47.

35. Sometimes a director also has to teach. Other examples of instances when I have used affective memory techniques with nonprofessionals include: laughter for the college student playing Peter in *The Zoo Story*. (The student attended my Ripon College and later my Lee Strasberg Theatre Institute acting classes); tears resulting from agony and despair for the adult playing Jerry in the same play (for Fond du Lac, Wisconsin, Community Theatre state, regional, and national competition winner); fear and trembling for the young man playing Jive, a character thrown into prison in *The Cage* (also a state, regional and national competition winner); pain with tears resulting from the loss of a loved one for the actress playing Nellie Forbush in *South Pacific* (Sharon King had attended one of my University of Wisconsin, Fond du Lac Center, acting classes but was naturally very recep-tive and talented); emotions based on stark terror for the actress playing Susy in *Wait until Dark*; a feeling of depression for the actress in the last act of *The Last of the Red Hot Lovers* (when the character of Barney opened the door and the audience saw her, they roared every night); torment, loneliness and anguish for the man in *The Dirty Old Man* (this play was another contest winner starring my daughter and Dr. Howard Mauthe in the Midwest. Several years later I directed the play for a professional theatre in Los Angeles); and high emotional moments from feelings of justification, righteousness and despair of Antigone and hopelessness for Haemon for the Ripon College students in *Antigone* (the students were in my acting classes at Ripon College as well as later at the Lee Strasberg Theatre Institute, Los Angeles. So he could secure a top agent, I did an audition with "Haemon" [Richard Parker Clemons] where I used an affective memory for the role of the mother in *Butterflies Are Free*. I chose an event concerning my own son. I fused the emotion of an affective memory with that of the role resulting in tears due to feelings of love, compassion and hurt for the son.). All of the last four examples incited

deep emotion resulting in tears of various degrees from the actors. Since I have directed student, amateur and professional plays and television productions numbering over 200, the list of affective memories working to fuse with specific roles could go on indefinitely.

36. Originally, the event was a dance instructor slapping a chair and shouting. For the fourth time, the circumstances began as before with her tap dancing in the same place, with the same music, clothing and group, but she changed the end of the event to a time when the instructor was sitting on the back of a chair, rather than on the seat, and not shouting.

37. July 23, 1980. By the term literal emotion I believe Strasberg meant emotion during a rehearsal or performance resulting from the actor's reaction to the circumstances of a scene or to his current needs or life situation. Strasberg distinguished this type of emotion from "remembered" emotion, that is, emotion generated through the senses or affective memory. Remembered emotion is something that the actor can create and repeat. Strasberg often cited a well-known example of remembered emotion: "One actor may say to another, 'hit me, hit me, if you don't hit me, I won't get the feeling and be able to respond.' That's not acting. If an actor is hit, he's going to fall down. Where is there acting in that? The idea is that one actor appears to hit another, and the way in which he hits is filled with power, tension and reality, so it is believable. The actor being hit reacts, or falls down, with force and feeling, as if he has been hit. He feels hurt and pain, but has not been touched. That's acting. Vakhtangov would call the kind of emotion involved in this situation remembered emotion, not literal emotion." Vakhtangov, too, encouraged actors not to use literal emotion, but rather to use remembered emotion.

38. Schechner, "Working with Live Material," p. 132.

39. Hethmon and Strasberg, p. 111. Thus, if an actor says an affective memory isn't working anymore, as in a production after several performances, it is usually because the actor begins to anticipate. Strasberg claimed, "If I work with the actor again, [the affective memory] would still be there." Strasberg class, July 23, 1980.

40. Ibid. At another time Strasberg admonished, "If the exercise is not properly done, it can fail you when you try to do it. This has happened to people in long runs, and when I ask them to go through the exercise carefully and clearly as I guide, it happens as fully as ever. The process of reliving and re-creation is stimulated within . . ." (Strasberg class, Los Angeles, July 13, 1981).

41. Strasberg's teacher Maria Ouspenskaya had twelve keys, twelve really outstanding productive memories. The keys can be six, twelve or whatever. Golden keys of affective memories are invariably in the past, for conditioning factors that create emotional responses are created early in life. "The further the actor goes back in years, the better it is" (Strasberg, July 23, 1980).

42. Lee Strasberg class, Los Angeles, May 4, 1981.

43. Shelley asked Lee this question shortly after she consented to write the foreword for this book in 1979. She told the story when moderating at the Actors Studio in March 1980 and again May 7, 1982, verifying that she learned the correct term "just a couple of years ago." During the same session Shelley also told the story of working on a film with George Stevens. Stevens played certain music for her, which had a relationship to Shelley's past and led to memories resulting in the emotion Stevens wanted. After learning affective memory work from Strasberg, Shelley told George on their next film together, "You do not need to play music for me anymore. I can do it myself." She admitted, however, "I play music sometimes now, just so the crews and those around me will be quiet, so I can concentrate" (May 7, 1982).

Part 2, chapter 6, Other Exercises

1. Witten by Noel Coward. My daughter and I wrote the following instructions for the script: Memorize the following lines without regard to meaning. We will then give the meaning (the circumstances or intention) in class through improvisation of a situation.

2. Seminar by Shelley Winters, July 19, 1981.

3. Viola Spolin. *Improvisation for the Theater* (Evanston: Northwestern University Press, 1963).

4. Robert Lewis, *Advice to the Players* (New York: Harper and Row, 1980).

5. An example could be "Hoopvye ploski, stav neevya, pleko, plash bool cloo blash shal dal ploo," etc. Some actors just say la, la, la or speak in a kind of foreign language (e.g., Danny Kay's Russian or sounds suggesting German or French).

6. Strasberg faculty meeting, The Lee Strasberg Theatre Institute, Hollywood, June 27, 1978.

7. Ibid.

8. Robert H. Hethmon and Lee Strasberg, *Strasberg at the Actors Studio* (New York: Viking Press, 1965), pp. 214–15.

9. Ibid., p. 212.

10. Strasberg faculty meeting, June 27, 1978.

11. Hethmon and Strasberg, p. 162.

12. Ibid., p. 162.

13. The student is asked to choose a simple song, such as a nursery rhyme, which comes easily and naturally, so he does not need to remember words. A simple song leads to a better exercise, but there are no laws about the choices. At times, something can be learned about the student from his choice of song. The instructor may get an image of someone who wants to be his own person if he makes an ambitious choice.

14. Hethmon and Strasberg, p. 163.

15. Lee Strasberg made similar comments numerous times to various actors.

16. Hethmon and Strasberg, p. 123.

17. From documented notes of a Lee Strasberg class.

18. The actor should learn control over his body in this exercise. The actor may, however, discover impulses that make it difficult to maintain physical control and stand still.

19. Notes from Lee Strasberg classes; repeated frequently.

20. Notes from Lee Strasberg class. Sometimes the teacher interrupts because of something going on, and the instructor wants the student to make contact with it, or to make some note to the student. At times a teacher tells the student about the sound he just finished and talks a little bit about what just happened in the exercise. Other times a student will go on with the entire exercise and an instructor won't say anything until it is completed. The instructor's attack varies according to the student's needs.

21. Hethmon and Strasberg, p. 164.

22. Ibid., p. 165.

23. Strasberg faculty meeting, June 27, 1978.

24. Ibid.

Part 2, chapter 7: Improvisation

1. "Some comics make very good actors because they [have]learned to think onstage

and improvise at that moment when something happens" (Lee Strasberg class, July 27, 1981).

2. Lee Strasberg, July 27, 1981.

3. Mitch Tuchman, "Dialogue on Film: Dustin Hoffman," *American Film: Magazine of the Film and Television Arts* (Washington, D.C., April 1983), pp. 26, 71.

4. *Montgomery Clift* (film), Italy, 1983, Four Star Theatre, Filmex, Los Angeles, Sunday, May 1, 1983.

5. David Galligan, "Robert Duvall," *Drama-Logue* (Los Angeles, California, June 2–8, 1983), p. 14.

6. Kazan's habit of asking the author to revise was legendary, but no author (including Miller, Williams and Robert Anderson) ever said he regretted any of Kazan's changes. Williams, in fact, rewrote the entire third act of *Cat on a Hot Tin Roof.* Kazan got along well with playwrights—a key to his ability to get them to change their scripts. When he selected a play to direct, it was because he believed in it.

7. Robert H. Hethmon and Lee Strasberg, *Strasberg at the Actors Studio* (New York: Viking Press, 1965), p. 107.

Part 2, chapter 8: Preparing and Learning the Role

1. The term *script* applies to material written for stage or film.

2. Examples of verbs to find the character's spine or determine the action of the character include: to find out something, to demand, to have fun, to discover, to hide, to advise, to urge, to hold on to, to follow, to fight, to escape, to respond, to examine, to face up to, to chastise, to probe, to confront, to comfort, to persuade, to ask, to reproach, to forgive, to wait, to chase away.

3. Tyrone wants to maintain his position by dominating as a father, a man and a head of the house. Because of his neurotic fear of poverty, he is unable to relate to his family. At first he cannot admit his greediness and his faults. James Tyrone is basically a good man, who loves his wife and family, but his miserliness extends into his emotional relationships with them.

Mary Tyrone's obstacle to a material and emotional "home" is Tyrone, but nevertheless she can exist because of his need for her. She is at the mercy of her physiological dependence on drugs. Her needs are dictated by the inevitable aspects of the addict's cycle.

4. Edmund has to understand himself and his family in order to find truth and forgiveness. He tries to help his family by making them face the truth. Jamie tries to free himself from guilt by confessing his own sadism, sneering at the hypocrisy of others and denouncing everything, including the theatre, which has been so important to his father.

5. Kazan at the Actors Studio, New York, June 1981.

6. *Montgomery Clift* (film), Italy, 1983, Four Star Theatre, Filmex, Los Angeles, Sunday, May 1, 1983.

7. Robert De Niro, Los Angeles, November 24, 1980. De Niro elaborated: "I also did it [trained with La Motta, became a taxi driver, etc.] to have confidence, to feel I was right for this, that I did it right. When it's real, you'll know it."

8. Pat H. Broeske, "Louis Gossett, Jr., an Actor and a Gentleman," *Drama-Logue,* March 31–April 6, 1983, p. 15. *Drama-Logue* also reports how Robert Duvall researched some roles: "On *Tender Mercies* I went around with a couple of guys listening to accents. I gave a guy . . . a script and he sent me a tape of five or six guys reading my part until I found an accent that set something off in me . . . With *The Great Santini* I just went

down and hung around the Marines a little bit" (David Galligan, "Robert Duvall," *Drama-Logue* [Los Angeles, California, June 2–8, 1983], p. 15).

9. Barbara Saltzman, "Noted," *Los Angeles Times,* Saturday, April 2, 1983.

10. David Galligan, "Robert Duvall," p. 14.

11. Lee Strasberg, faculty meeting, Los Angeles, June 27, 1978.

12. Lee Strasberg, September 19, 1977. Strasberg also added, "Begin to think. Most actors memorize lines and do not know what they are talking about, so in our work we emphasize improvisation. What do you really mean with the line?"

13. Strasberg on Stanislavski, September 19, 1977.

14. Strasberg also liked actors to ignore punctuation marks or rewrite the lines without them in order to avoid talking in sentences.

15. A student did the *Our Town* role and I critiqued: "You are preaching, just saying words at the class, and not working specifically." When he substituted images of a beloved canyon for the Grovers Corners sites, his concentration became more involved and his acting more truthful.

16. Strasberg was working with my daughter in a two-week seminar in Wisconsin when this incident occurred. Subsequently, she was accepted as the youngest student in his New York professional classes.

17. If he talks or thinks of a dentist coming to a door offstage, he can specifically visualize a dentist he knows (e.g., a man with a moustache, dark curly hair, glasses, the features he remembers).

18. Actors Studio, Los Angeles, May 5, 1982. Shelley, at another time declared, "I saw my daughter's face when I looked at the actress playing my daughter." Actors Studio, Los Angeles, June 19, 1984.

19. Lee Strasberg, September 19, 1977.

20. De Niro continued, "When I say keep the scene simple, I mean in terms of external behavior, as it is in life. I mean not tearing up the scenery or retching, but an actor can still be intense in a scene. Whatever goes on in the mind can be whatever turmoil is needed. I have no set way of working on a part. Every part is different. The circumstances are different, the reason is different. I may have something in back of my mind to do. That's the main thing—that it's personal, works for me and [for the character]. As long as you make a choice that does something. If you don't do anything it's general as they say." (November 24, 1980).

Strasberg's viewpoint of "external" work is as follows: ". . . external is when you just go with words of a scene. [External] actors do not build any life separate from words of the scene. [An actor must] come onstage to fulfill his life as the character—not just the words of the author. The actor has to create the reality behind the words" (October 25, 1979).

21. Dick Cavett interview with Lee Strasberg, PBS, January 3, 1978. Strasberg continued, "Obviously, the spoken lines come out of something the actor is thinking, feeling, doing . . . Therefore, if he thinks of one thing, then a second thing, a third thing, a fourth thing, or maybe even a fifth thing, he can then go on twenty times, as he has thoughts, ideas and sensations which stimulate the way in which he speaks the lines. As soon as he becomes concerned with the lines, everything else begins to fade away. If there is a problem with words and the actor worries about the line, he can make the words unimportant—throw them away. The lines are not that important—much depends on the actor's behavior."

22. Shelley Winters seminar, Los Angeles, July 10, 1981.

23. Ibid.

24. De Niro, November 24, 1980.

25. Lee Strasberg on Cavett television show, January 3, 1978.

26. Lee Strasberg, May 4, 1981. Sometimes actors imitate other actors. James Dean admired and deliberately tried to imitate Marlon Brando. He was successful with the public, but other actors have been criticized for imitating. Strasberg spoke of Burt Reynolds: "When he imitated Marlon, it held him back. He started out trying to be Marlon, and now he has the message he's not. He should try to develop his own acting talent. He should have respect for his talent. Now that he is going on his own, I hope he will do things he's capable of doing. He is a good solid actor."

27. De Niro, November 24, 1980. De Niro further expounded, "An actor just finds something to keep him going. In a movie sometimes he has to find out where to use it like in a take. It's not like in a play. In a movie I have to do it (a way of smoking, drinking coffee or water) enough so it will be used. But on the other hand, it could be cut out, and you don't want to overdo it. When I worked on *Godfather II,* I worked a lot with video tape [Strasberg claimed this is dangerous for some actors, as they can become too self-conscious], as I had to move . . . in a way to connect [my role] to the other [*Godfather I*] film. I played it back to see how it would connect and watched myself. Then I said, 'Do more of this or more of that."

28. Shelley Winters seminar, Los Angeles, Monday, June 28, 1982. Shelley also advised students, "Spencer Tracy could steal any scene by listening and watching other actors. Don't go to lines. Go to thoughts, so the audience feels like they are peeking in. Also, when I prepare, I automatically think of something parallel in my own life and use affective memory. But an actor can get too involved in his own work and ignore what the playwright is saying. The actor needs to figure out what the playwright is saying to the audience and how he [the actor] fulfills the play the most."

29. Robert H. Hethman and Lee Strasberg, *Strasberg at the Actors Studio* (New York: Viking Press, 1965), p. 121.

30. Shelley Winters, Actors Studio, July 10, 1981.

31. Shelley Winters, Actors Studio, May 7, 1982.

32. Brando's sister Jocelyn disputes this story. She told me, "He was always himself when I talked to him on performance days. He has such super concentration that he doesn't need a lot of preparation. Marlon and Henry Fonda have the most super concentration of any actors I know." (Personal conversation with Lorrie Hull, March 1982).

33. De Niro, November 24, 1980.

34. A movie role for which Strasberg was nominated for the best supporting actor Academy Award.

35. July 1978.

36. Barbara Walters interview of Walter Matthau, ABC television, April 8, 1982.

37. Hethmon and Strasberg, p. 152.

38. Ibid., p. 146. Robert De Niro, too, confirms the value of simplicity: "The actor does not need to overdo. He makes simple choices yet has an intensity. If an actor is not sure about what he wants to do, he mistakenly goes to the obvious and 'acts' because he is not secure about who he is, so he starts to overact. Acting should be very simple and not involved and complicated in terms of behavior. People are very simple when they are relating to each other or by themselves" (De Niro, November 24, 1980).

39. Strasberg, May 4, 1981.

40. De Niro, November 24, 1980.

41. The Lee Strasberg Theatre Institute, Los Angeles, Monday, August 16, 1982, seminar conducted by Al Pacino. I asked Pacino about the Hickey-Hamlet monologues. Pacino

elaborated, "After performing the two monologues, my throat was dry, so I had a cup of coffee, and then did the monologues again as Lee suggested. Before I repeated them, people were asking, 'Who is that?' Lee teased, 'See, we take anyone!'"

42. Dick Cavett television show, January 3, 1978. At another time Lee, describing why he was a strict taskmaster with the multitalented Pacino, detailed the problems the modern actor faces. "After three months in a successful play, actors become bored doing the same things over and over again. In the old days they traveled and the stars acted with many different actors. The lesser actors acted with many different stars, so they learned different ways plays could be done. Because of the different mediums today, we get mush—not champagne. Brando, Pacino and others start in the theatre, then go to Hollywood and become stars. All who succeed are so unhappy. Success today does not go hand-in-hand with achievement. They go their island—like Marlon. Even the British acknowledge Marlon as a greater talent than Olivier. The movies are one of the greatest discoveries of man, for each frame can be perfect—like a painting that is perfect. But nothing can ever parallel the experience an audience gets in live theatre" (Lee Strasberg class, May 4, 1981).

Part 2, chapter 9: Class Scene Studies

1. My Teachers/Directors/Writers/Actors class operates somewhat differently. New material by the writers is constantly explored and presented in class as well as for projects for invited audiences.

2. Strasberg class, Los Angeles, May 4, 1981. Strasberg also suggested the "marvelous scenes in short stories of Irwin Shaw, Colette, Ernest Hemingway, Anton Chekhov and Guy de Maupassant." According to Strasberg, "A short story writer doesn't explain so much, gets the plot into his description and then gets into the dialogue."

3. Strasberg class, October 25, 1979. Strasberg concluded, "I then can show the actor where he went off and he'll understand."

4. In class Strasberg warned, "The teacher must help sustain the actor's logic and continuity and be sure he's really alive and not faking alive" (July 18, 1981).

5. Paradoxically, at times heat, cold or another sensation could be effective for a particular scene even though the sensory work is not connected with the scene. The audience need not know what the actor worked on if heat, cold or the sensation used gives the actor a quality he or the director wants.

6. Robert H. Hethmon and Lee Strasberg, *Strasberg at the Actors Studio* (New York: Viking Press, 1965), p. 290.

7. Strasberg expounded, "We have evolved procedures in training. An actor can concentrate on two, three, four or more objects [including sense memories], then add characterization, emotional memory and other things" (Lee Strasberg to his class, July 13, 1981).

8. The given circumstances mean everything that happened before the scene or play as well as the events in the play that affect the scene.

9. From a tape of Lee Strasberg (made in 1978) played for new students at The Lee Strasberg Theatre Institute.

10. Strasberg, July 21, 1978.

11. Ibid.

12. Strasberg, June 11, 1980. Strasberg continued, "I always watched Brecht to be sure I wasn't saying something wrong. I told the actors, 'A remembered reality is just as real. The memory of reality is not unemotional, but it draws attention to what is happening at

that moment, so it should be clear, real and believable.' I think I was right in the interpretation I was giving him [Brecht]." After rehearsals stopped, Strasberg received a letter from Brecht assuring him that because of the rehearsal sessions in Strasberg's apartment, Brecht for the first time felt he could work with American theatre people. When Strasberg in 1961 visited the Berliner Ensemble, Brecht's theatre, he attended many rehearsals. Strasberg was pleased that the Berliner Ensemble was using the narrative technique as Lee had rehearsed it many years earlier in Brecht's presence. Strasberg commented, "Obviously, our way of working must have made an impression on him. I was impressed with the sincere feeling and complete believability of the Berliner Ensemble. Brecht strived for a reality just like we do. When he directed his own plays, things were done quite differently from what he wrote. He got more of his 'epic' ideas across through production such as signs, choruses, etc."

In the *Encyclopaedia Britannica*, 15th edition 1974 Strasberg wrote: "Brecht mentioned some of the procedures of Stanislavsky he felt indebted to—the creation of the given circumstances that motivate the beginning of an event, the emphasis on creating the activity of the day that helps to define the actor's behaviour, and the individualizing of the characters that make up a mass. And he warns that 'we shall get empty, superficial, formalistic, mechanical acting if in our technical training we forget for a moment that it is the actor's duty to portray living people'" (p. 61).

It appears that Strasberg believed that Brecht directed his actors to make unsentimental choices but to be truthful in their portrayals. When I participated in a discussion before an audience in Monaco, the Monegasque head of protocol, who was also an amateur actor, claimed that in Brecht's works actors were to show (indicate) the characters' feelings and "distance" themselves from the characters. He felt that was Brecht's style. I argued, "Acting in any style could be based on the actor's truth. Indeed, acting based on the actor's truth is what fine actors have been doing for over two thousand years. Brecht wanted reality based on truthfulness from his actors." I told the preceding story about Strasberg and Brecht, which I had heard in a private conversation with Lee, concluding my response with, "I have read from Weber that Brecht claimed, 'Never believe anything I write. I'm constantly changing my opinion.'" The worldwide audience reacted with thunderous applause.

13. "Lee Strasberg," in Helen Krich Chinoy, ed., *Educational Theatre Journal* (December 1976): 550.

14. Hethmon and Strasberg, p. 293.

15. Ibid., p. 294.

16. Ibid., p. 296.

17. Ibid., p. 297.

18. Ibid., p. 340.

19. Ibid., p. 285.

20. Ibid., p. 278.

21. Ibid., p. 147.

22. Ibid., p. 336.

23. Examples of appropriate sources for directed scenes include: *Sweet Bird of Youth, Cat on a Hot Tin Roof, Blithe Spirit, The Rainmaker, Barefoot in the Park, Requiem for a Heavyweight* and simple two-character scenes (see appendix G for list). Short stories are not as good for directed scenes as for acting scenes (see also lists of simple scenes and advanced scenes suggested for actors, appendix G).

24. Some stars, such as Katharine Hepburn and Robert De Niro, are noted for influencing directors. Robert De Niro knows how he likes to work with directors: "The ideal

situation is when you want to do something to see how it works, the director is supporting an actor and everbody is working together and nobody is telling you what to do. No director can give it to you. That's for sure. Maybe they can give it to you in a cerain way—a movement or objective, support in a certain way. Kazan has so much enthusiasm; he generates this like a kid. I told him, 'I don't know if you are conning me or not, but even so, it's terrific.' He puts out that energy and gives it to somebody, so actors feel competent and don't have to worry.

"What you do might not be what directors thought it was. When they start to make you feel you don't have a mind of your own and start to tell you to do this and do that, if it's an important job—you get through it and that's it. It can be a bad situation or you might be overacting and he's trying to tell you to do less, but that's different and an actor can understand that . . . You don't want to be pampered but want to be on a good footing with everyone. You try to talk, but sometimes directors have it in their heads a certain way. In movies it is usually more flexible, but in a play, if you are working, taking your time, and they want a result, then it's hard. They'll say, 'That's not the way I thought— the way you are working—I want you to do this.' You really have to trust directors. That's the best situation—to be confident it will be okay—no matter what you do, it will be okay, and then you try harder—try something new and listen when they say 'Let's try this'" (Robert De Niro, November 24, 1980).

25. Martin Ritt, leader of Actors Studio Directors' Unit, Los Angeles, February 10, 1983.

Part 3: Directing

1. Strasberg remarked, "The preliminary work of the director is very hard to define" (Lee Strasberg Theatre Institute, Strasberg directing class, Los Angeles, May 12, 1981). Perhaps it is presumptuous to give advice on any aspect of directing. Nevertheless, after directing over two hundred productions, attending Strasberg directing seminars, observing Kazan direct, teaching directing classes, supervising other directors and conducting directing workshops in Monaco, Sweden, Indiana, Wisconsin, California, Yale, Arkansas, Nebraska and many other national and international theatre conferences, I was finally so bold as to start a Teachers/Directors/Writers/Actors class in 1973 at the Lee Strasberg Theatre Institute. Over the years this class presented many works by established playwrights as well as numerous scripts written by class members. The class also served as a testing ground for directorial techniques. All the above experiences have produced concepts that may be of interest and use.

2. Suggestions are *Kazan on Kazan* by Michael Ciment; *On Directing* by Harold Clurman; *Orson Welles* by Joseph McBride; *Directors on Directing* by Cole and Chinoy; *Directors in Action,* edited by Bob Thomas; *Stanislavski Directs* by Nikolai Gorchakov; and *The Vakhtangov School of Stage Art* by Gorchakov. See also books in appendix E which Strasberg suggested to his directing class and my recommended reading list for directors and actors, appendix G, 9.

3. Kazan's first concern was to capture the essential qualities in a play and catch them in a phrase. This idea then became the keynote of the production, and all casting, designing and rewrite suggestions were made in this light.

4. Elia Kazan, "Look, There's the American Theatre," *Tulane Drama Review* 9 (2) (T26): 71.

5. Miller himself wrote that the theme of *The Crucible* was "handing over of conscience

to another, be it woman, the state or a terror, and the realizatiaon that with conscience goes the person, the soul immortal and the 'name'" ("Introduction," *Arthur Miller's Collected Plays* [New York: The Viking Press, 1957], p. 47).

6. Strasberg directing class, May 12, 1981.

7. "Unfortunately, most directors do not stop to visualize scenes or what is happening in scenes" (Lee Strasberg, May 5, 1981).

8. Lee Strasberg directing class, May 12, 1981.

9. Lee Strasberg directing class, April 23, 1980.

10. Lee Strasberg directing class, April 9, 1980.

11. Lee Strasberg directing class, April 23, 1980.

12. Lee Strasberg directing class, April 9, 1980.

13. Ibid.

14. Lee Strasberg directing class, May 5, 1981.

15. The Lee Strasberg Theatre Institute, Hollywood, Calif., Thursday, July 28, 1971.

16. Leader of the Actors Studio Directors' Unit, Los Angeles, October 4, 1982.

17. Generally, the actor chosen conforms reasonably well to the physical attributes of the character to be portrayed. Age, size and sex are the primary considerations that make a characterization believable to an audience. But often a director is confronted with several individuals who fit the purely physical characteristics of the part. What then becomes important is the actor's talent and the psychological dimensions he can bring to the role.

18. Lee Strasberg directing class, May 12, 1981.

19. Mitch Tuchman, "Dialogue on Film: Dustin Hoffman," *American Film: Magazine of the Film and Television Arts* (Washington, D.C., April 1983), p. 70.

20. Strasberg, July 28, 1971.

21. "Dialogue on Film—Richard Attenborough: An Inquiry into the arts and crafts of filmmaking between fellows and promninent filmmakers held under the auspices of the American Film Institute Center for advanced film studies," *American Film: Magazine of the Film and Television Arts,* Washington, D.C., March 1983.

22. Package Publicity Service, 247 West 46h Street, New York, N.Y. 10036.

23. Mark Rydell, moderator of Actors Studio, Directors' Unit, Los Angeles, February 17, 1983. Rydell continued, "The creation of genuine experience is important. Once a director helps an actor with that and helps build behavior of a subtext, the text will come."

24. Tuchman, pp. 28, 69, 70.

25. Mark Rydell, after being nominated for best director for the 1982 Academy Award, professed, "A director turns people on. He gets the best out of them. He sets an environment in which artists can flourish, in which they feel a sense of trust, in which they can expose themselves with impunity" (*Drama-Logue,* Hollywood, March 18–24, 1982, p. 16). Rydell at another time told of Katharine Hepburn's belief that she should put out a fire in *On Golden Pond.* Rydell, the director, remained firm that the boy extinguish the fire for the intent of the script (Actors Studio, Los Angeles, June 18, 1982, Mark Rydell as moderator).

26. "Advice to Actors'" and "Advice to Directors" by Professor Loraine (Lorrie) Hull, available from the American Community Theatre Association, a branch of the American Theatre Association, 1010 Wisconsin Avenue, Suite 630, Washington, D.C. 20007.

27. Strasberg admired Ford: "John Ford was able to achieve wonderful results from actors which others could not get. One way was by taking away responsibility from actors. Clark Gable, before becoming a big star, was once dissatisfied with a take. Ford told him it was what he wanted, but he let Gable do it again. Gable did it but suddenly realized

Ford had not said, 'Action.' Gable asked, 'Aren't we filming?' Ford answered, 'I told you you could do it again.' Maureen O'Hara once stopped in the middle of a scene, saying, 'Not good enough.' Ford just said 'Next' and went on to the next scene. Ford got an ease from actors which other directors could not. He always took away from the actor a concern with what the actor tried to do, and we try to do this through relaxation" (Lee Strasberg, September 29, 1981).

28. Lee Strasberg, September 29, 1981.

29. Charles Champlin, "The Capra Credo: Keep 'em Guessing," *Los Angeles Times,* "Calendar," March 18, 1982.

30. Seminar by Shelley Winters, Los Angeles, Monday, June 28, 1982. Charles Champlin, writing about William Wyler in the *Los Angeles Times,* quoted Walter Mirisch, for whom Wyler made *Friendly Persuasion* and *The Children's Hour,* as saying: "No one came near . . . Willy in his ability to place his characters in their settings and make them move. They moved easily and logically; there was nothing theatrical or artificial . . . there might be three areas of action simultaneously—something in the foreground, in the middle distance, in the background, all related" (*Los Angeles Times,* "Calendar," August 2, 1981).

31. Jo Annmarie Kalter, *Actors on Acting* (New York: Sterling Publishing Co.), p. 192.

32. At times directors or authors (e.g., Kazan and Arthur Miller) will first read the script to the cast. The reader tries to get the point of the script across without indicating performances or striving for characterization or emotion. By the time the cast does the first reading, members have heard the entire script, are more relaxed and are able to listen more fully to the other characters.

33. In a 1968 documentary, "Direction of an Actress by Renoir," the outstanding French director directed an actress to read a script over and over without inflection at all. As he worked with the actress, she began to lose her slight affectation and became more truthful and believable. This is another example of a director's initially asking an actor to rehearse lines simply and easily.

34. Not only did Strasberg have his cast in the Pulitzer Prize winning *Men in White* visit a hospital to recreate the reality of the operating room and the hospital but the group also worked on appropriate improvisations for the play.

35. Lee Strasberg directors seminar, Racine, Wisconsin, June 1967. Sponsored by the Wisconsin Idea Theatre and the University of Wisconsin Extension, Madison, Wisconsin.

36. Ibid.

37. Strasberg's theory was that at first the actor should concentrate on developing the inner line of the character without worrying about vocal projection. Once the inner line is established, the director may ask the actor to improve his projection (Strasberg's expression was "Give it more energy") in the last few weeks of rehearsal. If increased projection is demanded during early rehearsals, the actor may talk loudly but give no sense of truth and fail to grow in the role; I believe this is especially true for inexperienced or amateur actors. Some fine professional directors, however, encourage their actors to project from the beginning, even if the actors feel slightly false. These directors contend that this will not interfere with the actor's later development of a sense of truth in the role and that proper stage energy will eventually become second nature and no longer a problem. Having worked both ways through the years, I find that Strasberg's theory has been the most successful for those I direct.

38. Strasberg, Wisconsin directing seminar, June 1967.

39. Ibid.

40. Ibid.

41. Ibid.
42. Ibid.
43. Notes from Lee Strasberg class, October 25, 1979.
44. The Actors Studio, Los Angeles, with Martin Landau as the moderator, August 7, 1981.

Conclusion

1. Posted at the Lee Strasberg Theatre Institute, Los Angeles, on Lee Strasberg's death, February 17, 1982.

Appendix A

1. Vakhtangov, "Symposium of Lectures Given by Vakhtangov in the Studio," personal translation by Thelma Schnee for Lee Strasberg (New York, 1967), mimeographed and given to me by Lee Strasberg. The Group Theatre had translations of Vakhtangov's writings which Strasberg studied carefully. Arranged by B. E. Zakhava, the director of the Vakhtangov Theatre, notes from the diary of Vakhtangov were translated for the use of the Group Theatre, and made available to me by Lee Strasberg.
2. Robert H. Hethmon and Lee Strasberg, *Strasberg at the Actors Studio* (New York: Viking Press, 1965), p. 410.
3. *Stanislavski's Legacy,* edited and translated by E. R. Hapgood (New York, 1958), pp. 170–82.
4. Constantin Stanislavski, *An Actor Prepares,* translated by E. R. Hapgood (New York, 1936), pp. 94–104.
5. "Professional Acting Training as Summarized by Lee Strasberg," *Educational Theatre Journal* (Washington, D.C.: American Educational Theatre Association), November 1966.

Appendix B

1. Robert H. Hethmon and Lee Strasberg, *Strasberg at the Actors Studio* (New York: Viking Press, 1965), pp. 308–309.
In an interview with Lee Strasberg for the *Tulane Drama Review,* Strasberg made the following assertions about differences between Stanislavski's and Vakhtangov's influence on his work:
There is a theoretical difference between the way Stanislavski sometimes approaches the work and the way we—or the pupils of Stanislavski, especially Vakhtangov, by whom we were influenced—phrased the thing. He [Stanislavski] defines things for the actor, but doesn't clearly enough define for the actor the need to create a character other than himself. [Stanislavski asks, "If you were the character?"]
On the other hand, Vakhtangov says, "If you had to do such and such a thing, as Othello does, what would have to happen to you, what would motivate you to do that? In other words, he places the aesthetic intention first and then uses the technique as a way of carrying out the aesthetic intentions. When that is not done, often, even in Stanislavski's productions, the work makes the reality descend to the level of the actor rather than helping

the actor to ascend to the level of the character. You see, work on a part helps create the
reality and so we must be careful to bring the actor to the reality of the play by motivating
him to act as the character acts. The thing that is valuable in the Vakhtangov method is
that once your approach to the actor is set—you don't set exactly how he is to achieve his
role; that you leave to the actor's creativity and imagination—he himself combines with
this artistic intention, so that you get what you get in a photograph, where the positive
and the negative are equal. This is an important consideration, because often the work is
quite true, aesthetically true—I mean it isn't the fault of the work—but the director will
do certain things wrong and mislead the actor. . . .

What kind of logic can I, the actor, get which will help me to give the author's or the
director's logic? My logic must fuse with the intended logic of the play. . . . The actor has
to build for himself something that will help him; he has to find a believable core, an
essence in the part that can be done. . . .

In any play that needs a heightened reality you must find a subtext, such as Vakhtangov
found for *Turandot* . . . Affective memory is a basic element of the actor's reality. Vakhtangov emphasized that in acting we never use literal emotion . . . It should always be
only remembered emotion . . . Therefore, Vakhtangov stressed the idea of affective memory as the central experience with which the actor works. (Richard Schechner, "Working
With Live Material: An Interview with Lee Strasberg," *Tulane Drama Review* 9 (1) (T25,
Fall 1964): 129–32.

2. Hethmon and Strasberg, pp. 309–11. For further discussion of Shakespeare in our
theatre today, plus a discussion of style and classic plays, see Hethmon and Strasberg,
pp. 305–22. Strasberg believed that "rightly understood, style is not opposed to realism.
Style is a measure of expression, not a part of expression. . . . There is only the best
expression that the actor can give to a reality that he has explored and understood for
himself." He recognized the elements in the Shakespearean theatre different from our
own and felt that we should keep, maintain and use those elements. Strasberg also liked
actors of today to create the behavior with a modern sense of reality and conviction that
is at the same time right for the play. Strasberg told Actors Studio members: "In our
theatre today we are not just in a rut so far as facing the problem of Shakespeare and
most classic plays is concerned. We are in a real dilemma. On the one hand we feel, 'No,
we lack style. We lack form. [Style could be considered the outward form of the play].
We cannot move and cannot talk as actors of these plays would act and talk!' And when
you tell me that, I agree with you. I, too, believe that to be able to act and talk like
Shakespeare's characters which means to have intelligence, wit and emotional facility and
mercurial emotions and the ability to maintain emotion over a long period along with
words that pour out quickly and fully and intelligibly, is very difficult. . . . Caught as we
are in this dilemma, it is important for us to remember that the approach to Shakespeare
can only be in terms of Shaw's statement that classic characters are classic because they
are the kind of people who created our arts, our sciences, our politics, our wars. They are
people dealing with large problems of life. They come to these problems with deep sensitivity and deep intelligence. And therefore, no matter how alive the actors may be, no
matter how much the tone rings out and the words clatter easily and intelligently along, if
they play a scene from one of Shakespeare's histories so that I can't somehow believe that
these were the people who created the great English empire, to me it is not Shakespeare.
To me it is an imitation of other good actors rather than representation of life. Because
we are aware of the strength of the verbal pattern, we are sometimes fearful that we will
get caught up in the Shakespearean phrase, but there is really no need to fear. The phrase,
after all, is the embodiment of the thought. One thought can have fifteen adjectives,

depending upon the author's ability to find adjectives that are expressive. One of the keys to Shakespearean language is that in his time minds worked a little more quickly and a little more actively than nowadays. . . . The concept of good speech today implies impersonality and politeness, whereas the Elizabethan concept embraced vividness of thought, of feeling, of sensation, of expression and behavior. The ability to dance and to sing and to fence was necessary to the classes of people with whom Shakespeare came into contact. We need not be afraid of that. I understand the fear of getting caught up in the vocal or verbal pattern, but keeping the thought going with Shakespeare's words through all of Shakespeare's phrases is the key to a lot that Shakespeare says. . . . In Shakespeare there is the fullness of sensation that resulted from the fact that in his period things were being said fully. . . .

"There is a classic tradition in acting. Just reality is not classic. Just theatricality is not classic. The classic tradition combines the sense of theatricality with depth and strength of feeling. Theatricality plus reality characterizes the classic tradition in acting. . . . Therefore I bemoan the artificial or purely vocal approach because it will never really come to grips with greatness of soul and thought and feeling and wit. Only the tone becomes great—and often only large and beautiful and melodic—and you do not understand what is happening on the stage.

"Classic plays deal with these great people, but even the small people in classic art have been seen not by an ordinary person but by a Michelangelo. He filled them with his passion and his vision so that they seem somehow more than ordinary mortals, and we must never permit ourselves to fall into simply bringing these people down to the ordinary level of reality in order to make them human.

"Don't forget that even in ordinary plays I bemoan that approach. The purpose of this work is not to make everything casual and ordinary. On the contrary, our purpose is to fill everything with the utmost possible significance, to bring out the most important and fullest and most dramatic responses of the human being. . . . To create the leap of the soul and the leap of the imagination that brings one into these classic situations and environments and to create that as fully as the ordinary little things the actor does, requires an inner technique that is equivalent to what a painter does when he paints from an ordinary model a character that is somehow different. . . .

"Plays like the Restoration comedies or George Bernard Shaw's comedies or Noel Coward's comedies are difficult because we realize that they are not like Tennessee Williams's, and accordingly they are played with an approach entirely different from that employed with Williams, an approach called 'style'. . . . We assume that their plays are written on one note and cannot have any other notes or levels or elements. That is not true of any art. . . .

"The demarcations being made in the theatre today are deadly. 'This is a real play,' and 'This is an historical play,' and 'This is a French play,' and each has its style. No. They come out of different contents. They come out of different backgrounds. They portray different manners and customs. They show different behavior. They have different patterns of rhythm and of sound and of habit and even theatre. But there is never just a different style or form whereby the French play is in the French style, and the English play is English style, and Shakespeare is Shakespearean style. The essential thing that combines all the elements of theatre and that goes through all the history of theatre is the human being and his living presence. This has not changed in the five thousand years of human endeavor of which we know.

"These theatrical demarcations are dangerous when they apply to the end result we wish to achieve. Yes, a French play does have something different from an English play. But that something is not done differently. You do not play a French piece on one violin and a German piece on another. You play both on the same violin. We seem to make these formalized differences almost because we don't really perceive the intrinsic differences that stem from meaning, from content, from experience, from what the author was getting at, from the world that the author was part of, and from the theatre that the author worked in. . . .

"Classic plays are plays that have caught images and experiences of man at certain periods. But a classic is not a classic just because it caught a local historical moment. A classic is a play that, coming out of its own time, has caught something that lives on for all time, that has a universal meaning and content. . . .

"The first work that is done for the actor in training him for classic plays is the first work that is done for any actor in training him for any play. The basic craft of the actor is the ability to incorporate a character on whatever level is required. That craft is basic to all characters, Greek, Elizabethan, Spanish, commedia dell'arte, whatever you wish. That is not the kind of thing commonly thought of as classic acting, but it is the kind of thing that is thought of as great acting under any circumstances and under any conditions, classic or modern. . . .

"The additional work the actor needs for training in classical acting is the development of such basic skills as are required for moving like the characters. . . . They wore the costume of their time, and this costume sometimes made them behave differently. . . . You go toward the classic play or any play with the intention of trying to find out what the author wants. . . . Obviously there can be differences as to what the author has in mind, but unless you bring back Molière and Shakespeare from the dead, there is no way to settle those differences."

3. Both formulations were explained by Strasberg in his discussion on p. 229 from the *Tulane Drama Review.*

4. Especially inspiring was Vakhtangov's advice to the actors playing masks in *Turandot.* It was such that he and his students agreed the latter portion of the following quotation was necessary for all actors, artists, musicians or writers: "They should be able to speak naturally and realistically, that is easily but not lightly, wisely but not obtusely, eloquently but not grandiloquently—in a word, they should be able to talk with dignity on any theme and to any person. . . . I mean to *talk*—to talk cleverly, easily, succinctly, eloquently, but without any oratorical prattle, finding words that immediately express your thoughts, possessing a stock of vivid examples to cite by way of comparison. You must talk without affectation, without coquetry . . . without overdone humility, without false modesty and naturally, without impertinence. To be able to do this you must train yourselves not to think only of ordinary things. You must learn to converse with yourselves (loudly or silently) about anything. Watch people, in their conduct, their psychology. Pay attention to what's happening around you. Learn to see the beauty in life, but don't ignore its ugly side either. Learn to make comparisons, to draw pictures of life in your mind and to take part in them. You must train your mind to grasp the ideas of all centuries and ages of all the countries of the world, to understand all existing customs and traditions. You must always ask yourselves what could make the world beautiful and harmonious, what you must fight against and what you must champion." Nikolai M. Gorchakov, *The Vakhtangov School of Stage Art,* translated by G. Ivanov-Mumjiev, edited by Phyl Griffith with assistance from A. Gazlyev (director of the Vakhtangov Museum) (Moscow: Foreign Languages Publishing House, 1959, p. 143).

5. Ibid., pp. 64, 84. Vakhtangov continued his advice to directors:

Now, about the general amount of knowledge that a director should possess. I needn't explain that he must know everything about the play he is directing. How and where to get the necessary reference material is one of his jobs, that is, the ability to organize himself and his knowledge. . . . I'll ask you to improve your knowledge of literature, paintings, of the history of the theatre.

You should read, read and read. Starting with the newspapers and ending with the latest journals and publications. . . . Reread the classics. You must write down in your journals what you have read during the week, what paintings you have studied, what you have learned about the old and modern theatre. Moreover, once a week you must devote two or three hours to good music. It doesn't matter how you do it, but you must listen to music, for without that you'll never be good directors. You need not understand all the finer points of a musical work, its composition, theme, rhythm and other specific qualities and properties. But you must absorb music, inhale it as if it were air of the most salubrious kind that cleanses your thoughts of nonsense. When you listen to music, learn to dream, let your imagination soar to unexplored spheres, feelings and relationships.

And lastly, how does a man working in a theatre come to be a director? Through his great love of the theatre, I think. The director is interested in the play, the characters, the dressing-rooms, colleagues, plus the building in which the theatre is housed with all its rooms, cellars, attics, workshops, and what most important, its *stage*. For the actor, the stage is chiefly the part facing the audience. For the director, it is the entire space with the wings, flies, traps, footlights and all the machinery. And the *audience*. If the director doesn't know, love and respect the audience, if he works not for the audience but merely to satisfy his own ambitions, then he'll never have a real theatre. He may have something like one, but it will never be a theatre with a capital T. . . .

All I've just told you. . . . It's the result of what I've seen and of what I've been taught by Adashev, Stanislavski and Nemirovich-Danchenko. It's the result of our experience at the First Studio, especially in its organizational period, when we had Sulerzhitsky with us. Of course, some of the ideas are my own (pp. 64–66).

6. Carroll Baker, *Baby Doll* (New York: Arbor House Publishing Company, 1983), p. 153. In 1983 Dustin Hoffman made practically the same statement about a professional film crew contributing to the creativity of a movie (see part 3).

7. Gorchakov, p. 203.

8. Ibid., p. 129.

9. Ruben Simonov, *Stanislavski's Protégé: Eugene Vakhtangov* translated by Miriam Goldina (New York: Drama Book Specialists, 1969), pp. 146–50. Reprinted by permission of Drama Book Publishers, 824 Broadway, N.Y. 10003.

10. William L. Kuhlke, *Vakhtangov's Legacy* (Ann Arbor, Michigan: University Micro-films, Inc., 1965), pp. 99, 12.

11. Gorchakov, p. 206. In 1927 *The Dybbuk* was performed in the United States as it was directed by Vakhtangov for the Habima Theatre. Raikin Ben-Ari writes of Broadway's reaction to the Habima Theatre: "The Habima's appearance on Broadway led to heated discussions in New York Theatre circles. People were either excited about us or thought us crazy. In either case we aroused the spectator. And to our way of thinking, this was a great achievement—one for which Vakhtangov had told us every theatre should strive." Raikin Ben-Ari, *Habima,* translated by A. E. Cross and I. Soref (New York: Thomas Yoseloff, Inc., 1957), p. 190. In the last years of his life Ben-Ari attended sessions moderated by Strasberg at the Actors Studio.

I made practically the same statement about "arousing the audience" at International Theatre Conferences where I participated in panel discussions. This was *before* I realized that Vakhtangov had this philosophy fifty years earlier!

Appendix C

1. Michael Schulman, "Backstage Behaviorism," *Psychology Today* (Del Mar, California, June 1973), p. 51.

2. Ibid., pp. 51, 52.

3. Ibid., p. 54.

Appendix F

1. Paul Gray, "Stanislavski and America: A Critical Chronology," *Tulane Drama Review* 9 (2) (T26, Winter 1964): 38, 41.

2. Oscar G. Brockett, *The Theatre: An Introduction* (New York: Holt, Rinehart and Winston, 1969), pp. 308–09.

3. Edward Dwight Easty, *On Method Acting* (New York: Allograph Press Corp., 1966), p. 8.

4. Robert DeNiro, November 24, 1980.

5. Conversation with Loraine (Lorrie) Hull while filming *The Arrangement,* Warner Brothers, Los Angeles, 1968.

6. Michel Ciment, *Kazan on Kazan* (New York: The Viking Press, 1974), p. 37.

7. *Los Angeles Times,* "Los Angeles Times West Magazine," October 20, 1968, pp. 33, 38.

8. New York Actors Studio, November 20, 1981. At a previous event Kazan stated, "[Strasberg] is recognized today as the foremost authority in this art and his work has made the Actors Studio a force in the world of the Theatre" (Actors Studio Masked Ball Benefit Program, October, 1978).

9. *Los Angeles Herald-Examiner,* syndicated article by Harold Heffernan, March 1976.

10. William Glover, "There's Method in the Madness of World Famous Actors Studio," *Milwaukee Journal,* January 24, 1965, part 5, p. 5.

11. Theodore Hoffman, "Stanislavski Triumphant," *Tulane Drama Review* 9 (1) (T26, Winter 1964): 16–17.

12. Robert C. Jennings, "The Method Goes to College," *Los Angeles Times, October 20, 1968, p. 38.*

13. Ibid.

14. Ibid.

15. From the film Acting: Lee Strasberg and The Actors Studio, by Herbert Kline.

16. Shelley Winters, Actors Studio moderator, March 8, 1977.

17. Paul Newman and Rod Steiger on a fifteen-minute film played in New York at Strasberg's seventy-fifth birthday party, 1976.

18. Ibid.

19. "An account of the Actors Studio," *Sight & Sound* 26 (3) (Winter 1956–57): 133, quoted by Rogoff, p. 137. Gordon Rogoff, "Lee Strasberg: Burning Ice," *Tulane Drama Review* 9 (2) (T26, Winter 1964). Statements by *TDR* contributors were challenged in a letter to the *TDR* by Lee Strasberg. The following statements are excerpted from Strasberg's letter:

"The production [*The Three Sisters*] received such reactions as Jerry Talmer in the *New York Post:* 'Lee Strasberg proved that he could direct a play—if the right play—with all the creative truth and strength a human being can command . . . I do not think I have ever seen 16 or however many actors walking a stage with more valid and interrelated inner lives than those Mr. Strasberg has elicited from his brilliant cast.' Douglas Watt in the *Daily News*: 'The Actors Studio Theatre production of *The Three Sisters* is a stunning achievement . . . serving notice that there is still room for artistry in depth. Lee Strasberg, the Studio's artistic director, has staged the play—first venture in this capacity in some years—and he is the true hero of the occasion.' Norman Nadel in the *New York World-Telegram*: '*The Three Sisters* conveys an abudance of meaning and feeling beyond anything you might suspect from a reading or from most productions of this classic.' Howard Taubman in the *New York Times*: 'Under Lee Strasberg's direction, the Actors Studio Theatre is doing the best work of its youthful career . . . there is an admirable sense of unity in the production.' This reaction was reinforced after the visit of the MAT, when some compared the two productions to our favor. One of the most favorable reactions came from a reviewer abroad, uninvolved in the quarrels about the Method, who, comparing mine with other productions she had seen, including the MAT one, stated: 'Once or twice in a decade a theatre production of a great classic achieves such a radiant fusion of acting and direction that it passes into legend, its nuances of characterization and mood seeming to illuminate not just for the moment, but for limitless future recollection, the dramatist's conception of life . . . It is only now, 28 years later that I have seen a production which, besides being almost perfectly cast throughout, equals that of St. Denis in its marvelous evocation of changing mood and season and the nuances of human relationships, of gaiety, hope and frustration, that parallel the springs and autumns of the Russian landscape" (Audrey Williamson in *The Scotsman*). Lee Strasberg, "Letters: Strasberg vs TDR," *Tulane Drama Review* 2 (1) (T33, Fall 1966): 234–39.

20. Glover, part 5, p. 6.
21. Ibid., p. 6.
22. Jennings, p. 32.
23. Ibid., p. 33.
24. Richard Schechner, "Reality Is Not Enough: An Interview with Alan Schneider," *Tulane Drama Review* 9 (3) (T26, Winter 1964): 118–19.
25. Toby Cole and Helen Krich Chinoy, *Actors on Acting* (New York: Crown Publishers, 1954), p. 621.
26. *Time,* December 16, 1974.
27. John Gassner, *Directions in Modern Theatre and Drama* (New York: Holt, Rinehart and Winston, 1965), p. 457.
28. *New York Times,* February 2, 1975.
29. *TV Guide,* December 7, 1974, p. 13.
30. Ezra Goldstein, *Dramatics* 3 (January/February, 1977): 44.
31. Ibid., p. 10.
32. *Footlights,* June, 1978, p. 14.
33. *The Christian Science Monitor,* Thursday, March 10, 1977, p. 26.
34. Among the Actors Studio Academy Award winners were Karl Malden, Elia Kazan, Eva Marie Saint, Joanne Woodward, Jo Van Fleet, Celeste Holme, Marlon Brando, Kim Hunter, Jerome Robbins, Shelley Winters, Anne Bancroft, Sidney Poitier, Patricia Neal, Martin Balsam, Walter Matthau, Rod Steiger, Estelle Parsons, Sandy Dennis, Cliff Robertson, Cloris Leachman, Robert De Niro, Jane Fonda, Bruce Dern, Ellyn Burstyn, Jack Nicholson, Lee Grant, Diane Ladd, Burgess Meredith, Christopher Walken, Sally Field, Dustin Hoffman, Maureen Stapleton, Jon Voight, and Robert Duvall.
35. Personal conversation with Lorrie Hull, July, 1973. *The Hollywood Reporter* ran a

feature article about Strasberg's opinions of the Moscow Art Theatre, labeling Lee Strasberg, "The man who made Stanislavski a Household Word in the United States."

36. UPI News Release.

37. Todd McCarthy, *Daily Variety,* "Heart Attack Kills Lee Strasberg, 80," Thursday, February 18, 1982, Hollywood, California.

Glossary

Action (in a director's work script): Can state the specific action of the scene. The action of the moment. Can state what each character is doing, silently or through speech, and what each character wants or intends to do. Some directors designate these work script actions through active verbs (e.g., to advise, to flirt, to tell alarming news, to accuse). The way in which the smallest actions come from and relate to the script's overall action denotes the inner life of the play (see *Intention, Objective, Spine*).

Action (inner or psychological): What the character wants; why he is there. Each character is motivated by something he wants although he himself may not be aware of what he wants and the script may not clarify it until late in the play. The actor must consider his character's situation and his relationships with other characters. Action can be expressed through active verbs in an actor's or director's planning (see *Intention, Objective, Spine, Choices*).

Action (outer or physical): The behavior of the character. The play between characters.

Activities: An actor's tasks and movement onstage. The physical activities that accompany action.

Adjustments: The manner in which basic action is carried out in performing a role. The form of an inner action's or goal's fulfillment. How the actor adapts to particular circumstances, environments, characters, etc. An actor adjusts to circumstances in the script or to circumstances he gives himself. Adjustments can be found in a script and via an actor's imagination to help the actor perform the correct reality (see *Justification*). A result of an adjustment is the attitude that colors the action in the circumstances of the scene.

Affective memory (emotional memory or emotional recall): When an actor re-creates sensorily his own emotional experiences and fuses them with his character's (see part 2, chapter 5).

Animal exercise: An exercise in which the student tries to create the movements, responses and inner life of an animal as accurately as possible. A good introduction to character work (see part 2, chapter 4).

Beat: A short segment of a script which has a complete purpose. (Also called unit, sequence or section.) Each script can be broken down into beats. Some directors visualize a play as one major unit broken into dozens of subunits or beats all interrelated and all pointing in one direction; others consider a beat a measure, the time between crises or a series of scenes within a scene. The beat can be one moment or several minutes (see *Unit, Tempo,* part 2, chapters 8 and 9, and part 3).

Blocking: The movement of the players during a scene. Integration of the players, set, sound, lights and all elements needed for the stage picture.

Choices: Actions or intentions selected by the actor. Can be under the guidance of the director and should be according to the circumstances of the script. An actor's performance can be determined by how he chooses his actions and how he states them to himself. A good actor makes strong creative choices based on an understanding of his character's feelings.

Combination exercises: Several exercises done simultaneously. After the actor is trained to concentrate and accomplish one sensory object at a time, he is next taught how to add more objects cumulatively and finally to carry all objects at once (see part 2, chapter 4).

Combination exercises with private moment: Combination exercises that begin with a private moment. Words are added along with other exercises that prepare the actor for the variety of tasks he will have to perform on the stage or before a camera (see chapter 4).

Composition: The physical arrangement of characters on the stage or screen. The pattern of the stage picture. Directors can study the works of great artists for ideas on composition.

Concept: The overall style of production. Director's concept is realized through props, costumes, scenery, music, movement, mood, acting— all aspects of the production. Actors make inner and outer choices based on the director's concept (see *Style*).

Emotional memory or emotional recall: Same as affective memory (see part 2, chapter 5).

Etude: An improvisation guided by the director on the theme or some event in the play. Each actor portrays his character in the play. A term particularly used by Stanislavski and Vakhtangov.

Event: The circumstances behind the written word. An individual situation in a script. Each event can be part of a sequence of situations.

Gibberish: Meaningless sounds substituted for recognizable talk. Forces the players to communicate. Breaks verbal patterns (see part 2, chapter 6).

Given circumstances: Everything that has happened prior to a scene, and in the scene that affects the scene and motivates and influences a character's behavior.

Groundplan: The plan of the physical surroundings of a scene. Like an architect's floorplan. Planned by the director in conjunction with the set designer. Building a model is even better than a drawing. The groundplan should indicate clearly locations of all doors, windows, fireplaces, arches, stairs and major pieces of furniture. Vertical aspects such as walls, platforms, steps, chairs, tables, cushions on the floor and other things for actors to stand, sit or lie on are included—anything that has height. The groundplan is arranged so the director can plan his stage pictures on more than one plane and achieve a variety of playing areas. Flexibility is essential; the director must be willing to change his plans because of what he discovers as he works with actors.

Improvisation: Spontaneous acting out of a basic situation in which the actors provide their own words, actions and movement without a written script (see part 2, chapter 7).

Inner action: See *Action*.

Inner monologue: A form of "speaking out" in which an actor expresses his personal feelings and reactions during a scene. He speaks out between the lines, in place of lines or during his partner's lines. What the actor is really experiencing is dealt with by the inner monologue. The inner monologue helps relieve anxiety, tension and stress when the actor speaks out and gets it into the work. Note the difference between this and the narrative monologue. The inner monologue and narrative monologue could be combined, as there may be a need for the inner monologue in the narrative monologue.

Intent: The main theme of the play (author's and director's intent). Some directors find the author's intent by studying and recording the action of the play. Kazan records the action of each act in three or four sentences. Also, each character's spine (see *Theme* and *Spine*).

Intention: Sometimes labeled action or objective. The sense of the play is carried forward through intention. The intention of the character can be expressed in terms of a verb that takes an object (see Action). The intention can be literally the same as the dialogue or can be very different from the dialogue. It is what the actor is really doing or intends to do on any given moment. Intentions create subtext.

Justification: The reason for a character's behavior. "What would motivate me to do it that way is the principle of justification" (Lee Strasberg). An actor uses his imagination to justify whatever is uncomfortable or whatever he himself would not normally do in a particular manner. An actor tries to justify necessary behavior, thinking or movement for the role. He can say to himself, "It is as if . . ." to justify what the director wants or what is required. This technique fosters an actor's belief in what he is doing and develops his faith in himself.

The Method: Originally another word for the Stanislavski system. More recently it has come to mean a type of actor training developed by Strasberg and others based on Stanislavski's definitions. A procedure of acting training which guides an actor in dealing with his own instrument. The procedure is not a set series of rules that have to be applied specifically.

Mood: The emotional effect on the audience. Feelings and emotions generated from the clash of forces in the action of the play. All elements of the production contribute to the mood: acting, lighting, sound effects, scenery, business, stage pictures, movement, etc. In their cumulative effect, moods set the tone of the play. A play is composed of many mood shifts, every unit or action having its own specific mood. The play's action is the source of the mood, and the characters' changing moods convey this. The tone of a production is the achievement of appropriate moods. Moods can be planned and recorded by a director through mood adjectives that describe a scene or what a character is feeling.

Motivate: To provide with a motive or motives. To motivate can be applied to an outer action or an inner urge that moves or prompts a person to action (see also *Movement* and *Action*). A director can mo-

tivate an actor by aiding him in creating objects of concentration—
emotional and physical.

Motive: Something that prompts a person to act in a certain way.
Prompting to action.

Movement: See *Blocking*. All movement should be motivated by the
dramatic action and justified from within.

Narrative monologue: The actor speaks out the character's thoughts and
feelings during rehearsal. This goes step by step and moment to moment as a rehearsal procedure. The narrative monologue is used especially when actors are not thinking as the character in a scene or
do not seem to know what they are doing. Strasberg believed it
stemmed from Stanislavski's concern with what is happening in a
scene. The narrative monologue is not based on emotion or drama
but involves an actor's discovery of and logic of the scene. The narrative monologue can give an actor colors and variety because it is
not based on an intense emotion.

Object: Anything on which an actor can focus his concentration (see
part 2, chapter 2).

Objective: Whatever the writer, director or actor wants to achieve. What
the actor wants through the action. For each actor there can be an
overall objective as well as smaller objectives within each scene (see
Inner action). The director's objective may be to fulfill the author's
intent, or the objective could be the statement the director wants to
make. The play's objective includes the objective of all the characters,
so it is usually quite general but unifying. In every play there is usually
one overall objective, sometimes called the spine or main action of
the play (see also *Intention*).

Particularization: A process in which an actor recalls some specific event
in his own life to use in his role (see part 2, chapter 8).

Pause: A silent gap where tempo values can be moving. What is not said
is often just as important as what is said; the momentary silence of a
pause tells the audience much.

Personalization: A process in which the actor recalls an actual person
he knows as a model for his partner or for what he is visualizing,
talking or thinking about in a scene (see part 2, chapter 8).

Private moment: Discovered by Strasberg. An exercise in which the
actor creates a feeling of aloneness while he is actually in the presence

of other people. The intention is to enable the actor "to feel private in public" (see part 2, chapter 4).

Rehearsal process: A logical sequence in rehearsals, and procedures used in rehearsals (see part 3).

Relaxation: A state in which the actor has rid himself of excess muscle tension as a prelude to full concentration (see part 2, chapter 1).

Rhythm: A pattern of movements and/or sounds. Regular recurrence of particular elements. A measurable tempo that is a result of a particular psychological state or life-style. The quality of an actor's inner state that manifests itself in a specific, measurable way. The pulsations of a play. The way in which a production moves or flows is determined by rhythm and tempo. Tempo and rhythm have an important effect on moods of the production, but moods can be imposed on tempo and rhythm as well (see *Tempo*).

Script: The written text of a play, motion picture or television production or any written work containing dialogue designated for specific characters.

Section: See *Beat*.

Segment: See *Beat, Unit*.

Sense memory: The ability to relive sensations and respond to imaginary objects. Sense memory is produced by recalling previously experienced objects, situations or events. One technique of teaching sense memory is through the various exercises that constituted Strasberg's method of work (see part 2, chapters 3 and 4).

Sensory exercises: Exercises aimed at the development of sense memory. The sense memory exercises begin with the imaginary creation of one object (such as a breakfast drink) having a muscular sequence in which all the senses are involved. The actor imaginarily creates simple objects that most people deal with daily so that the actor can begin to develop his ability to create reality for himself, his imagination and his ability to believe. The exercises then progress to the actor's re-creating sensations he remembers (see part 2, chapter 4).

Singing the words: A way of working to break verbal patterns of the lines.

Song and dance exercise: Exercise created by Strasberg; not really a song and dance (see part 2, chapter 6).

Spine (character's): The chief motivating force for each character from the character's own viewpoint. The character's overall action derives from the spine of the play (see part 3).

Spine (play's): The play's main action; a through action that pervades the whole play. What the writer wants to communicate. Sometimes called the overall objective of all the characters (see *Objective*).

Stages of rehearsal: Procedures for each day of rehearsal (see part 3).

Style: How the play is presented based on the director's concept. Refers to form and appearance. Includes all facets of production (see *Concept*).

Substitution: A process in which the actor recalls from his own life an object or situation he knows for the actual or imaginary object or situation onstage or seen offstage (see part 2, chapter 8).

Subtext: Inner thoughts, feelings and intentions not expressed in the dialogue. Problems and thoughts behind the words. Sometimes spoken out in an exercise; the actor speaks to or about himself.

Tempo: The external manifestation of rhythm. The speed or pace of the production as a whole or of a particular scene. Tempo may be increased by speeding up lines or movement, shortening pauses and using extended sound effects. The emotions and energies of the actors also affect tempo.

Text: The actor's dialogue and everything written in the script.

Theme: The idea of a play. What the writer wants to tell the audience. Most plays have a central theme that can be called the "spice of meaning." Can be an individual director's point of view, so there's not just a single possible theme. For some directors the theme is interchangeable with spine of the play and becomes the play's central event (see *Spine, Concept, Objective, Intent,* part 2, chapter 8).

Unit: Divisions in dramatic action in a script and all segments of a plot. Whenever a character shifts lines of talk or action in a new direction or the writer shifts the dominant focus from one character to another, a new unit is formed (see *Beat*). Units vary in size from two or three lines to twelve or more; sometimes they consist of a single line followed by silent activity or activity alone. Each unit has its own objective. The director asks, "Is it logical?" about the unit's objective and characters' actions. Some directors entitle the units and separate them in the text by drawing lines.

Selected Bibliography

"Actors Studio Acting Sessions Tapes" and Actors Studio Directors Unit Tapes. Wisconsin Center for Theatre Research. Wisconsin State Historical Library. Madison, Wisconsin.

Ben-Ari, Raikin. *Habima*. Translated by A. H. Gross and I. Soref. New York: Thomas Yoseloff, 1957.

Boleslavsky, Richard. *Acting: The First Six Lessons*. New York: Theatre Arts, 1933.

Brockett, Oscar G. *The Theatre*. New York: Holt, Rinehart and Winston, 1969.

Cavett, Dick. "Interview of Lee Strasberg." PBS telecast, January 3, 1978. (Notes taken by Loraine Hull)

Chinoy, Helen Krich, ed. "Reunion: A Self-Portrait." *Educational Theatre Journal* 28: 4 (December, 1976).

Ciment, Michel. *Kazan on Kazan*. New York: The Viking Press, 1974.

Clurman, Harold. *The Fervent Years*. New York: Hill and Wang, 1958.

———. *The Naked Image*. New York: Macmillan, 1966.

———. *On Directing*. New York: Macmillan, 1972.

Cole, Toby, and Chinoy, Helen Krich, eds. *Actors on Acting*. New York: Crown Publishers, 1954.

———. *Directors on Directing*. New York: Bobbs-Merrill, 1963.

Diderot, Denis. *The Paradox of Acting*. New York: Hill and Wang, 1957.

Freed, Donald. *Freud and Stanislavski*. New York: Vantage Press, 1964.

Gassner, John. *Directions in Modern Theatre and Drama*. New York: Holt, Rinehart and Winston, 1965.

———. *Producing the Play*. New York: Holt, Rinehart and Winston, 1953.

Glover, William. "There's Method in the Madness of World Famous Actors Studio." *Milwaukee Journal,* January 24, 1965.

Gorchakov, Nikolai M. *Stanislavski Directs*. Edited and translated by Virginia Stevens. New York: Minerva Press, 1968.

———. *The Vakhtangov School of Stage Art*. Phyl Griffith with A. Gazlyev, eds. Translated by G. Ivanov-Mumjiev. Moscow: Foreign Languages Publishing House, 1959.

Gray, Paul. "Stanislavski and America: A Critical Chronology." *Tulane Drama Review* 9: 2 (T26, Winter 1964).

Hethmon, Robert H., and Strasberg, Lee. *Strasberg at the Actors Studio*. New York: Viking Press, 1965.

Hoffman, Theodore. "Stanislavski Triumphant." *Tulane Drama Review* 9: 1 (T25, Fall 1964).

Hughes, Glenn. *A History of the American Theatre, 1700–1951*. New York: Samuel French, 1951.

Hull, S. Loraine. "Documented Notes from Lee Strasberg Classes," New York, 1966; Lee Strasberg Seminars, Racine, Wis., 1966–67; The Lee Strasberg Theatre Institute Strasberg classes, Los Angeles, 1971–81; Strasberg lectures and critiques at the Lee Strasberg Theatre Institute and Actors Studio, 1971–81; notes from Actors Studio sessions, Los Angeles and New York, 1971–84.

———. Personal conversations and interviews with Lee Strasberg, 1966–81. Documented notes from Lee Strasberg Theatre Institute faculty meetings, 1972–81, conducted by Lee Strasberg, Los Angeles.

Jennings, C. Robert. "The Method Goes to College." *Los Angeles Times,* Oct. 20, 1968.

Kuhlke, William Lonnie. *Vakhtangov's Legacy*. Ph.D. diss., State University of Iowa. Michigan: University Microfilms, Ann Arbor, 1965.

Lewis, Robert. *Method or Madness*. New York: Samuel French, 1958.

Magarshack, David. *Stanislavski, a Life*. New York: Chanticleer Press, 1953.

Moore, Sonia. *The Stanislavski System*. New York: Viking Press, 1965.

Munk, Erika, ed. *Stanislavski and America*. New York: Hill and Wang, 1966.

Newman, Edwin. "Interview with Lee Strasberg." NET telecast, November 1969. (Notes taken by Loraine Hull)

New York Public Library. Actors Studio Packet.

Rogoff, Gordon. "Lee Strasberg: Burning Ice." *Tulane Drama Review* 9: 2 (T26, Winter 1964).

Schechner, Richard. "The Bottomless Cup, an Interview with Geraldine Page." *Tulane Drama Review* 9: 2 (T26, Winter 1964).

———. "Reality Is Not Enough, an Interview with Alan Schneider." *Tulane Drama Review* 9: 3 (T27, Spring 1965).

——. "Working with Live Material: An Interview with Lee Strasberg." *Tulane Drama Review* 9: 1 (T25, Fall 1964).

——, and Hoffman, Theodore. "Look, There's the American Theatre" (an interview with Elia Kazan). *Tulane Drama Review* 9: 1 (T25, Fall 1964).

Schulman, Michael. "Backstage Behaviorism." *Psychology Today.* Del Mar, California, June 1973, pp. 51–54, 88.

Simonov, Ruben. *Stanislavski's Protégé: Eugene Vakhtangov.* Translated and adapted by Miriam Goldina. New York: Drama Book Specialists, 1969.

Stanislavski, Constantin. *An Actor Prepares.* Translated by E. R. Hapgood. New York: Theatre Arts, 1936.

——. *Building a Character.* Translated by E. R. Hapgood. New York: Theatre Arts, 1949.

——. *Creating a Role.* Translated by E. R. Hapgood. New York: Theatre Arts, 1961.

——. *My Life in Art.* Translated by J. J. Robbins. New York: Theatre Arts, 1952.

——. *Stanislavski on the Art of the Stage.* Translated and Introduced by David Magarshack. New York: Hill and Wang, 1961.

——. *Stanislavski Produces Othello.* Translated by Helen Nowak. New York: Theatre Arts, 1948.

——. *Stanislavski's Legacy.* Edited and translated by E. R. Hapgood. New York: Theatre Arts, 1958.

Strasberg, Lee. "Acting, Direction and Production." *Encyclopaedia Britannica.* 1967, 1972, and 15th ed., 1974.

——. "Letters: Strasberg vs TDR." *Tulane Drama Review* 2: 1 (T33, Fall 1966).

——. "Professional Acting Training as Summarized by Lee Strasberg." *Educational Theatre Journal.* Washington, D.C.: American Theatre Association, November 1966.

——, ed. *Famous American Plays of the 1950s.* New York: Dell Publishing, 1962.

Tuchman, Mitch. "Dialogue on Film: Dustin Hoffman." *American Film: Magazine of the Film and Television Arts.* Washington, D.C.: American Film Institute, April 1983.

Vakhtangov, Eugene. "Symposium of Lectures Given by Vakhtangov in the Studio." Personal translation by Thelma Schnee for Lee Strasberg and given to Loraine (Lorrie) Hull by Lee Strasberg. New York, 1967. (Mimeographed)

Vexler, Felix. *Studies in Diderot's Esthetic Naturalism.* New York: Russell and Russell, 1973.

Index

(Alphabetical lists of suggested authors and scenes for actors, youth and directors appear on pages 253–273, 284–289 and are not included in this Index.)